THE WOMEN OF
THE FAR RIGHT

THE WOMEN OF THE FAR RIGHT

SOCIAL MEDIA INFLUENCERS AND ONLINE RADICALIZATION

EVIANE LEIDIG

Columbia University Press
New York

Columbia University Press
Publishers Since 1893
New York   Chichester, West Sussex
cup.columbia.edu

Library of Congress Cataloging-in-Publication Data
Names: Leidig, Eviane, author.
Title: The women of the far right : social media influencers and online
    radicalization / Eviane Leidig.
Description: New York : Columbia University Press, [2023] |
    Includes bibliographical references and index.
Identifiers: LCCN 2023012021 (print) | LCCN 2023012022 (ebook) |
    ISBN 9780231210164 (hardback) | ISBN 9780231210171 (trade paperback) |
    ISBN 9780231558303 (ebook)
Subjects: LCSH: Right-wing extremists. | Women radicals. |
    Radicalization. | Social media—Political aspects. |
    Internet personalities.
Classification: LCC HN49.R33 L44 2023 (print) | LCC HN49.R33 (ebook) |
    DDC 303.48/4—dc23/eng/20230502
LC record available at https://lccn.loc.gov/2023012021
LC ebook record available at https://lccn.loc.gov/2023012022

Cover design: Noah Arlow
Cover images: Shutterstock

CONTENTS

THE WOMEN OF
THE FAR RIGHT

INTRODUCTION
"A New Chapter"

I n May 2019, then twenty-three-year-old Canadian Lauren Southern posted on her website, laurensouthern.net, a farewell message titled "A New Chapter." In it, Lauren[1] stated that over the course of four years, she had made deep friendships and embarked on adventures around the world, listening to stories of hope and loss.

Unless you knew about Lauren Southern's political activism, her farewell message revealed nothing about her political beliefs. Yet her departure from public life, despite having signaled a move away in the six months earlier, was a major loss of one of the alt-right's main celebrities.

The rise and fall of Lauren Southern reflect the ephemeral nature of the alt-right movement. After all, the alt-right had no clear leader, structure, or even ideology. It existed almost entirely online, and its adherents were vulnerable to censorship, suspension, and shadow banning. I emphasize that the alt-right needs to be understood in relation to the far right at large; the alt-right existed during a particular time and place (discussed in chapter 1), but the far right encompasses a much broader milieu that continues to live on.

What comes to mind when you picture the far right? Is it a violent mob of angry, young white men holding tiki torches and chanting, "You will not replace us?" Or a hooded figure accessing the dark corners of the internet to post hate-filled messages? Lauren's "resignation" announcement importantly makes us question the role of women in the alt-right, whose most visible faces were those of men: Richard Spencer, Milo Yiannopoulos, Stefan Molyneux, and Paul Joseph Watson are just a few prominent examples. However, these women, who are not just in the background but are actively helping to shape the far-right movement, go mostly unnoticed by those outside the far right.

The American and Canadian women who feature at the core of this book are Lauren Southern, Brittany Sellner (née Pettibone), Lana Lokteff, Rebecca Hargraves, Robyn Riley, Ayla Stewart, Lacey Lynn, and Lauren Chen, and a few others are mentioned in passing as supporting figures within the far right. Importantly, they are not the type of women you will find climbing the ranks of the conservative establishment in the hopes of one day representing the Republican Party in the United States. They operate separately from the network of mainstream conservatism institutionalized through organizations such as Turning Point USA (see chapter 6), PragerU, and BlazeTV, which are aimed toward a new generation of aspiring conservative leaders and spokespersons. With the exception of Lauren Chen, who crosses the far right and conservative spectrum, these influencers are not involved with these conservative organizations and prefer to engage in political activism that is more explicitly ideologically extreme. This distinction is not meant to disregard potential overlaps between conservatism and the far right—that boundary has become increasingly blurred through the recent mainstreaming of far-right ideas into conservatism since Donald Trump's rise—but rather to identify that the far right is fundamentally and overtly supremacist in its dehumanization efforts. These women thus mobilize within an adjacent milieu seeking to cultivate a long-term agenda of social and cultural change—that is, metapolitical change, not short-term gains at the ballot box. They're deeply embedded in helping to achieve a far-right utopia.

Although known by their online presence, some are connected to offline groups as well, such as Brittany Sellner, affiliated with the European youth-led Identitarian movement; Lacey Lynn, a member of the white-supremacist organization Identity Evropa (which later became American Identity Movement); and Ayla Stewart, involved in the Unite the Right rally in Charlottesville in 2017. Throughout this book, I ask: How is women's involvement different from that of their male counterparts? How do these women feel about the male dominance prevalent within the far right?

"Anytime the [press] mentions the alt-right, they always make it sound like it's a bunch of guys in the basements. They don't talk about how these guys have wives, and the wives are supportive, and the wives go to these meet-ups and conferences and that they're there," remarked Lana Lokteff in early 2017. "So, I think it's important for right-wing women to show themselves. I think it's good to be spokeswomen for our movement and to kind of sell it a little bit. This is propaganda; it's good marketing. The more of us who put out content can be highly impactful."[2] This book argues that the propaganda and marketing produced by far-right women plays a key function within the broader movement: normalizing and legitimizing far-right ideology for mainstream appeal.

These young, attractive women are taking to mainstream social media sites to recruit followers and build audiences for their cause. I call these women "influencers" because they serve as leading online personalities shaping and popularizing ideas within the far-right community. Compared to the dark web and fringe forums such as 4chan and 8kun (previously 8chan), which inspired the terrorist attacks in Christchurch, New Zealand, in 2019 and in Buffalo, New York, in 2022, forums where (mostly male) users hide behind anonymous avatars, these women prefer to spread their message on mainstream platforms such as YouTube, Instagram, and Twitter. Importantly, being an influencer isn't just discourse oriented. It is encompassed within a broader influencer *culture*. The media scholar Crystal Abidin defines influencers as "everyday, ordinary Internet users who accumulate a relatively large following on blogs and social media through the textual and visual narration of their personal lives and lifestyles, engage with their following in 'digital' and 'physical' spaces, and monetize their following by integrating 'advertorials' into their blog or social media posts and making appearances at events."[3] The far-right women featured in this book are self-styled vloggers (video bloggers), activists, entrepreneurs, and authors. They discuss issues such as dating and relationships alongside free speech, the "invasion" of migrants in Europe, and culture wars on university campuses. They travel the world to film documentaries and go on speaking tours. In this book, I show that it was the female leaders of the alt-right who helped mainstream the ideas of what was previously a fringe phenomenon by tapping into the practices of influencer culture to reach wide audiences.

After countless hours watching videos on YouTube and scrolling through Instagram profiles, I realized that what makes these women so appealing is how they present as relatable to viewers. They may be energetic, charming, and self-confident, but they are also remarkably down-to-earth and empathetic. These women discuss the troubles of finding love, desiring financial security, and making friends amid loneliness. They post photos of themselves traveling on vacations and at coffee breaks in cafés. They showcase their lives and lifestyles.

I contend that perceptions of authenticity and accessibility serve as the most powerful tools of the modern far right. As Lauren Southern said to fellow influencer Brittany Sellner in one vlog they did together in August 2017, "I think a big thing that people enjoyed about our videos was how natural we could just talk about life stuff, about relationships, about stuff that you would have just sitting down and talking about at a slumber party, except we're inviting people to join us with the camera." She continued, "And it's a lot of fun and really natural, and we had so many comments from people saying, 'We want to see you.'"[4]

Banal conversations held within the intimate format of YouTube vlogs conceal an effective strategy of far-right propaganda. These women broadcast from their bedrooms about the danger of Islam to the West or advocate for more women to become housewives in order to stem societal collapse wrought by "cultural Marxism" (a conspiracy theory that left-wing academics and activists are deliberately working to undermine Western culture with progressive values). They employ humor and satire along with clickbait headlines for their videos to entice more viewers. By articulating far-right narratives via webcams in the early stage of the alt-right's presence on the internet, these women helped propel the alt-right to prominence while still remaining within the confines of their homes.

This book demonstrates that the rise of far-right women influencers is as much a story about social media as it is about the increasing visibility of the far right. YouTube's algorithmic structure, which personalizes recommendations for viewing content, and Instagram's recommendations of accounts to follow provide users a targeted experience on these platforms. As I researched this book, from late nights to holiday breaks, push notifications popped up on my phone to suggest that I follow accounts ranging from far-right figureheads such as Colin Robertson (known by his pseudonym "Millennial Woes") to the former *Fox News* commentator Tucker Carlson and on several occasions to then president Donald Trump. I found myself quickly immersed in a digital apparatus that consisted not just of alt-right but of extreme-right, white-supremacist, neo-Nazi, Islamophobic, anti-Semitic, and conspiracy theory content.

Social media have been shown to have a radicalizing effect, although among academics and experts it remains contested as to how significant a role they actually play in an individual's radicalization experience. In a systematic review of the literature on online radicalization, the media scholars Alice Marwick, Benjamin Clancy, and Katherine Furl note that "the internet does not cause radicalization, but it helps spread extremist ideas, enables people interested in these ideas to form communities, and mainstreams conspiracy theories and distrust in institutions."[5] As has happened to anyone sucked into the YouTube vortex, watching one influencer's YouTube video instantly exposed me to related content on a multitude of far-right channels just a click away. I found myself in a digital rabbit hole where ideas about the demographic replacement of white people by Muslim immigrants and Western civilizational superiority were the norm.

But it's not just the search and recommendation algorithms that make social media platforms addicting and potentially dangerous. In fact, it is unlikely that an individual will simply stumble across these influencers through algorithms alone. Rather, I argue that these women influencers are effectively appropriating genres and practices of preexisting digital cultures—for example, self-help, food vlogging, and homemaking—as a vital means to retain followers and appeal to wide audiences. Through this practice of relatability, they are able to cultivate their personal brands within online spaces and foster a specific social and cultural identity that makes them immediately identifiable based on their political stances. As measured by views and subscriptions, their celebrity status on their YouTube channels—often featuring guest collaborations ("collabs" for short) on one another's channels—results in what media and communication scholars describe as *parasocial relationships*. Parasocial relationships are one-sided relationships in which fans feel as if they intimately know and are close to a celebrity after prolonged exposure. But whereas parasocial interactions usually consist of fans developing illusions of intimacy with the celebrity, here in the case of far-right women influencers the fandom culture transforms into a community where influencers respond to fans, while fans, in turn, participate in helping to shape influencer content via comments and likes. This type of performative ecology should not be confused with real authenticity, however; it is a deliberate strategy to gain followers even if the influencers frame it as genuine. As Tama Leaver, Tim Highfield, and Crystal Abidin importantly note about the nature of Instagram influencers, "Authenticity has become less of a static quality and more of a performative ecology and parasocial strategy with its own bona fide genre and self-presentation elements."[6]

On the nature of being a far-right influencer, Rebecca Hargraves (also known by her pseudonym "Blonde in the Belly of the Beast") stated in September 2018, "[We] aren't carefully crafted and curated. . . . We're real people, average people." She was placing herself in the same camp as her viewers, real people who "have been on a genuinely revelatory journey of understanding ourselves and the lies we've been told by [leftists]. We represent hundreds of millions of dejected and downtrodden Westerners that are being displaced and that are in danger of being silenced, just as you are trying to silence us right now."[7]

As I sunk down the rabbit hole, I saw this fine line between normalcy and extreme political beliefs displayed by influencers on a daily basis. Alongside Instagram photos of cuddling with puppies and perfectly manicured nails were screenshots of tabloid newspaper headlines about the sexual-grooming activities of Muslim gangs in the United Kingdom. Photos were shared in real time from far-right political rallies in Dresden and Chemnitz, Germany, in 2017 and 2018, respectively (the latter resulted in violence) as well as from antilockdown protests during the COVID-19 pandemic. I saw recipes for homemade berry jam in my Instagram feed next to selfies with armed Bulgarian militia groups carrying out border patrols to detain crossing refugees.

These far-right women influencers are adept at merging banal and political messages in everyday life. Captions such as "red lipstick nationalism"[8] and the hashtags #motd (makeup of the day) and #ootd (outfit of the day) are used in posts to announce new YouTube videos that promote the idea that a woman's sole purpose in dating in her early twenties should be for a heterosexual marriage. A post of a glamour shot taken on a boat in the Mediterranean Sea is captioned by a satirical comment about the media editing out photos of drowning migrants. Selfies taken using the "OK" hand gesture proliferated after its adoption by white supremacists in online memes and images, leading to its being listed as a symbol of hate by the American Jewish civil rights organization the Anti-Defamation League.[9]

I argue that not only the content created by these influencers can spur radicalization but also the easy access to these influencers. Gone are the days of infiltrating closed chat rooms via a computer and a virtual private network; now one only need follow or subscribe to an influencer through a phone app. This ease of accessibility makes the modern far-right strategy of recruitment and retention powerful. Access isn't just limited to social media networking platforms, either. There exists a vast underground of far-right commercial spaces: dating sites, merchandise-selling sites, cooking blogs, even a white-supremacist-owned coffee company.[10] Far-right figures also produce podcasts and books, which are promoted by fellow influencers who invite the authors to appear on interviews or who provide reviews on their channels. This book explores the vast ecosystem of far-right entrepreneurism as it intersects with social media influencer culture.

The impact of female leaders in the far right can be more insidious than most people realize. In 2020, the trial was underway of Philip Manshaus, a twenty-two-year-old Norwegian man who had murdered his adopted stepsister from China and attempted a mosque shooting outside Oslo the previous year. Manshaus entered the courtroom and immediately gave a Nazi salute. It was revealed during court testimony that Manshaus holds National Socialist views in addition to beliefs in conspiracy theories and was inspired by the Christchurch terrorist attack in New Zealand a few months earlier.

What was left underreported in the media coverage of the trial is that Manshaus was also an avid viewer of Red Ice TV, a white-nationalist media outlet cofounded by Lana Lokteff and her Swedish husband, Henrik Palmgren. According to Cathrine Thorleifsson, an anthropologist of the far right, Manshaus "framed homosexuality as deviant and wanted to preserve the purity of the white race anchored in conservative Christian values and way of life. His goal was to find a wife and form a family to preserve the future of the white race."[11] In the weeks leading up to the attack, Manshaus became obsessed with finding a wife, having children, and settling down in a rural homestead with the aim to increase white birth rates in the West.[12]

We need to take seriously the potentially dangerous effects of these far-right women influencers as much as we do male right-wing terrorists. Although it is easy to spot the deadly consequences of terrorism, there's something much more sinister about how these women can appeal to young men and women to join their movement.

When the leading far-right figure Ayla Stewart satirically called for a "white baby challenge" on Twitter in mid-2018, she claimed that attention needed to be paid to the fact that "in 300 years, demographically, there will be no more white people. Our birth rates are so low such that there will not be any more white people. White people need to get on with having more white babies if we want to continue on with the legacy that our ancestors have handed onto to us."[13] When the Canadian YouTuber Lauren Chen made a video entitled "The Need to Breed: Falling Birth Rates in the West" in 2018, she cited humans' base biological imperative to reproduce and their duty to society to "preserve our culture, our Western Judeo-Christian, freedom-loving culture."[14] Such narratives of pending demographic replacement are prevalent among the far right, but their articulation by soft-spoken female voices provides a normalizing effect for the message—a strategy with a deep legacy for the far right.

As the journalist Seyward Darby writes in *Sisters in Hate* (2020), a book based on the lives of three women of the far right, "Women have been in backrooms and classrooms, chat rooms and newsrooms, boardrooms and bedrooms. Far from being incidental to white nationalism, they are a sustaining feature."[15] This book shows the integral roles such women play in promoting the contemporary far right.

Researchers of the far right often remain distant from the people they study. But "if we stand too far back from racist groups and fail to look carefully at the women and men in organized racism, we are likely to draw politically misleading conclusions," writes the sociologist Kathleen Blee. "Superficial studies simply caricature racist activists and make organized racism a foil against which we see ourselves as righteous and tolerant."[16]

With this book, I aim to challenge the misrepresentations and common assumptions about women in the far right, not only in terms of who they are, what they do, and how they act but also in terms of how those factors inform our response. For three years, I immersed myself in the world of far-right women influencers, becoming a follower, subscriber, and viewer. I wanted to experience the minutiae of their digital selves in real time, whether they were announcing a pregnancy or a new book or talking explicitly about saving the white race.

Entering the world of these influencers in pursuit of understanding them and their mindset was totally consuming. At one point, when Brittany Sellner's Instagram profile was suspended, I quickly searched all her social media accounts to see if she mentioned her Instagram profile being down. Had Instagram finally taken the step, as other mainstream social media platforms had done, of suspending or censoring her profile? Or had Brittany recognized the fake profile I had created as a follower and consequently blocked me? A few months later, I logged onto my fake Instagram profile and saw that Brittany's account had been restored. Her most recent post revealed that her account had been suspended for three months because she had mentioned her husband, Martin Sellner, leader of the Austrian branch of the far-right Identitarian movement, and posted photos of him.[17]

The ephemeral nature of social media material is a specific challenge. In academia, we are used to negotiating routes of access. The process of gathering data from our informants can be tricky, and we must abide by strict ethical guidelines to protect anonymity and confidentiality. I had to go through a months-long process to secure ethical approval from the national ethics review board before I could begin any data collection on these influencers. Although the high standards of academic-ethics approval can be frustrating to meet, such guidelines are rigorous to help establish scholars' credibility. They ensure that future research will be carried out in nonmanipulative ways. The process took unusually long because I, unlike most academic researchers, was not securing informed consent from the women I was studying—even though all the information I was accessing was publicly available. I would instead be "lurking"—watching YouTube videos and gazing at Instagram posts rather than interacting directly with my informants. The primary methodological approach I used to study the influencers in this book was digital ethnography. I immersed myself in their daily digital lives and became embedded in an online culture with its own distinct vocabulary, humor, and sarcasm as well as its own visual presentation and aesthetics. To supplement my digital ethnographic findings, I also interviewed experts (e.g., academics, counterextremism practitioners) to gain a better understanding of various aspects of that culture, ranging from female-supported misogyny to far-right fashion and clothing to their experiences of online governance and regulation used to counter the far right. In addition, I interviewed a so-called former supporter of the alt-right who had been radicalized and was now undergoing a deradicalization journey.

By making the case that I could easily lose access, get blocked, or, worse, become a target for far-right harassment if discovered, I was eventually able to get my research approved by the ethics board without needing consent from the influencers I was studying. Many people have asked me if I have interviewed these far-right women.

My answer is always the same: no, but I don't have to. They have already revealed their life stories online, and I doubt that I would solicit anything new from trying to interview them about their backgrounds. Instead, this book analyzes how they present themselves to their online *audiences*. These far-right women have chosen to be public figures. This *publicness*, I argue, is key. It is a strategy of branding oneself while still promoting a political movement.

Over time, tracking these influencers gradually began to feel personal. Studying this world meant taking an active part in it, being a part of it. It meant getting notifications on my personal phone to follow accounts I had connected to using my fake profile. And having a fake profile meant posting the occasional photo taken from my real life in order to seem active. Being able to distinguish between my "real" online identity and my "fake" one became increasingly difficult throughout the research process. There were also times when I was relating to these women in the most unexpected ways. Like Brittany, I love really spicy Thai cuisine. (I was definitely not expecting this answer from her during an AMA, or "ask me anything," vlog.)[18] I soon discovered that Lauren Chen is a *hapa*, a term used to describe someone with mixed East Asian and white heritage, the same as my ethnic background. When Rebecca Hargraves described growing up in an affluent school district in an American suburb with predominately white and East Asian upper-middle-class families, it struck me that we could easily have been classmates.[19] All of these small details led me to see our common attributes as they shared their life stories on social media.

Despite our clear political differences, I felt a relatable connection to some of these women and an interest in continuing to follow them. In part, I was facing the same life obstacles at the same time as they were: all of us were young adult women seeking to find our voice and identity, to assert ourselves, to feel empowered and valued (paradoxically feminist goals for them). Although we had different pursuits, their stories of self-fulfillment and accomplishment were a common bond between us. Even as someone who can spot the signs of radicalization, I found it easy to become absorbed in these women's world. And here lies the crux of the problem: these influencers are integral to normalizing the far right in the twenty-first century through their visible social media performances.

In the following pages, I detail the all-encompassing nature of my three-year journey following far-right women influencers. At all hours of the day, I would receive notifications on my phone alerting me of their new Instagram posts, including Instagram Stories that required that I view them within twenty-four hours or else risk missing material for data collection. On some days, I would spend hours watching back-to-back YouTube videos recommended by Google's algorithm. The influencers presented themselves as relatable and accessible women who documented the most mundane aspects of their everyday lives, but they subtly (or sometimes explicitly) infused these moments with far-right propaganda.

This book traces a narrative of the lives of far-right women influencers. It starts with a puzzle in chapter 1: Why are women involved in the far right, and what exactly was the alt-right? Understanding the roles that women play in far-right movements requires unpacking the history of their contributions to racist and white-supremacist organizations. The alt-right was just the latest iteration of this legacy, repackaged for millennial audiences. The remaining chapters of this book look through the lens of the experiences of someone who joins the far right: first the recruitment to radicalization (chapters 2 and 3), followed by group-building propaganda (chapters 4, 5, and 6), and, finally, countering the far right (chapter 7) and scenarios of exiting that world (conclusion). This narrative arc is bolstered by insights into the influencers' backgrounds to signify their steps in this process.

In chapter 2, I argue that part of what made the alt-right (as a representative of the contemporary far right) so successful is that it relied on social media to recruit and radicalize followers. Some special platforms were created by and for alt-right supporters, but most of the adherents depended on mainstream sites such as You-Tube and Instagram. I show how the influencers featured in this book have entirely amassed their audience through the latter, contending that mainstream platforms provide opportunities for exposure and amplification to project far-right messages for widespread appeal.

Chapter 3 explores the core of recruitment and radicalization efforts through their tailored approaches to both men and women. Most noteworthy is an intense focus on antifeminism as these influencers devote hours of content discussing the degrading consequences of feminism on modern society and advocate for a return to traditional gender roles based on femininity and masculinity. An important consequence of this worldview is that young women are expected to become wives and mothers as their duty to further the cause, which I expand on in chapter 4. Given this central emphasis on domesticity, some women in the far right have overlapping ties with other online communities, such as tradwives (short for "traditional wives"), which presents a slippery slope for the visibility of far-right propaganda.

In chapter 5, I highlight that far-right entrepreneurism serves to build in-group identity by selling merchandise and profiting off commercial products and services. Far more lucrative, however, is how they gain income revenue from sponsors and advertisers directly by means of social media platforms' financial models. As markets have expanded, so too have global connections. Chapter 6 contends that the far right is becoming not only more mainstream but also more global. These influencers have gained recognition abroad for their political commentary and activism, ranging from protesting in the streets to filming documentaries based on current events. Their impact surpasses the early days of webcam vlogging. At the same time, far-right women internationally have contributed to the movement's global reach and present the new, younger faces of activism.

In chapter 7, I discuss approaches to counter the far right, both online and offline, in the hope that we can develop better collective solutions that place human dignity and rights at the core of our responses. A joint effort among tech companies, governments, and civil society must attend to the ways in which gender informs different avenues of engagement and participation both within the far right and in our responses to it. Finally, the conclusion considers whether exiting the far-right scene is, in fact, tenable for these influencers and the inherent paradoxes of women's participation in a political movement that devalues their involvement. It also reflects on the ethical dilemmas and risks of doing research on the far right as a field of study.

Ultimately, this book shows that far-right women are marketing themselves in their most authentic and accessible form while promoting a hateful ideology. This intimate and entrepreneurial strategy, when combined with far-right views, serves as an important recruitment, radicalization, and propaganda tactic with gendered dimensions. A central component of this success lies in the visibility afforded to these far-right women influencers on social media platforms, where the publicness of their influence is widely shared with and promoted to mainstream audiences.

1

THE ALT-RIGHT VERSUS
THE FAR RIGHT

T he nature of the [alt-right] movement is that you can't
define it, but you know it when you see it," stated the
Canadian YouTuber Lauren Chen in 2016.[1] There are few
books published about the alt-right, and even scholars who have
been researching the far right for decades are still somewhat at a
loss when it comes to specifically defining the alt-right.

The alt-right did not constitute a political party, nor was it an
organization with a formal membership list. It did not have designated leaders, although figures such as the white supremacist Richard Spencer and the British YouTuber Paul Joseph Watson emerged
as prominent voices. Much alt-right activity took place online, but
its effects emerged offline, as exemplified by the deadly Unite the
Right rally in Charlottesville, Virginia, in 2017.

Perhaps what makes defining the alt-right so elusive is that it
had no clear ideological agenda, unlike previous far-right organizations and groups that created a consolidated message through
pamphlets, manifestos, magazines, and other literary, audio, and
visual material. In this same vlog, Lauren pointed to two issues on
which alt-right supporters shared common views: they were against

third-wave feminism (and what she called "social justice warrior stuff"), and they were critical of Islam. Yet Lauren didn't think that these two issues were enough to qualify support for the alt-right because she believed many people supposedly share those views. Instead, she attributed the "focus on Western nationalism" as a core feature of the alt-right.

Lauren categorized the alt-right into four tiers of what she described as "increasing extremism." (As she elaborated her point, a music soundtrack reminiscent of the type used for cute baby or puppy videos played in the background.) Tier 1, according to her, is "Western nationalism," or those whom she described as "pro-Western but not pro-white," because although race does play a role in this tier, it is apparently not the central focus. For Lauren, "there are a number of nonwhite people who identify with the alt-right," given that, she claimed, "it's not a racial issue. Instead, it's a social issue." People in this tier may be accepting of legal immigrants who "assimilate and contribute" to Western society. Lauren didn't specify what counts as assimilation or contribution by immigrants. Nor did she acknowledge that historical systems of immigration and citizenship were shaped by institutionalized racial policies in Western societies.

Tier 2 constitutes those who promote "pro-white nationalism" and "associate the West specifically with Caucasians." They believe that white nationalism isn't inherently racist because "taking pride in your own race and being proud of your own heritage doesn't mean you have to think other races are bad; you just happen to think your own race is fine." Here Lauren was falsely equating white pride with the identity politics of "social justice warriors" and describing the reaction of some in the alt-right who believe that progressivism has demonized white people and consequently see the need for "advocacy on behalf of Caucasians" in the name of all ethnicities being represented equally. This mindset is a reactionary backlash against the demand for recognition by minority communities who have faced systematic discrimination and are seeking equality and dignity.

Lauren then described tier 3 of the alt-right, or "racial homogeny and determinism," in which, it is argued, ethnicity should be a defining feature of who we are. She explained that people in this tier are "really into racial identity, almost like a tribalistic way." They desire racially homogenous societies and are against reproductive "race mixing." This attitude ties into the concept of racial determinism, which is the idea that race determines behavior based on genetics. Ultimately, it is the belief that race shapes a society's culture. Research, however, has discredited the idea that genetics solely determine behavior and points to social behavior as the most likely explanation for differences.[2]

Lauren concluded her vlog with a description of tier 4: "white supremacy and anti-Semitism." She admitted that "this is where everything you've heard about the alt-right being bad is true, at least in part." Those in tier 4 believe in racial determinism and take it a step further by advocating that "the white race is genetically superior to all others, and in their minds white cultures are better because white people are better." Spurred by eugenics, which became popularized with twentieth-century colonialism and imperialism, this theory holds that certain racial groups (specifically white European populations) are genetically superior; it has been debunked as scientific racism. Anti-Semitism within the far right is also quite prominent, ranging from disgruntlement about Jews being in positions of power to the belief that there exists, as Lauren described it, a "global Jewish conspiracy theory [sic] hell bent on world domination." This supposed conspiracy is frequently referred to by the name "Zionist Occupation Government," or ZOG.

Following these categorical descriptions, Lauren answered some anticipated questions from her viewers, such as "Is being alt-right the same as being right wing?" (short answer: "no") and "Where did the alt-right come from?" (more complicated answer: it is "a reactionary movement to the current antiwhite, antimale, anti-Western propaganda that we've seen coming out of social justice activism"). As I discuss later, the alt-right had far deeper roots in previous far-right organizations. Importantly, Lauren stressed a few times during the video—as well as in the description box—that despite what some on social media might label her, she did not identify as being part of the alt-right but was merely interested in it. Yet as I show throughout the book, "being part of" versus being "interested in" the alt-right is a slippery slope.

Lauren's own category definitions highlight that the alt-right was complex and widespread, with diverging and at times conflicting ideological beliefs. But it was precisely these gray areas that provided an effective means for those either to be "in" or "out" of the movement. The influencer Ayla Stewart (known by her pseudonym "Wife with a Purpose") described in 2018 how at one point she was part of the alt-right but then no longer identified with it after an incident involving Richard Spencer claiming that Easter is a pagan holiday.[3] A devout Mormon, Ayla was personally offended based on her religious beliefs and thereafter stopped using the label *alt-right* by association. Yet today Ayla continues to believe in alt-right principles, and her preference for racial self-determination could be considered to fall within tier 3, according to Lauren's classification system. Others, such as the Canadian influencer Robyn Riley, have always rejected the label *alt-right*. She instead self-describes as "right-wing," although her content suggests otherwise, with frequent allusions to race tribalism and reverence toward Western civilization.

Lauren's claim that she wasn't part of the alt-right is somewhat true. Most of her views fall more on the conservative than the far-right end of the political left–right spectrum. By criticizing third-wave feminism and the politically correct, or PC, left and advocating for traditional gender norms, Lauren occupies the liminal space between alt-right and her preferred label: *conservative*. However, for others such as Rebecca Hargraves and Robyn Riley, identifying as a conservative includes spewing overt white nationalism. Herein lies the difference between women in the far right and the women of mainstream conservatism, according to the sociologist Kathleen Blee: "[The distinction between the former and the latter] is not [the former's] conclusion that the family is dying but their choice of the party responsible for its downfall."[4] Yet although Lauren may have chosen not to self-identify as alt-right, several of the views she advocates for can be easily placed within her definition of tier 1. She has created several videos arguing that "Muslims do not share Western values, especially when it comes to women" and similarly accused migrants of the 2015 "refugee crisis" of raping European women.[5] Adhering to prevalent narratives within the far right, Lauren holds Muslims and the political establishment—that is, "enemies"—responsible for the downfall of the heterosexual family and Western (white) society.

Further, Lauren has argued that migrants should be assessed not just on their skills but also on "the culture where they're from";[6] this was her response to the United Nations (UN)—which she views as an international body having "anti-Western, globalist sentiments"—urging Canada to take in more asylum seekers. The term *globalist* is a far-right dog whistle used to refer to the so-called ZOG conspiracy, in which Jews are allegedly on a crusade to destroy Christian civilization with the aid of the political left and racial and sexual minorities. Whether Lauren intended its usage in this manner is unclear, but it indicates how deeply the slur has spread from the far right into wider conservative circles.[7] Relatedly, Lauren has vlogged with a poster in the background displaying the words "#FreeTommy," a campaign created by the alt-right in response to the imprisonment in 2018 of Tommy Robinson, a former leader of the anti-Muslim organization English Defence League, which again shows the gray boundary between conservatism and the far right.

I argue that the best way to characterize the alt-right is by distinguishing it as a *movement*. This characterization accommodates figures such as Lauren Chen and Ayla Stewart as occupying different positions on a wide spectrum. More specifically, the alt-right was a loose coalition of supporters that functioned largely without a membership list, was based online, and had a transatlantic geographical reach. Regarding the last characteristic, some would consider that the alt-right was by and large an American phenomenon. However, the extremism researcher J. M. Berger counters this claim by showing that the alt-right's online presence, although American in origin, quickly spread into an international network.[8]

So how does the alt-right compare to previous and current far-right movements? Is ideological ambiguity unique to the alt-right? What about its organizational structure? I turn to past research on the far right and specifically on the roles of women in these movements before providing some reflections on what makes the alt-right distinct within the broader far-right landscape. To clarify, I take the alt-right as a starting point to situate the origins of the far-right women influencers featured in this book, many of whom rose to prominence as thought commentators and activists within the alt-right. Although the alt-right is now largely defunct, it represents a time in which far-right politics gained increasing resonance within the United States and the United Kingdom and was spearheaded by digital activism on platforms such as YouTube, Twitter, and Facebook. The burgeoning popularity of the alt-right can be attributed to its growth as a cultural movement, which intersected with mainstream conservative politics to propel it into visibility. These far-right women influencers can thus be considered both alt-right and far right in the sense that their political careers originated in the alt-right, but their ideologies represent the broader contemporary far-right movement.

Altright.com was founded in 2017 by the white nationalist Richard Spencer, who claims to have coined the term *alt-right* (an abbreviation of *alternative right*) in 2008.[9] An earlier version of altright.com appeared in 2010 when Spencer launched *The Alternative Right* webzine. Spencer has long been active in far-right politics, particularly through his role as president of the National Policy Institute, a think tank based in Virginia that pushes a white-supremacist agenda, which is clear in its motto: "For our people, our culture, our future." Along with Spencer, the website was cofounded by Daniel Friberg, a leading figure within the Swedish far-right scene and owner of the publishing house Arktos Media. The alt-right's aim was to serve as an umbrella movement for a wide range of far-right adherents, popularized following Donald Trump's presidential election victory in 2016. It is important to note the close temporal relationship between the alt-right and Trump's ascent to the White House, which brought the alt-right into mainstream visibility. Toward the end of the Trump presidency, the alt-right movement largely fell apart into various factions and gave rise to a vast network of alternative groups such as antigovernment extremists, militia and sovereign citizens, QAnon, the Proud Boys, and online trolls. Together, these groups would take part in the insurrection at the U.S. Capitol on January 6, 2021. Thus, whereas the alt-right was a phenomenon that dominated North American far-right politics from 2016 to 2019, the contemporary far-right milieu persists in various mutations. Nonetheless, understanding what the alt-right was and why it became successful can help us understand the context in which the women influencers in this book operated and that jump-started their political activism.

Soon after the term *alt-right* started circulating in media headlines, books about the alt-right tried to diagnose this new phenomenon. In *Making Sense of the Alt-Right* (2017), the political scientist George Hawley describes it as fundamentally racist as well as "atomized, amorphous, predominately online, and mostly anonymous." Others are more skeptical of the label *alt-right*, such as the sociologist Kathleen Blee: "My concern is that the term *alt-right* has been part of the rebranding effort here in the U.S.," she told me, "in which groups like Identity Evropa [later known as American Identity Movement] have sought to distance themselves from the ideas of Nazism and the Ku Klux Klan in public, while embracing those ideas in private spaces."[10] Members of the American Identity Movement, for instance, stormed Politics and Prose bookstore in Washington, DC, during Jonathan Metzl's book talk for *Dying of Whiteness: How the Politics of Racial Resentment Is Killing America's Heartland* (2019). These white-nationalist protestors stormed the reading and chanted, "This land is our land," before taking off.[11] Patrick Casey, the leader of

American Identity Movement, parted ways with Richard Spencer in 2017, which caused a fissure in the movement. Casey had also previously worked for Red Ice TV, co-owned by Lana Lokteff. In November 2020, he announced that American Identity Movement had been dissolved and was undergoing "strategic reorientation."[12] By then, Casey had become a leading figure for the new online coalition Groypers, or Groyper Army, which promotes an "America First" white-nationalist agenda.[13] Casey's story illustrates that several internal factions operate within the mutating American far-right scene, and the alt-right was often used as an identifier because it lacked a toxic group history. In reality, the alt-right built upon the legacy of far-right politics but was rebranded under a new label, as Blee points out.

The term *alt-right* is controversial, not least because it was used to legitimize white supremacism and neo-Nazism under a much more acceptable umbrella term; some would also self-identify as the "dissident right." It is why experts of the far right are cautious to label organizations according to how their members view themselves. For instance, if individuals call themselves "nationalists," do they belong to a nationalist rather than a far-right organization? Throughout this book, then, I acknowledge that the term *alt-right* is problematic and contextualize it as part of the modern far-right landscape. I use *alt-right* specifically when referring to a particular time and place—namely, the dominant far-right political scene in North America approximately from 2016 to 2019—or when referring to a particular person known for their de facto leadership in the alt-right, such as Richard Spencer. Otherwise, I generally use the term *far right* to signify ideological beliefs and practices that remain constant within this milieu.

I classify the alt-right as a *reactionary* movement, with the core of this reaction as the reproduction of far-right ideology. Far-right ideology includes three elements: nativism, extreme nationalism, and authoritarianism. *Nativism* is the idea that people "native" to a land have a right to claim its territory; the irony here, of course, is that white European settlers are not native to North America. *Extreme nationalism* refers to the idea that nations should be constituted by ethnicity (ethnic nationalism) or sometimes by culture (cultural nationalism). The boundary between ethnic nationalism and cultural nationalism isn't clear-cut, and far-right organizations often use the latter as a strategic ploy to seem more legitimate to an external audience. Finally, *authoritarianism* is about maintaining the status quo and social hierarchy (i.e., white/Western political and economic dominance) through law and order. These three elements, when combined, characterize almost all far-right movements.

A brief note on the term *populism* is apropos here because it is frequently used adjacent to and sometimes as a substitute for *far right*. Scholars define *populism* as fitting into two camps. The first camp advocates what the political scientist Cas Mudde calls a "thin ideology" of "the pure people" versus "the corrupt elite" and of politics representing the general will of the people. It is a thin ideology because it depends on a "thicker" ideology, such as nationalism, to function.[14] According to this definition, populism can manifest on both the political left and the political right. Left-wing populists—such as Senator Bernie Sanders and Congresswoman Alexandria Ocasio-Cortez—view corporations and big-business-friendly politicians as the corrupt elite and the pure people as the working class and marginalized communities. Right-wing populists, in contrast, view the political and (mainstream) media establishments as the corrupt elite due to their supposed leftist orientation and the pure people as composed of "native" inhabitants. Right-wing populists use buzzwords such as *our history* and *our heritage* to signal their disapproval of leftist politicians and media figures who advocate for multiculturalism, which the populists view as destroying "our" ("native" or white) culture. Former U.S. president Donald Trump and Congresswoman Marjorie Taylor Greene are notable right-wing populists. The second camp defines populism as a style, such as charismatic leaders who seem more "authentic."[15] Trump might once again come to mind as fitting this description, but others such as the former president of Brazil, Jair Bolsonaro, and the prime minister of Italy, Giorgia Meloni, are also ideal examples. The term *populism* is often used as a placeholder to describe the far right, which results in confusion for most people. Similarly, the terms *Nazi* and *fascist* are also littered across many media articles about the far right, but these categories are more specific to organizations stemming from a historical period (albeit periodization of fascism is open to interpretation).[16]

More recently, contemporary far-right actors focus on anti-Islam and antifeminism as paradigmatic issues. As the sociologist Hilary Pilkington writes about current trends in the British far right, "While a highly conservative understanding of gender roles and concern with the reproduction of the 'native' population, typical of classic extreme parties, might alienate women, the framing of anti-Islam ideology and the protection of western traditions of gender equality and LGBT rights might extend some appeal."[17] In the past decade, a few far-right parties have visibly promoted women and/ or LGBTQ+ individuals in an effort to appear more legitimate and less toxic to a mainstream audience. Take, for instance, the former leader of the National Rally party in France, Marine Le Pen, or the openly gay leader of Alternative for Germany, Alice Weidel, both of whom have argued that Islam is a threat to Western civilization because it is oppressive toward women compared to the West's (supposed) gender equality.

The sociologist Sara Farris calls this new shift in discourse "femonationalism": the association between the far right and certain feminists on the shared basis of anti-Islam and anti-Muslim sentiments.[18] This alliance promotes a discourse of women's rights and gender equality in comparison to Muslim women's oppression by and their need to be "saved" from Muslim men. The far right uses these gender-equality claims to justify their racist agenda, distracting outsiders from their deeply misogynist and patriarchal culture.

Similarly, the far right engages in what Jasbir Puar calls "homonationalism," or the use of nominal LGBTQ+ rights, to promote racist and xenophobic positions, especially against Islam, which is portrayed as homophobic and intolerant.[19] The gay Dutch politician Pim Fortuyn put forth this argument against immigration and multiculturalism in the 1990s and early 2000s. Homonationalism has more recently been vocalized by the British far-right lesbian activist Anne Marie Waters, who is also founder of an organization called Sharia Watch UK. Yet, despite such claims, the far right remains overwhelmingly committed to heterosexuality and sees people within the LGBTQ+ community as perverted and LGBTQ+ rights as secondary to the promotion of male–female romantic relationships.

In her study of women and LGBTQ+ supporters of the English Defence League, the far-right grassroots movement founded by Tommy Robinson (real name Stephen Yaxley-Lennon), Pilkington finds that despite the group's appeals to these minorities, displays of masculinity and heterosexuality continue to be the default.[20] Sexism and double standards against women are prevalent in the group, and its members express rampant homophobia despite the official group message. Discriminatory behavior experienced by women and LGBTQ+ members is often overlooked or considered trivial. Rather than promoting gender equality and LGBTQ+ rights, these far-right activists are exploiting such issues as women's and gay rights to "defend" themselves against the "real" enemy—Islam.

Although femonationalism and homonationalism are trends seen in the European far right, at least within populist far-right parties, they are rare within the North American far right. The American alt-right, compared to its European counterparts, was much more conservative on social issues relating to gender and sexuality. With the minor exception of gay celebrities such as Milo Yiannopolous, the alt-right was predominantly homophobic and transphobic. The far-right women influencers featured in this book, for example, would never consider a same-sex marriage to be morally acceptable—they discuss only heterosexual relationships.

Concerning femonationalism, the alt-right did promote the idea that Muslim women are oppressed by Muslim men and that respect for women is solely a Western value. This false narrative, however, was not created out of the alt-right's association with feminists. When Lauren Southern confronted participants at a march to end violence against women in the United Kingdom in late 2017, she asked them, "Would you rather have women's rights or Islam?" All of the respondents looked at her puzzled, and many became angry, asking why she would pose such a ridiculous question and accusing her of being ignorant. Out of the dozens filmed, only one older woman replied, "Women's rights."[21] If the women at this rally are representative, only a minuscule number of feminists would align with the alt-right on gender equality in uniting against Islam.

In another instance, the influencer Robyn Riley shared an Instagram Story of a Twitter screenshot of findings from a study, supposedly "independent analysis," conducted in Sweden on "the demographics of sexual assault & rape" showing that "men of non-European origin commit 84% of 'serious' rapes despite only making up around 10% of the population." The study, conducted by an amateur researcher who identifies with the far-right Sweden Democrats party, makes false claims that "Africans are most likely [to] commit rape, whereas Middle Eastern/North Africans are more likely to commit aggravated rape." Robyn responded to this unreliable study: "Feminists who shriek about rape culture but leave this out are cowards and morons."[22] Not only did she believe the heavily biased study to be true, but she also criticized feminists for permitting what she called "rape culture" perpetuated by Muslim men.

Indeed, negative representations of Islam are rife across the media produced by these influencers. Lauren Chen warned feminists, "Guess who doesn't like the child-free lifestyle? Islamic cultures who, by the way, are not so friendly towards women's rights." By claiming that Islamic cultures are oppressive toward women—a false dichotomy because Christian cultures have subjugated women throughout history—she was partaking in the fearmongering that if the West does not see an increase in birth rates, a Muslim invasion is imminent. "If no one is breeding and we have to import migrants, that affects everybody. If I'm someone who holds Western values dear, which I do, and everyone who has Western values all of a sudden stops breeding, this new ideology comes in and takes over, that affects me."[23] She also seemed to be implying that if feminists don't wake up, they'll soon find themselves oppressed by Muslim men. This "new ideology" she referred to is Islam in the form of Muslim migrants. It's clear that Lauren was supporting a xenophobic, racist political agenda and that, overall, the antifeminist stance of the alt-right surpassed any potential alliances with feminists over concerns of the perceived threat of Islam.

Finally, the alt-right had close ideological and organizational overlaps with its European equivalent, the Identitarian movement, also known as Generation Identity. The Identitarian movement mobilizes primarily as street-based activism, especially on-the-ground protests, although it heavily relies on social media to recruit young people and circulate campaign propaganda.[24] Modern-day Identitarians descend from a far-right intellectual movement of the 1960s known as the Nouvelle Droite (New Right), which channeled its ethnonationalist ideas through the French think tank Groupement de recherche et d'études pour la civilisation européenne, or GRECE (Research and Study Group for European Civilization). GRECE intellectuals developed and advocated the concept of ethnopluralism, or the idea that territorial regions should be separated and inhabited only by ethnic groups "native" to that region—in other words, that Europe exclusively belongs to "white" Europeans, and so non-European (nonwhite) immigrants should be repatriated.

To achieve popular support for their ideas, the Nouvelle Droite and GRECE favored a strategy of metapolitics—cultivating long-term social and cultural acceptance of its ideology in society—rather than seeking to enact change primarily through elections and political parties. Today, the Identitarian movement promotes a pan-European nationalist identity, following the intellectual legacy of its parent organization. There are thus several similarities between the alt-right and Identitarian movements with regard to ideology and the goals of metapolitical activism (discussed in chapter 6).

In reproducing far-right ideology, the alt-right was not unique in terms of its ideas, but it offered an opportunity for a subset of individuals to gain notoriety: women and even, ironically, women of color.

For years, scholars have been addressing the misconceptions that most of us hold about people involved in far-right groups. Although they are often depicted in the media and elsewhere as uneducated, lower class, and ignorant, the reality is that many people who join such groups are quite the opposite. Although some join as disaffected youth, members also often come from wealthy suburbs and middle-class families.[25]

Much like men, women who become involved may not have pre-existing ideological beliefs that fit within the far-right worldview of these organizations. Rather, they can develop such views *after* joining and associating with these groups. In *Inside Organized Racism* (2002), a pioneering study of women in extreme-right and white-supremacist organizations in the United States, such as the Ku Klux Klan, Kathleen Blee provides a glimpse into their everyday lives. She details how these women are recruited into and remain within these organizations. In many ways, my exploration of the world of far-right women influencers echoes Blee's findings from two decades ago. There are ideological echoes when Blee writes that these women described having "been stripped of their culture, heritage, history and pride."[26] These words appear again and again among the far-right women influencers I discuss. As Brittany Sellner explained in mid-2019, "I simply believe that everyone has a right to cherish and preserve their own homelands, ethnicities, and cultures."[27] For Rebecca Hargraves, "pride" and "a deep-lasting reverence and loyalty to Western civilization" are paramount.[28] Robyn Riley, meanwhile, regularly posts Instagram photos of European sculptures and buildings with captions such as "Europe belongs to Europeans," "The West is decaying before our eyes," and "Never apologize for who you are or where you came from."[29]

Other demographic aspects have also remained very much the same over the past twenty years: most of these women are educated, are not poor, were not raised in abusive families, and, perhaps most importantly, did not follow a man into the far-right movement.[30] The last point is especially pertinent for understanding women in the far right today. For example, the prominent influencer Brittany Sellner is married to the leader of the Austrian branch of the Identitarian movement, Martin Sellner, but, importantly, became involved in political activism before she met Martin. One figure whom Brittany cites as a source of inspiration is her father, who has long been active in right-wing politics, at one point even ran for governor of Kansas.[31]

Others, such as the Canadian influencers Lauren Southern and Robyn Riley, likewise credit their fathers as role models. In 2016, Lauren described her "phenomenal father" as "one of the biggest influences in my life,"[32] while Robyn reignited a closer relationship with her politically conservative father as she became more receptive to the alt-right in 2016.[33] Although their fathers are not part of the far right per se, they lean right, and this initiated the women's interest in conservative politics. Although Robyn doesn't divulge much information about her Slovenian husband, she does indicate that he supports far-right ideas by revealing that he is knowledgeable about the deceased philosopher Julius Evola, a major intellectual influence on European neofascism.[34] Notably, most of these far-right women cite becoming initially interested in politics through watching male figures online (see chapter 2).

Personal aspirations can play an important role, too. The journalist Seyward Darby describes Ayla Stewart as "a seeker": "Throughout her life, Ayla had been in zealous pursuit of meaning; [the far right] was just her latest aspiration." Lana Lokteff, in contrast, is an opportunist seduced by power and influence. "She is a stage manager as much as she is a performer. She dictates what her audiences see, and she doesn't want anyone to peek behind the curtain,"[35] Darby noted when she tried to get access to Lana's private life. Lana prefers to control the narrative, to play the game, rather than provide an unfiltered picture.

Another prominent figure within the far right who has appeared on Lana's podcast is Michelle Malkin, an Asian American woman descended from Filipino immigrants. Michelle is a well-known conservative journalist and author who made regular appearances on *Fox News* but slowly began transitioning from the Republican establishment spotlight to the extreme right. In addition to publicizing her anti-immigration and Islamophobic views, she stirred controversy when in 2020 she openly aligned with Holocaust deniers (Groypers), which led to mainstream conservative organizations disavowing her.[36] Soon after that, Michelle appeared on Lana's show, where she described the "demographic demise" within the United States as being the result of open immigration, which is causing "multicultural rot" and "white guilt, which is plied every single day in every cultural Marxist, leftist institution." She used catchphrases commonly found within far-right conspiracy theories. She asserted that "there's nothing wrong with—and I don't apologize as somebody who has nonwhite skin—defending the idea that America should maintain its historic demographic balance."[37] In other words, Michelle believes that white nationalism should be the foundation of the United States—a view that is clearly antithetical to her own family origin. An interesting aspect of their conversation was that Lana repeatedly identified Michelle as "Asian," whereas Michelle called herself "American." So although far-right figures such as Lana claim that they are open to nonwhite nationalists, their language and behavior reveals otherwise.

Similarly, Lauren Chen, who was born in Canada and raised in Hong Kong before moving to the United States to attend university, grew up in multiracial and multicultural environments and leverages her biracial identity to speak out without fear of being called a racist. She has been criticized as a "token minority," a term used to describe the lone person of a different racial minority in an otherwise (white) homogenous group of people. So-called token minorities are often used politically to represent the ideas or interests of a group of people based on their race.

Lauren has spoken explicitly on the topic of tokenism, describing it as a category that "as a biracial conservative woman, I even fit into." She explained in 2018 that "in the eyes of the left, token minorities are just pawns that conservatives use as a facade of tolerance. And they're the political equivalent of 'I can't be racist, I have a black friend!'" She tried to point out the problem with this logic: "What that actually means is that the views or arguments of these token minorities don't actually need to be taken seriously."[38] Rather than taking into consideration the arguments of token minorities, Lauren argued, the political left is more focused on aspects of their race, gender, and so on. Hers is a strawman argument, however, because the main issue here is not phenotype versus the content of an argument. Rather, it is that people in such token minority positions are often manipulatively used by the political right to advance causes that have been historically exclusionary, and their recent inclusion is commonly symbolic, to avoid accusations of racism. The content of their arguments rarely deviates from established ideological talking points.

In this same vlog, "The Problem with 'Token Minorities,'" Lauren reflected on her personal experience in this area: "What has really shocked me is the number of people out there, these supposedly tolerant progressives, who have accused me of trying to impress white people and men with my views, as if they're not really my own." She argued that the real threat to the political left is that conservativism is not just for straight, white, old men. In fact, she claimed that "conservatism is spreading among young people, among women, among nonwhite voters—and they can't call all of us tokens right?" Yet she failed to recognize that the reason why people who look like her were only recently adopting this political ideology is that their participation was only recently permitted.

The political right has always had a small number of prominent figureheads who do not fall within the white, male demographic. Lauren and Michelle are just the latest iterations. However, they and people who look like them constantly need to justify their support for a political ideology that for most of its existence simultaneously excluded them from the picture and included them in the category of "inferior peoples." The fact that they *are* the exception points to, if anything, the argument that systemic racism is still a lingering issue in the political right. The promotion of spokespersons such as Lauren and Michelle in order to appear diverse helps build an image of legitimacy for the political right to avoid accusations of homogeneity. At the same time, it is crucial to point out that persons of color can and do support structures such as white supremacy if it promotes their self-interest.

That Lauren Chen does stand out from the other far-right women influencers on the issue of race and representation reveals some fissures within the far right at large. Compared to Ayla Stewart, Rebecca Hargraves, and even Michelle Malkin, who equate pride in Western civilization with white culture, Lauren sees libertarian ideals and values such as democracy and freedom of speech as defining the West. Yet these abstract notions originated in a context where they were not universally experienced by all people but rather enjoyed by a privileged few. It has taken centuries of continued political efforts by the marginalized to ensure their inclusion in the democratic process, and even today such marginalization persists.

Women have long contributed to far-right movements, spreading ideology and propaganda (see chapters 3 and 4), but the alt-right presented a unique moment for these women to capitalize on potential visibility. Along with shifting political dynamics starting in 2016, the increasing popularity of social media platforms for users to seek out information and commentary created a demand that political influencers could supply. Far-right women leveraged their position into public-facing roles.

The far right constantly needs to adopt new strategies in order to promote its old message: pour old wine into new bottles. I argue that what made the alt-right distinct from previous far-right movements was its emergence and evolution in parallel with technology—it was based almost entirely online.[39] Social media proliferation has been a gold mine in this regard. The nature of our social relationships, although still fundamentally face-to-face, has greatly altered since the rise of internet use. We communicate through messaging apps, learn new skills via video tutorials, discover topics on shared posts, and are entertained through streaming services.

Since the 1990s, the far right has been a pioneer in utilizing information and communication technologies to recruit and mobilize supporters.[40] Starting with Web 1.0 websites and online forums, such as the American neo-Nazi website Stormfront.org founded in 1996, the far right relied on these online spaces to spread propaganda and connect with like-minded individuals around the world. Blee noted this reliance in 2002: "Computer bulletin boards, chat rooms, and Internet websites are becoming increasingly popular ways to distribute racist propaganda."[41] Twenty years ago, networking online was still in its infancy, but now our daily lives revolve around social media use.

In the 2010s, with the rise of Web 2.0 embodied by social media, the far right quickly adopted mainstream platforms such as Facebook, Twitter, Reddit, and YouTube and later took advantage of the popularity of fringe platforms such as Gab (a microblogging Twitter-alternative site) and the imageboards 4chan and 8chan. The "chansphere" in particular became well known following the horrific Christchurch and El Paso terrorist attacks in 2019 when the shooters uploaded their manifestos onto 4chan and 8chan shortly before carrying out their attacks. On these sites, an online subculture rooted in glorifying violence, misogyny, and hate intermingled with extreme-right ideas. "As a creature born and raised on the internet, [the alt-right] values trolling and internet pranks not just as sideshows or light diversions, but as key forms of political action," writes the journalist Mike Wendling on the emergence of the alt-right on these platforms.[42]

More recently, the far right prefers chat apps such as Discord and Telegram to avoid detection by security services and law enforcement. In these messaging channels, more extreme content is being shared between users.[43] Discord was particularly instrumental in helping to mobilize and coordinate the Charlottesville rally in 2017, and Telegram became a major vector of communication leading up to and during the U.S. Capitol insurrection on January 6, 2021.

The fact that the alt-right was actively recruiting by means of online channels should be seen as a natural extension of its efforts as a far-right movement. Today, more young people are joining not due to friends or personal contacts but on their own initiative via social media, as the extremism researcher Julia Ebner observed from infiltrating the U.K. branch of the Identitarian movement.[44] In the next chapter, I detail the contemporary far right's special relationship to technology and how platforms such as YouTube played an instrumental role in spreading its propaganda. This online origin was a golden opportunity for far-right women influencers seeking receptive audiences.

2

DOWN THE RABBIT HOLE
My Red Pill Journey

T his idea that a bunch of millennials with webcams filming in their bedrooms are radicalizing millions of teenagers is preposterous," Rebecca Hargraves stated in September 2018. "They've come to this corner of the internet because they're witnessing the cultural problems that we discuss, and that has influenced them."[1] For the alt-right and far right, radicalization and influencer culture are inseparable, and women have been at the forefront of this process.

Few will have heard about the Red Pill Women subreddit or even about Ladies Only on the neo-Nazi website Stormfront. These forums are filled with posts by women sharing dating and relationship advice and tips on how to be a good wife to a husband. They exchange cooking recipes, weight-loss strategies, and general health and beauty tips. As the media scholar Jessie Daniels notes, online forms of communication within the far right are largely "interactive and participatory" rather than dictated top down from movement leaders to members.[2] These chat forums can be attractive to women looking for friendship and intimacy. After having infiltrated the Red Pill Women subreddit, the extremism researcher Julia Ebner observes how such spaces are "socialisation hubs" for women seeking comfort and support. Discussions concerning self-improvement and betterment appeal to what Ebner calls the "endless chase of the ideal self."[3]

At first glance, Red Pill Women doesn't seem political. It's "not organized primarily around white nationalism, or questions of race or immigration, but rather around sexual strategy, gender roles, and relationships," writes the historian Alexandra Minna Stern. But elements of far-right ideology quickly emerge through "conversations that explore outright rejections [of] or retreats from feminism and liberalism; these are key elements of stories about brainwashed SJWs [social justice warriors] who finally see the light."[4] In this space, left-wing politics is viewed as a cult that drives a herd mentality, and escape is possible only by reverting to the traditional gender roles promoted by the far right.

This book is not about the closed chat rooms and forums where far-right women discuss domestic strategies and exchange recommendations. Rather, I demonstrate how the ideas voiced in these closed forums are being represented publicly by far-right women influencers on mainstream social media platforms. The best place to start is YouTube. "YouTube is one of the internet's top breeding grounds for far-right extremism," Ebner writes. "The fact that its algorithms do not distinguish between 'conservative' and 'far-right' does not help."[5] A prime example of this is how in 2018 the Canadian far-right influencer Robyn Riley described the origins of her ideological journey: "I was kind of feeling more comfortable flirting with alternative media, conservative media on the internet."[6] Similarly, when I was searching for far-right influencer content, I was being recommended videos on the channels of the conservative pundits Ben Shapiro and Dave Rubin and the former *Fox News* host Tucker Carlson.

In conducting my research, I was immersed in what the media scholar Rebecca Lewis calls the "alternative influence network": a network of reactionary YouTubers who "build audiences and 'sell' them on far-right ideology" within a fully functioning media ecosystem.[7] These YouTubers, notes Lewis, engage in two key practices. The first is that they reject traditional news media in order to build credibility and trust with their viewers through participatory culture. The second practice entails providing a specific social identity for themselves and their audiences by representing themselves and their viewers as social underdogs in a counterculture. As YouTubers, the far-right women influencers in this book engage in these two key practices.

Lewis writes that a crucial aspect of understanding the appeal of YouTubers within the alternative influence network is how they build trust with their audiences by stressing their relatability, authenticity, and accountability—that is, by adopting microcelebrity tactics to gain and retain followers. Microcelebrities have niche audiences, who often see themselves as public figures but use intimacy through extensive disclosure of their personal lives in order to appeal to fans.[8] The media scholar Theresa Senft coined the term *microcelebrity* in 2008 when she was researching "camgirls," young women who broadcast their lives to the public on the internet.[9] Senft found that camgirls were engaging in a new style of online performance revolved around building up their popularity based on personality. Much like traditional celebrities such as actors and sports stars, microcelebrities also gain popularity and fame but lack the same type of resources (e.g., mass media) enjoyed by traditional celebrities. As Crystal Abidin, a pioneer in the study of influencers and internet celebrities, and her colleagues Tim Highfield and Tama Leaver note, influencers intentionally and actively engage in microcelebrity practices. They fulfill four criteria to achieve this status: they "usually engage with positive self-branding strategies (as opposed to playing with notions of shame and scandal); manage a public visibility that is sustained and stable (as opposed to being briefly viral or transient); groom followers to consume their content aspirationally (as opposed to accumulating hate-watchers or audiences who tune in only with the desire to watch them fail or gawk at them); and can parlay their high internet visibility into an income that is lucrative enough for a full-time career."[10]

Far-right influencers can be considered microcelebrities in the sense that they are well known within the far-right online community and meet these four criteria in their online performances. As YouTubers, they produce vlogs that feature monologues about serious topics intertwined with personal stories, usually filmed in intimate settings such as bedrooms and living rooms. With this format, these influencers convey their authenticity and accessibility to viewers, "inhabiting a virtual space that is simultaneously public and homebound."[11] They engage with their audience by asking questions and soliciting recommendations at the end of their vlogs, and they respond to feedback in the comments section. It's no mistake that YouTube's slogan "Broadcast Yourself" ideally fits the microcelebrity dynamics.

Many far-right women influencers first created their YouTube channels in 2015 and 2016 during the early days of the alt-right, launching their political activism by commenting on issues such as feminism and identity politics. Lauren Southern, for instance, rose to popularity by vlogging about her experience taking a gender studies class at a university and soon thereafter was invited by Ezra Levant to be a journalist for the newly founded Canadian far-right news outlet Rebel Media.[12] Her first video for Rebel Media was titled "Why I'm Not a Feminist," which turned her into an overnight sensation with millions of views and boosted her into the political spotlight. She was offered her own show called *Standoff with Lauren Southern*, which would feature videos of Lauren confronting feminists at protests. However, she later returned to actively making YouTube videos after leaving Rebel Media.

These influencers create and produce their YouTube vlogs for optimal attention. The average video length is fifteen minutes (although some do have a runtime of up to an hour) and features clickbait titles and thumbnails, such as "ACCORDING TO 'SCIENCE' " and "Why Is Dating Becoming so Difficult?" These influencers exploit strategies to make their content viral, such as choosing purposefully offensive video titles or using trending hashtags appropriated from progressive social justice movements in order to "hijack" search engine optimization. Their vlogs' format is formulaic, usually an influencer sitting in a bedroom or living room, using a microphone or earbuds, and facing a web camera. Most of their videos feature monologues but sometimes consist of a dialogue—colloquially known as a "collab"—with another influencer either face-to-face or on split screens.

These vlogs are particularly interactive—despite the broadcasting format—given that influencers aim to be responsive to their viewers. They often crowdsource for comments and questions on the video topic, ask for recommendations on future content, and encourage thoughts and reflections in the comments section. These influencers also solicit donations from viewers, usually to their Patreon and PayPal accounts (see chapter 5), and ask viewers to become followers on their other social media accounts on Instagram, Telegram, and Twitter. Further, as livestreaming has become an increasingly popular medium, these far-right influencers livestream videos with an open chat displaying reactions from viewers in real time. The spontaneous and casual filming of livestreams as unedited material, compared to edited vlogs with scripts and high-quality recording, contribute to audience perceptions of authenticity and accessibility. These practices of the vlogging genre are key to far-right women influencers' propaganda efforts.

When I began researching the influencers for this book, YouTube became the primary platform to gather data because it has played an important function, especially early on, in launching and maintaining these women's political careers. Over time and more recently, Instagram has been just as fundamental in shaping their status and cementing their participation in influencer culture. The biggest advantage of Instagram is the emphasis on visuals, where these influencers engage in the practices of digital cultures and genres, such as selfies and food vlogging, to capture snapshots of their day-to-day life. I argue that what makes these far-right women influencers distinct from other far-right figures is their branding efforts to curate their lifestyles for audiences by merging their personal lives with political ideology through visual representation.

For instance, the culture studies scholar Ico Maly writes that Brittany Sellner's Instagram account gives her followers "more insight in 'the back office' of her political activism and seemingly giving unfiltered access to her private life. This influencer practice is commonly understood as 'networked intimacy.'" Networked intimacy helps "bind audiences to the influencer and create a perception of authenticity."[13] I highlight throughout the book that far-right women influencers use *networked intimacy* techniques to build and maintain their microcelebrity status and personal brands.

In Brittany's case, "Instagram was now regularly used to give her fans a look behind the scenes of her activist life," especially when she was traveling for political protests or editing videos for her YouTube channel. "Most pictures were now carefully staged and stylized to contribute to her brand," Maly notes.[14] In other words, Brittany's Instagram account complements her YouTube content, so that she leverages both platforms to cultivate an image. This leveraging contributes to what the media scholar Theresa Senft describes as the "presentation of self": presenting oneself slightly differently to different online audiences but remaining somewhat consistent in one's persona.[15] I argue that far-right women influencers, relying mainly on visual social media platforms, exploit these self-presentation tactics across platforms to generate the perception of authenticity to their audiences.

While influencer culture on Instagram has been critiqued for presenting a staged practice of authenticity, often through intentional and scheduled posts—what Abidin terms "calibrated amateurism"[16]— the adoption of Instagram Story became a key medium for these influencers. Unlike Instagram posts, which remain permanent unless deleted on a user's feed, Instagram Stories are ephemeral, disappearing after twenty-four hours, and only the sharer knows who has viewed the Story because there is no public "like" or "comment" button, which has traditionally fueled social media visibility. The media scholars Penny Triệu and Nancy Baym have found that while sharers still engage in a form of online self-presentation in such ephemeral content, the social pressure is lower because of the lower expectations regarding responses. Further, the private aspect of Instagram Stories means that responses can develop into one-on-one conversations, which help people feel closer.[17] The potential for Stories to initiate direct interaction thus offers unfiltered radicalization and recruitment possibilities between far-right women influencers and their followers.

Far-right women influencers use Instagram Stories to share unedited images (e.g., selfies absent of glamorizing filters), preferring snapshots of day-to-day activities such as cooking, homemaking, and wearing the OOTD (outfit of the day)—content that, I argue, assists in cultivating the perception of authenticity. But what highlights these sharers as far-right influencers is that they also share disinformation, conspiracy theories, and hate speech on Stories, taking advantage of the fact that increased privacy with self-deleting content offer opportunities to share material that is less publicly visible and rarely flagged by users or platforms as problematic. In addition, the visual element of Stories can be easily distorted to bypass automated content-moderation tools (see chapter 7).

Instagram as a platform has been underresearched in studies of the far right, especially its Stories function. This book is the first to illustrate how far-right women influencers are weaponizing Instagram as an influencer practice to effectively promote their ideology while engaging in personal branding to seem authentic and relatable. When combined, Instagram and YouTube are powerful visually oriented platforms that amplify the messaging of far-right influencers to broad audiences.

Following the deadly Charlottesville rally in 2017, and after Facebook implemented stricter hate speech policies in response to the Christchurch attack in 2019, governmental authorities and law enforcement demanded the shut down many far-right user accounts on mainstream social media platforms, thus leading to these users' migration to other, usually closed, platforms or to the creation of so-called alt-tech initiatives not reliant on Big Tech companies.

What exactly is alt-tech? Julia Ebner usefully highlights three types of alt-tech platforms. The first are what she calls "platforms created for extremists and used by extremists,"[18] which would include the dating sites WASP Love and Patriot Peer (alternatives to mainstream apps such as Tinder and Bumble), the crowdfunding site Hatreon (an alternative to Patreon), and the video site BitChute (an alternative to YouTube).[19] Also included in this list are alternative streaming sites such as the white-nationalist Red Ice TV (whose slogan is "The future is the past").

Ebner characterizes the second type of alt-tech platforms as "ultra-libertarian platforms, platforms created by libertarians or commercially driven developers, which tend to operate in the name of free speech and tolerate extremist content."[20] These platforms include the microblogging sites Gettr, Gab, and Parler (which became popular after Twitter censored leading far-right figures but was removed from Amazon's cloud-hosting service and from the Apple and Google app stores after the U.S. Capitol insurrection in 2021);[21] Minds (an open-source social network similar to Twitter); the image messaging boards 4chan and 8kun (previously 8chan); and Rumble (similar to YouTube and promoted as "immune to cancel culture"). In 2019, after having been banned from Google Chrome and Mozilla Firefox web browsers, Gab launched the browser extension Dissenter, which allows Gab users to comment on any webpage visible to other Dissenter users. Gab also launched an encrypted chat app in 2020, which law enforcement has already identified as an organizing tool for extremists.[22]

In this second category, one of the most popular new platforms to emerge is Odysee, a video-streaming site with a user interface like YouTube's. Odysee is particularly unique in that it is built entirely on blockchain protocol, which is open source and lies outside of the Big Tech monopoly. Significantly, any content posted onto blockchain is impossible to remove or change, which poses serious regulatory concerns for governments, law enforcement, and civil society. This immutability feature can be an attractive option for extremist actors looking to exploit it to spread propaganda and recruit followers.[23] Odysee has become an increasingly popular platform among the far right the past few years, so much so that Lauren Chen announced that she "actually joined Odysee's team as a brand ambassador," citing the platform's lack of censorship and its policy of allowing content creators to keep a large percentage of their earnings from members' direct donations.[24]

Ebner describes the third type of alt-tech platform as "hijacked platforms, platforms created for entirely different purposes that have been hijacked by extremists but proactively work with the authorities to ban these [extremists] from using their services." Discord and Twitch (initially designed as a chat app and a livestreaming service for gaming, respectively) and Telegram (a partially encrypted instant-messaging app) are notable examples.[25] The latter is especially popular among the far right and experienced a spike of new user downloads following the U.S. Capitol insurrection when right-wing extremists were kicked off Twitter, Facebook, and Parler. Although Telegram largely takes a lax approach to platform regulation, in an unprecedented move in early 2021 the company blocked dozens of public channels (operating as one-way broadcasts) for inciting violence and for violating the terms of service.[26]

Nearly all far-right women influencers continue to rely on mainstream social media platforms to disseminate their message and to crowdsource donations. They might cross-post their YouTube content onto their BitChute accounts or screenshot their Twitter posts to share on Telegram, but these influencers will not completely transition off mainstream social media platforms for a couple of reasons. First, tech companies don't consider the content they share to be extreme because of its framing and presentation, with occasional minor exceptions of violating hate speech policies. Their material thus remains on these sites, rarely getting flagged for offensive content (discussed in chapter 7). Second, far-right women influencers rely on a mainstream audience to spread their message and recruit potential followers. Exclusive use of alt-tech platforms might help retain current followers but drastically reduces the possibility of acquiring new followers. This aspect is especially important for engaging in what the alt-right called being "red pilled." In the next section, I show that mainstream platforms such as YouTube played an integral role for far-right women influencers to share their red-pilling journeys with mass audiences.

"I can't really pinpoint to one specific thing that caused that to happen; it was like a domino effect," stated Robyn Riley in September 2018.[27] A year earlier, Rebecca Hargraves described a similar experience: "Like most people, it wasn't a definitive event that caused it."[28]

Far-right supporters don't dramatically adopt far-right views overnight. The process of radicalization and recruitment (or vice versa) into far-right movements often happens incrementally. As the sociologist Kathleen Blee writes, the process for far-right women is gradual, sometimes taking years; the retelling of their "journey" can be convoluted, contradictory, and they can sometimes go so far as to "reshape stories, even memories, of their past" to fit their present activism.[29] "Whenever she told the story of her life," writes the journalist Seyward Darby about Ayla Stewart, "Ayla described a gradual awakening—a realization that the media and America's raging liberal culture had taught her to hate herself, her femininity, and her race."[30] It is most likely that Ayla was framing her radicalization journey according to her current political beliefs as a way of situating and understanding her past self.

In listening to their radicalization stories on YouTube, I found that many of these far-right women influencers first became interested in politics by watching male YouTubers. Rebecca specifically mentions Black Pigeon Speaks, a Canadian neo-Nazi based in Japan, as well as the alt-right figures Milo Yiannopolous and Gavin McInnes and the prominent American conservative pundit Steven Crowder, whom Lauren Chen also cites as an inspiration. In a vlog symbolically titled "Origin Story," Robyn attributed Jordan Peterson, the Canadian psychologist and intellectual darling of the far right, with having "red pilled" her. "I was seeing reality the way it is, as opposed to seeing it through an ideology," she narrated in August 2018, describing the process almost like a rebirth.[31] Robyn's experience is not unusual. As the historian Alexandra Minna Stern writes, "Common are accounts of women red pilled after watching Jordan Peterson videos explaining why feminism doesn't make women happy or why leftism is the great scourge of modern society."[32]

The term *red pill*, used frequently among the alt-right, derives from the film *The Matrix* (1999), in which the protagonist, Neo, is offered the choice to swallow either a red pill, which will reveal to him the "truth," or a blue pill, which will cause him to forget the recent past and return to a life of ignorance. For the alt-right, the red pill stands for what the media scholar Bharath Ganesh has called "the beginning of a process of radicalization," in which the "truth" manifests as the demographic replacement of white majorities in Western countries by immigrants and Muslims, which is orchestrated as a master plan by the left-wing political and media establishment.[33]

Both Robyn and Rebecca have created YouTube videos dedicated specifically to the topic of their personal red pill journeys—what I refer to as "red pill vlogs." There are distinct similarities between the two women's experiences. Both went to college, where they took liberal arts courses such as gender studies and mostly self-identified as liberal and feminist. After attending university, they lived in diverse urban areas and entered professional occupations. Rebecca pointed to working in the high-stress finance sector, having no social life, and drinking as "really the most important part of my red pilling." Seeing her female colleagues work eighty-hour weeks in a corporate job in Seattle at the expense of happiness and a family life was deeply upsetting to her. Meanwhile, Robyn was facing difficulty in a bad relationship and sought a way to transition to a better life.

Each embarked on a journey of self-improvement with a mindset of accepting personal responsibility. Along the way, they found confidence in voicing unpopular political opinions through watching the male YouTubers. They "have inspired me to say what I'm thinking and not be afraid of the repercussions," Rebecca claimed in her first YouTube video in February 2016. "These things are the truth . . . to save Western society, which I see crumbling," she added.[34] Their stories are ones of resilience as much as of a reawakening. And yet in sharing their journeys, they use far-right ideology to explain the reasons for their past unhappiness.

The far-right influencer who goes by the pseudonym "Lacey Lynn" (Lacey Lauren Clark) has a somewhat different red pill story. Unlike Robyn and Rebecca, Lacey didn't go to college and made the decision in high school—when she began dating her future husband—that she would be a "homemaker." Like the others, Lacey felt ostracized by friends and family members for her political views once she opened up to them. In her own words, "The more and more red pilled I became, the more difficult I found it to survive at socializing."[35] For a while, Lacey felt isolated after moving straight from her parents' home to her own home in Texas, where she didn't have any friends and was raising two young children while her husband traveled frequently for work. She eventually found a community at a local church and a group of mothers who also homeschooled their children.

"Then the internet happened," said Lacey in her vlog "Red Pilled: Losing Friends." "The good thing about the internet is you can find friends who are like-minded, and they may be spread out in different areas, but you can develop friendships and hopefully meet people offline." She created what she considered meaningful friendships online, which she saw as just as important as offline friendships. This was critical for Lacey because she felt as if she were losing more friend and family relationships as time went on.

Like Robyn and Rebecca, Lacey eventually felt validated for her convictions despite her shrinking social circle. "I was finally at a place where I felt like I was becoming a normal, functioning, capable adult," she affirmed in telling her story. Because of this, Lacey felt resolved in her actions and beliefs, even if they resulted in social alienation. Going forward, Lacey was determined: "Right now, as it stands, I'm rebuilding my community." And she called upon others to do the same. "Communities and families are worth fighting for, even if you have to be completely stripped away from who you thought you were, beaten down and rebuilt again," she commented. "That's what we have to do with our communities. They've been stripped down and beaten down, but we have to rebuild." By framing her choices as a moral compass to correct society's ills, Lacey was encouraging her viewers to follow in her footsteps so that they could also "rebuild" themselves and their communities.

The consequences of these women's transition to the far right are far from smooth, though they justify it as worth the challenges. Robyn, who now has tens of thousands of subscribers to her YouTube channel, related in a video titled "I Lost All My Friends in the Culture War" in September 2018 her painful experience of losing former university friendships. Misty-eyed, her voice shaking, she described feeling betrayed by the very people she once considered her second family: "My old friends who are still liberal can't see what I'm doing on social media outside of the confines of their own perspective, which puts me in a category of someone who is propagating hate speech, someone who has been radicalized, someone who believes in conspiracy theories, someone who probably has no credibility, someone who is being misled by unreliable sources, someone who has been manipulated by men in my life, someone who has probably internalized misogyny—I would imagine is something running through their heads." With her head held high, Robyn renounced her old friends. "When strangers are more supportive of what I'm doing on here than old friends, then maybe it's time to let go."[36] No doubt it is easier to let go when you can frame your cause as worthy to tens of thousands of supportive strangers.

The experience of losing her old friends clearly hurt Robyn. Nonetheless, she feels that it is important to speak out about her political views, using tactics of networked intimacy to come across as "authentic" and real to her audience. Robyn feels as if she's found her true self, and she wants her viewers to know that the process of doing so can be difficult, with the potential cost of social alienation.

"I think I'm currently going through something that a lot of people can relate to," she stated in "I Lost All My Friends in the Culture War." "It's something that feels very much like unchartered territory and that there aren't really many resources out there available to help you through this kind of experience or situation." By sharing her experience, Robyn hoped that others would find the strength to gain what she called "self-respect." This "sense of moral worthiness," as Kathleen Blee describes women radicalized in the far right,[37] gives purpose to these influencers.

Rebecca, meanwhile, stated in her first vlog in February 2016 that she had wanted to create videos for years but didn't out of fear of "social repercussions, or losing my job." Like Robyn, Rebecca felt as if she had always been a bit alienated by her viewpoints: "It is socially crippling, it is professionally crippling, . . . and not having an outlet to talk about these things is frustrating."[38] She echoed these anxieties in her second vlog a few weeks later, expressing her worry of getting caught making these videos and facing possible termination from her job.[39] However, the next year Rebecca revealed that YouTube was her main source of income.[40] She did not reveal whether she left her previous employment voluntarily or involuntarily. Some of these women may not hold membership in an offline far-right group, but they have experienced social and economic ostracization. It is telling that many of them initially chose a pseudonym when they first started their YouTube channels—Lauren Chen went by "Roaming Millennial," Rebecca by "Blonde in the Belly of the Beast," Robyn by "Critical Condition," Ayla Stewart by "Wife with a Purpose," and Elora by "the Blonde Buttermaker."

Red pill vlogs are a prominent genre on YouTube, but far-right women influencers express their radicalization journeys differently on Instagram, often orienting their stories through the aesthetics of influencer culture on the platform. In a before-and-after selfie photo post, Robyn described the "before" photo of her as in a period of "under-eating, in a bad relationship for 7 years, heavy smoker, feeling numb inside, lost," but the recent "after" photo as showing her in a time when she is "eating healthy, married and pregnant, off all drugs, feeling joy and gratitude for my life, saved." The "old" Robyn had dyed pink hair, a nose ring, and baggy clothing. The "new" Robyn is a natural brunette, free of piercings, in modest but feminine clothing.[41]

Robyn called the change a "glow up" in the post's description, a pop-culture term originating from the beauty-blogging community that refers to a mental, physical, and emotional transformation to improve one's appearance, often over a period of years. As Robyn pointed out in the same post, "These pics were taken 4 years apart and it didn't happen overnight! You've got to put in the work for the reward!!" With "glow up," an emphasis is placed on routines and lifestyle changes revolving around health. The process also centers on building self-confidence and discovering one's preferences, values, and passions. The ultimate aim of a glow up is a rebranding of oneself—a perfect analogy for red pilling. "If it could happen to me it can happen to anyone!" Robyn wrote.

At first glance, Robyn's message isn't political in nature. Stories of personal glow ups are scattered across the internet; millions of Instagram posts use the hashtag #glowup. Research shows that Instagram is a popular platform—especially because it is image based—for users to express personal difficulties in order to build social support and a sense of community.[42] But using coded language in her post, such as "find your femininity and embrace who God made you to be!" and "de-programming is a long process," Robyn hinted at far-right narratives regarding essentialist gender roles and red pill experiences. However, it is only by having insider knowledge about the subtle cues of far-right propaganda that one can detect how a personal story is simultaneously a political message of radicalization presented through networked intimacy.

A recurring theme across Robyn, Rebecca, and Lacey's red pill stories is how these influencers create validation for their life choices. Framing the process as finding their "authentic" and "honest" selves distracts from the hateful ideology of the far right. Gaining a sense of "self-respect" and building confidence in one's opinions are attractive to vulnerable young people, but for these influencers these gains come at the expense of dehumanization and "othering." Their far-right propaganda is highly effective at turning personal grievances into a "worthy" cause. Women influencers are at the helm of manipulating susceptible viewers into believing that joining the far right will bring them happiness, which in turn will lead to the betterment of society overall. They continue to exclude, however, those who do not fit within the far right's prescribed vision, such as ethnic and sexual minorities.

Not everyone shares their personal story. "Lana [Lokteff] didn't share her life story in detail or describe an emotional transformation," writes Seyward Darby about her interview with Lana. "Then again, why would she? Lana wasn't in the business of filming testimonials in her kitchen. Red Ice had been in the alt-news game for almost a decade; it had slick website graphics, good sound equipment, and other trappings of a real media operation."[43] Lana already had an extensive alt-tech propaganda outlet, meaning she could circumvent the vlogging format used by other far-right women influencers on mainstream platforms. This outlet also offered her privacy and the aura of professionalism.

But that greater privacy doesn't mean Lana's efforts at recruitment are ineffective. Darby narrates their conversation: " 'I ask girls all the time, "How did you find us?," ' Lana told me, referring to the women she knows on the far-right. 'They search around online. They'll find some of the bait and some of the memes out there, and kind of go down this little rabbit hole, and they find us. And then they realize, "Oh my God. There's all these people that thought like I do. Now I can be vocal." ' " The vast far-right ecosystem is more accessible than ever before. And Lana exploits this accessibility by having female guests on her show, all with different background stories but shared elements: "They had all felt lost, besieged, empty, probing, insecure, frustrated, or unmoored. White nationalism had transmuted their grievances or anger into a lofty purpose," writes

Darby.[44] Lana provided them the perfect spotlight to jump-start their far-right careers.

For most far-right women influencers, platforms such as YouTube and Instagram provide exposure to share their radicalization stories. Using strategies of networked intimacy, whether vlogging through a webcam or posting transformation selfies, these influencers are able to broadcast their personal experiences and merge them with ideological testimonials.

When sifting through recruitment vlogs, I found a YouTube video by Rebecca from 2017 geared toward her male viewers on how to red-pill women. She gave advice on what she thought are the best ways for men to red-pill their wives, girlfriends, sisters, and so on, after crowdsourcing suggestions on Twitter for her next video topic. She started off by reflecting on her own experience and what she thought convinced her to "see the world realistically," arguing that instigating a mental shift is difficult because of the alleged "disproportionate societal advantage" that modern women have today owing to feminism, liberalism, and globalism. As a starting point, Rebecca recommended that men initiate the red pill process on impressionable women by addressing the power that all women allegedly have but pointing out that women are also "woefully unhappy"—the men will get extra points if they can back this claim with a "garbage leftist [news] source" so that the woman in question won't be resistant to the idea. She falsely claimed, "Women are unhappy because they are rejecting their instincts and are misfit for a masculine lifestyle, and they grin and bear it because they have a tendency to believe that everything is OK."[45]

Rebecca alerted her male followers to exercise caution in the next step: testing a woman's susceptibility to "hard truths" before making an onslaught. She reminded her viewers that "unlearning" (echoing Robyn's experience of "deprogramming") a lifetime of liberal indoctrination is a process and can take time, even years.

She recommended YouTube as an instrumental tool, citing prominent YouTubers such as Black Pigeon Speaks (whom she heeded that "for the average woman I think that might be a little bit too hardcore"), British alt-right personality Paul Joseph Watson, Canadian white nationalist Stefan Molyneux, as well as fellow female influencer Lauren Southern. Rebecca suggested taking a supplementary offline approach by asking thought-provoking questions and presenting data to back claims made against feminism. But the key is to do this incrementally, "so as not to strain your relationship" and "push her mental boundaries slowly," or else she will get defensive.

Most important, Rebecca stressed to lead by example: "Be a strong man who promotes traditional gender roles. Share information with her that you find interesting or important. Challenge her worldview when necessary. Have mutually understood expectations of her role as the woman and the nurturer in the relationship." Over time, she asserted, women will become more conservative if traditional gender roles are reinforced, and this will lead to awareness of their femininity.

The themes Rebecca discussed in recruiting women—femininity, traditional gender norms—are an important foundation to understanding the core values of the far right, which I explore in chapter 3. But why would she receive such high demand from male viewers on how to red-pill women? In other words, who has been and is the audience of these far-right women influencers?

A quick glimpse through comments on YouTube videos gave me some indication that a disproportionate number of men make up this audience. Lauren Chen confirmed this assessment. "I was looking at my YouTube channel analytics the other day, and 85 percent of my viewership is male," she said in April 2017.[46] Robyn was in a similar situation. "I know I have a pretty large male audience right now, but my goal is to at least get to a sixty–forty split with women," she hoped. "I really want to be able to interact with women and encourage the kind of womanhood that I believe is long term most positive for the success of most women."[47] I was intrigued by these statistics. Wouldn't these women influencers naturally appeal to women? Why else would they make videos discussing topics such as dating and female friendship if not to recruit women for the far right?

Perhaps one reason why these far-right women influencers are so popular among men is that they symbolize a lifestyle that young men can aspire to if they join the far right. "As adept media personalities, they assure listeners, many of them men, that many white women are committed to traditional life, gender essentialism, and the restoration of the primordial patriarchy," reflects Alexandra Minna Stern.[48] Join us, they say to young men, and you will discover a world where you can meet young, traditional women who share your political beliefs. It is the potential of companionship within this community that seduces young men.

This was made abundantly clear to me while I was listening to the *New York Times* podcast series *Rabbit Hole*, which is about how society is changing as the distinction between online and offline gets increasingly blurred. The first few episodes feature the story of Caleb Cain, a young man who was radicalized into the YouTube alt-right universe as he became obsessed with watching videos for hours every day. As I listened to Caleb's radicalization process, his experience did not strike me as particularly unique or new. His journey as an active consumer of far-right narratives fit the findings of earlier research on joining far-right movements. Only this time, it was an algorithm rather than a friend who led him into the rabbit hole.

But then Caleb mentioned why he was partly drawn to the alt-right figure Stefan Molyneux (who is now banned from YouTube): "And he had a wife who would come on stream with him . . . they'd talk about their life together." He continued, "[He] talks about how much he loves his daughter. I want all that stuff! I want a family like that! 'Cause that's what I wanted my whole life. I wanted a stable family. Well, if I just keep watching more and more, I'll be like Stef."[49]

Hearing Caleb describe his desire for a loving family, as represented by the Molyneuxes, reveals how women in the far right, even if they're not as visible as the influencers, can have a powerful

effect. Caleb's longing for stability and affection is precisely captured in far-right propaganda, especially by women influencers
who promote the idea of a strong nuclear family. As Caleb started
watching more videos on YouTube, he eventually came across Lauren Southern, whose content he watched often. "She was beautiful;
she was my age," stated Caleb. "I was like, who's this? And I was like,
she's really owning the libs [liberals], giving them facts and logic."[50]
He was initially drawn to Lauren because he found her to be an
attractive woman his age, but it was her confidence and arguments
that won him over. Like Lauren, other far-right women influencers
use the same tactics to appeal to and recruit male followers: first
with their appearance and then with ideology.

I reached out to Caleb for an interview, and he told me about other
far-right women influencers he was actively watching back then,
such as Robyn Riley ("I remember her first video of her red pill experience," he mentioned), Brittany Sellner (then Pettibone), Rebecca
Hargraves, and the British YouTuber Tara McCarthy. He came across
these women via collabs. "When I was watching them, they were all
on the streams with everybody else," he stated.[51]

"What were the topics that you enjoyed listening [to] on their
channels?" I asked Caleb, wondering if they were gender- or politics-
based discussions.

"Probably the same topics the men talked about," he replied. But
"whenever Lauren [Southern] would talk about anything involving
feminism or women, you [would] get a sense of authority because
she is a female."

Caleb described how back then he had "a very traditionalist view
of gender," and figures such as Lauren reinforced that worldview. "I
was pretty adamant on traditional gender roles," he continued. "I saw
it as a really essentialist thing that was like, this is what Western civilization was built on, these family structures. If we destroy them,
everything falls apart. It was like a very existential threat; that's
why there's always an urgency."

Tropes of societal degradation and the need to restore order by
starting with the nuclear family unit have long existed in far-right
movements, and they were typically reproduced in the talking

points of the YouTubers Caleb watched. "I remember that Lauren and Brittany Pettibone would talk about birth rates a lot more than the male creators would, or they would talk about motherhood a lot," he said. "But I don't think any of those topics were necessarily drawing men in, if not, like, the fantasy. That's what it was all about."

Caleb's last point confirms my suspicion that the reason why these far-right women influencers have a high male viewership is they function as honeytraps for the male gaze. "I think that, for men, those content creators are probably interesting because they're attractive," Caleb verified. Although exploring the audiences of these influencers through comments on their YouTube videos or followers on Instagram would have been interesting angle to pursue, I decided not to do so—not only out of ethical concerns (and thus abiding by the set ethics approval) but also because I instead wanted to draw attention to how these women produce and amplify narratives within the far-right milieu.

In my conversation with Caleb, I brought up a related issue: "What would be the purpose of these women as the faces of the alt-right if not to recruit men?"

"Yeah, I guess so," agreed Caleb. "These movements kind of need to have women in them. I mean, why would anybody want to join a movement if there's no women?" A movement without women is doomed to fail, indeed.

Far-right women influencers importantly appeal to both men and women as targeted audiences by tailoring their content, although antifeminism is a shared core message, which I discuss in the next chapter. For many of these influencers, embracing this ideological point of view is the first step in their and possibly their followers' red pill journeys. As this chapter illustrates, sharing their personal radicalization stories to a mass number of viewers is made possible through the networked advantages of mainstream social media platforms. By further presenting themselves online through the microcelebrity strategies of relatability and authenticity, these influencers effectively legitimize and normalize far-right ideology alongside personal branding.

3
FEMININITY NOT FEMINISM

I do know what feminism is; I've been in the belly of the beast. I was deep, deep, deep in feminism and the world of feminism, and I chose to leave. I'm a recovering feminist," proudly stated Ayla Stewart in her vlog "Feminism—My History with It" in 2015.[1] Few would know that Ayla (born Erin Donnelly)[2] holds a master's degree in women's spirituality. In fact, her graduate thesis explored the sacredness of motherhood and home birth within the Mormon and Amish communities, and her bachelor's thesis in anthropology looked at the spiritual traditions of the Navajo and Hopi and how they related to women's equality and roles within their tribes' governance and social structures. It may come as a further surprise that one of the most vocal female proponents of the alt-right had once performed in *The Vagina Monologues*.

As Ayla narrated her past in the vlog, she described how her "woke," "intersectional" classmates in her master's program reacted negatively to her embrace of being a mother and her intellectual interest in stay-at-home mothering as a feminist issue. "I was pegged early on as being baby obsessed, as mother obsessed," she claimed and accused fellow students and faculty of feeling "ashamed" and "guilty" for their motherhood. A few years later in her life, Ayla no longer declared herself a feminist and now asserted in her vlog that feminism has "gotten even worse" since then.

Lauren Southern, meanwhile, gained internet notoriety by documenting her experience of taking a women's studies class at the University of the Fraser Valley in British Columbia. The first videos on her YouTube channel provided updates on the class discussions while she attended the course "undercover," thus building networked intimacy with her viewers early on through establishing trust and in-the-know relationships aligned with reactionary politics.[3] By trying, in her own words, to "expose" her fellow students for their so-called groupthink beliefs and behaviors, Lauren claimed that embracing the ideology of feminism results from institutional coercion that begins from a young age. According to her, by the time young women enter university, they take courses such as women's studies because they believe that it's requisite within what many in the far-right call "social justice warrior" (commonly referred to as SJW) "indoctrination." Fields such as women's studies directly extend from "Marxist" thought in academia, stated Lauren, which is the foundation of the SJW movement. Like Ayla, Lauren described Marxism as the "radical" bubble of "deep-end feminism." At several points in her videos, Lauren did satirical impersonations of feminists commenting about the patriarchy.

Both Ayla and Lauren focus on one common theme: feminism hates men. Ayla rejects feminism for being "disparaging towards men" and a man-hating movement. Feminism, according to Ayla, neglects men's biological instincts of providing protection, being strong, and being providers for the family unit. Lauren agrees, falsely claiming that feminists have many negative attitudes toward men. "One of the big reasons I didn't like feminism was because I had so many good men in my life. To see them being portrayed as evil rapists and misogynists and bad for women really angered me," she stated recently in mid-2022.[4] For Lauren, the most radical feminists hate men, and given the supposed lack of self-criticism within the "social movement," these issues are not addressed for fear of the ideology collapsing. Lauren and Ayla further complain that their opinions are not represented in and lie outside mainstream discussion, so they face stigma for criticizing feminist ideology.

Far-right women constantly ridicule and satirize ideas that have become popular with feminism, such as patriarchy, oppression, and misogyny. These notions, they argue, are merely feminist and SJW exaggerations to advance an (allegedly) cultural Marxist agenda that seeks to disrupt—sometimes quite literally—the nuclear family and, by extension, society at large. "Modern day feminism isn't in fact about equality at all but rather about wanting to destroy everything that's healthy and normal," said Brittany Sellner in early 2020. "There used to be a time when we had strong, tight-knit communities with a high level of trust among the residents." Today, she believes, that's changed. "Communities have become atomized and hostile; almost every child comes from a broken family."[5] Yet what Brittany considers a "healthy and normal" past is a myth. Lack of reproductive rights, domestic abuse, and restrictions on the freedom to express sexuality were widely experienced and brought forth into public recognition as a result of feminist and LGBTQ+ movements. Brittany's worldview reflects Kathleen Blee's findings from interviewing far-right women nearly twenty years ago: "The women's understanding of the politics of their movement also leads them to describe the movement and themselves in very different terms. Rather than burning with ideological passion or a desire to spread racist ideas, they feel hopeless about the 'degenerate' society that surrounds them and the possibility of changing it."[6]

Despite their feelings of despair, contemporary far-right women influencers advocate for a "solution" derived from the past. "We need to return to an era of feminine women relying on and submitting to their masculine husbands," according to Rebecca Hargraves.[7] Brittany takes a similar stance: "Focus on fixing the nuclear family and to rebuild the communities that have been damaged."[8] Rebecca and Brittany's responses are not new. As the gender studies scholars Gabriele Dietze and Julia Roth have noted, "The fields of gender, family, and sexual politics are heavily loaded with emotions—fears, passions, impulses to protect—which right-wing populist actors trigger and transfer into affective patterns."[9] Both Brittany and

Rebecca are appealing to the emotions of their viewers through the medium of networked intimacy, urging them to summon their courage and take back control of what has been lost. According to them, traditionalism can provide for women what feminism can't—a life of marriage and motherhood. As Lauren Southern summed up the issue in 2017, feminists say, "We think it's stupid to look at that traditional life: graduate, get married, have a white picket fence, family. We think that's so basic, lame," to which she responded, "But those are amazing, terrific ups and downs."[10]

These far-right women perform femininity instead of feminism. It's a performance because femininity (or masculinity) is something that is imitated and learned, not something one is born with. Gender studies scholars distinguish femininity and masculinity as a social construct because each is behavior that is performed based on observation over time. People born female or male learn (or are expected) to act feminine or masculine, respectively, based on role models in society and their upbringing. These far-right women, however, view femininity as a "natural," biological condition based on sex. These influencers rarely, if ever, challenge traditional notions of femininity as tied to reproductive abilities. For them, only two genders exist (i.e., the masculine and the feminine), and each is determined by sex (i.e., male and female). Men are presumed to act masculine, and women to act feminine. The idea of a nonbinary gender—that one can identify as neither exclusively masculine nor exclusively feminine—is inconceivable to the far right. Women not adhering to feminine qualities and men not adhering to masculine qualities, they argue, disrupts the "natural" balance, or "equilibrium," between the genders. Feminism, they believe, is at the root of this disruption.

In 2020, the Canadian government charged a young man for a terrorist attack motivated by "incel" ideology. This was the first time that an individual was charged with terrorism on this ground.[11]

Incels, or "involuntary celibates," are young men who believe that they are unable to access or form sexual and romantic relationships with women because of supposed genetic factors such as physical appearance, women's evolutionary preference for masculine men, and social structures that give women the privileged access of choice.[12] According to incels, in the "sexual marketplace" 20 percent of attractive men are monopolizing 80 percent of women for sexual relationships (known as the 80/20 rule). Incels thus hold a deeply misogynistic worldview, treating women like sexual objects and feeling entitled to do so.

Terrorist attacks had been carried out by incels before 2020, such as the notable perpetrators Eliot Rodger—who in 2014 opened fire on and rammed his vehicle into passersby near the University of California, Santa Barbara, campus—and Alek Minassian in the Toronto van attack in 2018. These young men represent what has become a large online subculture of self-identified incels on platforms such as 4chan and Reddit.[13]

Following the incel terrorism charges in Canada, far-right women influencers responded to the young man with empathy. "If more than anything, this story just goes to show how broken and fractured the relationships between men and women are becoming," stated Lauren Chen upon news of the ruling.[14] Far-right women are repeatedly pushing the narrative that societal chaos is the result of progressive movements such as feminism disrupting traditional gender norms.

"I think it is fine to call them terrorists," she continued, but "oftentimes we dismiss how broken dating culture has become, and I think with these incels—and incel isn't just a subculture, right?—the term conjures up images of this angry, upset man, but there are tons of other guys out there who, even though they may not be the 'typical' incel, are still not successful with women and still frustrated in a lot of ways." This argument is illogical. Although there may be many men who are not "successful" with women, this does not make them incels, who hold violently misogynistic views toward and believe they are sexually entitled to women.[15]

But this was not the first time that Lauren had defended incels. More than a year earlier, she falsely stated that "promiscuity and the decline of monogamy are responsible for the growing amount of incels," with "people favoring casual sex over long-term relationships."[16] There is no evidence to support the claim that sexual liberation or changing relationship commitments has resulted in a rise in the number of incels. Equating right-wing or conservative men's sexual desire with making them incels, Lauren asserted that "this results in defining the morality and value of men on how well they deal with women or the degree to which they embrace a feminist, gynocentric worldview." Not only is this an incorrect statement given that right-wing and conservative men are not being branded as incels, but Lauren was also making this association most likely just to promote fear among her disproportionately male viewers (see chapter 5). Aside from these two points, defining the morality and value of men on how well they treat women—or half the population—doesn't seem like an unreasonable request.

This sympathetic response to misogyny-based violence is prevalent within the far right. For instance, Brittany Sellner has made vlogs with titles such as "The War on Men," in which she discusses male resentment, anger, and social isolation as a false consequence of feminism. "It comes as absolutely no surprise to me at this point that movements like the men's rights movement have gained such popularity," she said in late 2019. "Men are tired of being shamed of their inherent qualities, such as masculinity."[17] Once more we see that far-right women influencers unquestionably view men as inherently masculine and women as inherently feminine.

There is an overlap between incels and the broader "manosphere" movement, which connects misogyny with the far right and alt-right. Other major factions under the manosphere umbrella include the men's rights movement (MRM), which argues that there is structural discrimination against men; the father's rights movement, relating to what is seen as discrimination against men in child-custody and family law; the Men Going Their Own Way (MGTOW) movement, which calls for men to completely separate themselves from a supposedly feminist-controlled society; and the pick-up art-istry (PUA) movement, which teaches young men how to seduce women for sexual success and thus to treat women only as sex objects (although the latter is not looked upon favorably by these far-right women influencers). There are smaller communities within the manosphere, such as the gamer/geek, TradCon (traditional Christian conservatives), and NoFap (no masturbation) communi-ties. The one element that unites all these branches of the mano-sphere is a shared antifeminism.[18] They believe that feminists dominate all aspects of society and by extension have repressed men and their "natural" masculinity.

Male supremacism is the underlying ideology driving the mano-sphere, but it is also fundamental to the alt-right and far right. "It's not a question of overlap between male supremacism and the alt-right but rather [of] male supremacist ideology being a major intrin-sic part of the alt-right," Alex DiBranco, director of the Institute for Research on Male Supremacism, told me. You can't separate the foundational component of male supremacism from the far right. Alex continued, "One of the distinguishing aspects of the alt-right is the overt hostility toward women, that less 'benevolent sexism' appears that is usually found in patriarchal traditionalism, includ-ing white supremacist groups." Because the contemporary far right sometimes comes across as being less sexist than other movements, "there seems to be a trend in which the alt-right and far right are often defined solely by their racism and xenophobia."[19] Neverthe-less, many alt-right actors built their brand on misogyny and anti-feminism as well as on racism.

On the flip side, there appears to be a female-ally parallel uni-verse to the manosphere. It's not a direct equivalent, though, largely because this world has not been fully mapped out. In writing this book, I hope to offer a starting point for charting out this umbrella movement of women-supported misogyny. On the one hand, you have tradwives (see chapter 4), who adhere to traditional domestic roles. On the other hand, you have far-right and alt-right women who believe in traditionalism but are more politically orientated in their goals. Also included in this network mapping are conservative women, who believe in cultural facets of traditionalism but are not as politically extreme as the far right. One can additionally position women within the Christian right or religious right who hold strong traditionalist views.

Lana Lokteff exemplifies a far-right women influencer who bridges the manosphere and women-supported misogyny, using antifeminism and pro-men arguments under the banner of set gender roles, while scapegoating immigrants and the political left for causing societal degradation. She seized the opportunity to promote this agenda at an early stage. "As she was shaping [her podcast] *Radio 3Fourteen*'s identity, the digital manosphere was expanding," writes Seyward Darby. "With antifeminism, red-baiting, and anti-Semitism, the telltale signs of Lana's foray into white nationalism were accumulating."[20] Soon thereafter, Lana would be advancing conspiratorial claims that the West was undergoing a white genocide orchestrated by feminists and a Jewish elite to lower white birth rates and encourage mass immigration—a process known among the far right as the "Great Replacement" (see chapter 6).

In another instance of far-right women supporting "our" men, one of Robyn Riley's YouTube viewers asked her what she thought of Nick Fuentes, a white-nationalist commentator who leads a loose coalition of internet trolls called the Groypers. She was expectedly positive in her assessment: "I think what they're doing is necessary, and it's really refreshing to see a bunch of young men who are willing to just stand up for what they believe in." She continued, "For such a long time, I feel like, especially in America, it's been kind of difficult for the dissident right because there haven't been any men who are willing to say, 'You know what, this is something I'm going to do. I'm going to take responsibility. I'm going to be a leader. I'm going to organize, and I'm going to do something good for my community and my country.' "[21] Clearly, she advocates that men act upon their "natural" masculine roles as aggressive leaders of the far right. Acting upon that masculinity also means defending "traditional" values, which the Groypers do in extremely misogynistic, homophobic, and transphobic terms.[22]

"We've seen people like Martin Sellner doing that in Europe with great success, but it hasn't really been until the America First [Fuente's] guys have really got the ball rolling that we've seen it in America," Robyn continued. "So, yeah, I think they're doing great work." This "great work" led to Fuentes getting banned from YouTube in 2020 for violating the platform's hate speech policy and later from the livestreaming site DLive after it was revealed that he participated in the storming of the U.S. Capitol on January 6, 2021.[23] Robyn made her comments about Fuentes in the week following the insurrection, a clear signal that far-right women stood behind their men's violent actions.

In a surprise twist, I came across a livestream hosted by Robyn and Rebecca Hargraves on their YouTube channel Motherland, featuring an unexpected guest—Roosh V (Daryush Valizadeh). A former PUA who sold books and travel guides giving men tips on sexual strategies, Roosh announced that he was renouncing his old ways and had found salvation through Christianity (although he has received heavy criticism for being an imposter).[24] Watching this conversation unfold between them, I witnessed an ironic alliance between two women who promote the sanctity of femininity and a former leading personality of the manosphere who was once banned from entering the United Kingdom because he publicly promoted rape. Yet the livestream presents like a vindication: Roosh is redeemed by two prominent far-right women.

One key difference between far-right women influencers and the manosphere is that despite a shared antifeminist outlook, the former lament the breakdown of traditional gender roles that have led to societal decay, whereas the latter advocate for violent entitlement to women. Thus, promiscuity (favoring men's desires) is promoted within the manosphere but not by far-right women. Both Brittany and Lauren Chen attribute society's alleged antimen attitude to dating or hook-up culture. According to Brittany, dating "was understood between two people back then, even a few decades ago, that it was a fit for marriage. Nowadays that's been erased and replaced with hook-up culture, so apps like Tinder or going to the bar or club."[25] She didn't acknowledge that perhaps dating in the past was permissible only if it led to marriage, thus significantly restricting people's sexual activity based on prescribed social norms. She also claimed that the increasing social trend of rape allegations as well as increasing public accusations of sexual harassment and assault because of the #MeToo movement has led men to be afraid of approaching women.[26] Rather than prioritizing the concerns of women who have been the victims of sexual assault, Brittany took a sympathetic stance toward men who have been asked to consciously change their behavior toward women.

In her reflection on the incel terrorist attack in Canada, Lauren also pointed to contemporary dating culture to understand the perpetrator's motivation. "We often talk about how dating, sorry, hook-up culture, hurts women. At least in the conservative community we do. I don't think we spend enough time talking about how it hurts men," she said. "And what we see is that with these incels, there's this popular talking point among men's rights activists of the pareto distribution in the dating for men; it's like 20 percent of the men get 80 percent of the women, or something like that." Despite her limited knowledge of incels, she was still aware of the 80/20 rule popularized by that community. Because of this disparity, she concluded, "a lot of men are feeling left out and disenfranchised."[27] Once again, Lauren portrayed all men as sympathetic with the beliefs of incels, thus normalizing the deeply violent and misogynist behaviors promoted in the manosphere.

Ironically, the sponsor for Lauren's video on the topic of incels was a company that provided home testing kits for personal health, and she was promoting the male hormone test. "Did you know that globally sperm counts have dropped by 50 percent in the past four years? That means that globally men are producing less testosterone and experiencing hormonal imbalances as a result," she warned. "The only way to find out that this is happening to you is to get tested." The same company produced tests for women on fertility, progesterone, and ovarian reserve, but it's revealing that Lauren chose to advertise a test for men instead. The fact that most of her YouTube viewers were male and that she made a video reacting to incels' violence by highlighting sympathy for men's needs suggest that these women influencers can be highly persuasive yet are still often overlooked for their impactful role in the formation of misogynistic views within the far right. Far-right women influencers help construct archetypes of masculinity and support antifeminist attitudes while remaining in a position of privilege and visibility within the movement.

As "evidence" to support their view of femininity and masculinity, interestingly, all the far-right women influencers consistently promote scientific articles. In each video about feminism, dating, or relationships that I came across, there would be dozens of screenshots taken from media articles and academic studies highlighting high rates of depression and loneliness. These influencers falsely attribute these conditions to societal decay and the breakdown of the nuclear family due to feminism.

"When women do more chores like doing dishes and doing the laundry, and men do more chores like taking out the garbage or repairing the sink, couples reported having a happier sex life," Lauren Southern interpreted from the findings of an academic study published in the *American Sociological Review*. "So traditionalism is better for your marriage, better for your happiness, and better for your sex life," she concluded,[28] despite the fact that academic experts have criticized the study in question for drawing upon a data source that is more than two decades old.[29]

Brittany employs the same tactic by frequently citing research findings in multiple videos attacking feminism. In one vlog about fatherhood, she provided statistics from the U.S. Census showing that households with an absent father are more likely to be poor;

from the U.S. Department of Education revealing that children are more likely to do well in school with fathers at home; from the U.S. Department of Justice that children with fathers in the home are less likely to be incarcerated; and, finally, an academic study published in the *Journal of Marriage and Family* that children are more likely to use drugs in father-absent homes and less likely to be sexually active when they live in homes where the father is present.[30] When showing these data, Brittany claimed that society doesn't care about fathers anymore and that this attitude can be attributed solely to feminism and single motherhood. She did not, for instance, consider the role of structural conditions such as poverty, employment, and excessive criminal sentences as potentially mitigating factors for father-absent homes.

Using scientific articles is a well-adopted strategy for far-right recruitment, as Rebecca revealed in her how-to-red-pill women video (see chapter 2) or when citing an academic study in the *American Economic Journal* concerning women's decreasing happiness. According to Rebecca, women today are expected to succeed at home and work, what she described as the "idiotic concept of having it all."[31] Yet the study that Rebecca referred to has been criticized by other scholars in the field, who have found that not just women but both men and women have experienced similar decreases in life satisfaction.[32] Thus, it is incorrect to assume that feminism is solely responsible for women's unhappiness; rather, a combination of social, political, and economic factors simultaneously affect both women and men.

One trope that these influencers often repeat is the sexual market value (SMV) of women. The basic idea is that women are born with a high sexual value based on fertility and beauty that decreases as they get older and can no longer bear children. Far-right women claim that if a woman has multiple sexual partners, this exponentially decreases her SMV. Men, in contrast, are born with a low SMV, but it increases as they earn more income over time—a trait that is considered supposedly attractive to women because they desire a family and the household financial stability provided by men. These influencers popularize the idea of SMV as a natural state of gender relations.

"You are extremely valuable, but that value diminishes over time," Lauren Southern told her women viewers in 2017. "I mean, your sexual market value and your desirability as a potential partner in life." Because of that diminishment, she encouraged women to get married and have children early, which she claimed is "statistically one of the highest predictors of happiness in a woman's life," but, she cautioned, "your chances of having either of those things diminishes over time as you push them back for partying, for work, for education, or for finding yourself, whatever it may be." Lauren encouraged young women to not go to college or through a process of self-discovery. Rather, they should get married and start having babies as soon as possible. To back up her claim, she cited an academic study published in the *American Economic Review*, "Career, Family, and the Well-Being of College-Educated Women."[33]

However, she didn't read that article very well: the study actually points out that there's "no evidence of greater life satisfaction or greater emotional well-being" among women who have achieved both a successful career and a family. In other words, although women who have both a career and a family report not having greater happiness, that doesn't mean that they don't have an *equal* amount of happiness to women who have just a career or women who have just a family. Further, the study acknowledges that women who have both a career and a family believe the combination will "improve on aspects of their life such as sense of purpose, sense of control, prestige, or social status," aspects that are not necessarily captured in measurements of happiness.[34] This is an important caveat because it calls into question how happiness, which may differ from person to person, is measured. Nonetheless, far-right influencers continuously perpetuate the combined myth of SMV and happiness in traditional gender roles by misrepresenting academic research as evidence.

On the topic of dating, in 2019 Lauren Chen cited a study published in the *Journal of Personality and Social Psychology* that men report being more attracted to a woman's physical attractiveness, whereas women prefer a man's social status when selecting a potential romantic partner. "Thank you, science!" she exclaimed. "Generally speaking, men do care more about looks, and women do care more about something like wealth."[35] Upon closer inspection, I find that the authors of the study disclose that they measured only people described as at "the low end of social status and physical attractiveness"[36]—that is, not people at all levels of social status and physical attractiveness. Those at the lower end of social status and physical attractiveness may have less economic and social resources, so they find their options to be limited and thus rely on what is available to them. Some women may seek traits such as financial security provided by men, and some men may desire fertile women for their child-bearing abilities, but far-right women claim these preferences to be the result of the evolutionary impulse toward survival of the fittest. However, even if this claim were true from a biological determinist standpoint, advances in modern society mean that, for most people, depending on these resources to survive is no longer necessary. As an exception, those on the low end of social status and physical attractiveness are more likely to rely on these evolutionary traits to survive. The mating preferences detailed in the study are thus not generalizable to the entire population, as Lauren claimed.

Lauren Chen also cited another study in *Evolutionary Psychological Science* that finds that women care about men's physical attractiveness, sometimes at the expense of a less desirable personality. "What's interesting about that study is that it focused on looks and personality traits, but not actually something like wealth or social status," she commented. But given how the study measures personality traits, Lauren dismissed it as "subjective" and open to interpretation, compared to what she described as an "objective" trait such as "social status" (which is also, ironically, subjective). The takeaway, according to Lauren, is that "if you are a guy who is on the unattractive side or less attractive, the fact is you can still make up for those shortcomings physically by enhancing things like wealth or social status." On the flip side, "For a woman who's considered unattractive, you just have fewer options because men are more visually oriented."[37] Once more, Lauren sought a confirmation bias.

These far-right influencers cherry-pick certain academic studies on gender to fit their agenda, a strategy employed for metapolitical aims. As Ico Maly writes about far-right YouTubers, they "carefully construct an aura of 'evidence-based' discourse to construct their very own idiosyncratic political narrative on the basis of assembling facts, fiction, lies, and news taken out of context and re-entextualized in a very different narrative."[38] This type of media literacy conforms to YouTube's community guidelines while also allowing these influencers to establish credibility as authoritative figures. Likewise, the media scholar Francesca Tripodi describes this strategy as "scriptural inference" among conservative Christian and far-right groups, a media literacy practice of close reading of texts to find truth and "do your own research" that "bolsters their mistrust of mainstream media and supports their need to 'fact check' the news."[39] In short, these women influencers present their interpretations of scientific "evidence" that seems to fit into their worldview in order to advance the far right's mission, and their viewers don't question it because they assume it to be credible truth.

We all, of course, have an inherent bias in our personal interpretation of knowledge. We understand information in a way that fits our point of view. But these influencers do so in a manner that doesn't acknowledge the complexity and nuance of phenomena such as happiness and depression or omits crucial factors such as systemic inequalities in explaining issues such as absent fathers. They create a simplistic black-and-white narrative—a feature of all radical movements—that is much more manageable to sell as far-right propaganda and easier to comprehend for audiences.

The reason far-right women influencers focus on issues such as feminism and cultural Marxism and consequently propose the nuclear family unit as a solution to the societal breakdown caused by these leftist attitudes or use academic studies to bolster their claims is part of a greater strategy I alluded to in chapter 1: driving a metapolitical agenda to change mainstream social and cultural values. The far right and the alt-right in particular engage in "a cultural or ideological war for hegemony."[40] Rather than focusing on short-term electoral gains, these activists are set on a long-term plan to mobilize on ideas. They hope that this metapolitical strategy will eventually cause a shift in public consciousness attuned to their message. When delivering that message through networked intimacy techniques, such as "exposing the truth" to their audiences in vlogs, these far-right women influencers can speak directly to the masses with just a click.

Besides the tactic of using scientific articles, far-right women influencers appeal to religion to argue in favor of traditional gender norms. In particular, these women weaponize Christianity to reach a different audience.

Brittany Sellner identifies as Catholic, having also attended private Catholic school as a child.[41] Her Instagram page features her lighting candles at the church altar and visiting local chapels as well as world-renowned basilicas. Other photos of religious artwork and architecture evoke the notion of Western Christian civilization. She frequently refers to the decline of religiosity in her YouTube monologues, which she attributes to young people's unhappiness. "I believe our society's abandonment of God is the primary reason for its decay," she claimed in late 2019. She warned her viewers that declining church membership in the United States is a worrying sign because civilizations allegedly collapse when they lose religion: "Knowing God is real brings a moral framework to our lives, it gives meaning to our actions." Seeking fulfillment through marriage and starting a family can rectify this decline, she noted, if done with genuine purpose and joy in serving God.[42]

Expectedly, Brittany is also vehemently antiabortion, arguing that even if pregnancy results from rape or incest, abortion should not be permitted.[43] In response to the prochoice argument that abortion is a woman's choice because it involves her body, Brittany stated in one vlog, "The very premise is fallacious. It's not a woman's body; it's a completely separate human body growing inside her own." Brittany was considering only the well-being of the fetus, not the life of the woman, in this scenario. One of her Instagram posts featured her at a so-called March for Life rally in Vienna in October 2019, holding pink-and-white posters featuring images of babies, while pink balloons float in the background.[44] Her views closely align with the far-right nationalism that has arisen in European countries such as Poland, which is pro-Catholic and antiabortion in the name of "family values."[45] When the U.S. Supreme Court overturned *Roe v. Wade* in 2022, these influencers widely celebrated in their Instagram posts. "[Abortion] is always wrong. The circumstances of how you got pregnant, including but not limited to your financial situation, your mental health, and whether or not the father is a good person are not reasons that suddenly make the killing of an unborn child moral," wrote Robyn Riley in an Instagram Story connecting religiosity with morality.[46]

Rebecca Hargraves likewise points to her Catholicism for providing purpose in life; she had "returned" to the church through "rediscovering Christianity." Like Brittany, Rebecca also believes that Christianity can serve as a moral corrective for society. "It bound communities and nations together for centuries," she claimed in one vlog. "That is something that we are notably lacking, and I believe is at the heart of the failure of the America project—its loss of faith."[47] Yet the Pew Research Center documents that more than 70 percent of Americans identify as Christian, and although Christianity is indeed declining, the number of adults who practice non-Christian faiths is growing.[48] Thus, what bothers Rebecca is not so much that America has lost faith but that it is demographically shifting to a multifaith landscape. Further, a closer examination of the data on Christianity indicates that the number of white Americans who regularly attend church services has decreased significantly, a trend that likewise holds for Black and Hispanic Americans, although they still attend religious services at higher rates overall.[49] It's clear, then, that Rebecca was equating America's "loss of faith" with white American Christians' loss of faith. This resentment was later echoed by Congresswoman Marjorie Taylor Greene in 2022 in her call for a Christian nationalism that valorizes a mythic white Christian America.[50] Other far-right women influencers similarly refer to Christianity as a collective designation synonymous with Western civilization, whether it be in such phrases as "our Western Judeo-Christian, freedom-loving culture," which Lauren Chen uses in discussing our base biological imperative to reproduce as our duty to society, or in Lacey Lynn's advice to find community through your local church, a site that promotes what she sees as fundamental Western values.[51]

Although most influencers identify with Western Christianity, as I was writing this book, Robyn Riley began undergoing a process of conversion to the Eastern Orthodox Church. Although she was "raised in a traditional, Christian, conservative household"[52] (a sharp contrast to her liberal, feminist young adulthood), she revealed during a livestream in August 2020 that she lacked personal spiritual fulfillment in Protestantism and Catholicism and so turned to orthodoxy: "Personally, I feel like I'm being called to the Orthodox Church. That's what it seems like God wants for me."[53] She documented her experience of becoming an Orthodox catechumen in her Instagram posts, including snapshots of Bible study and her Orthodox-themed home decor. "My goal is to model for young women a wholesome, Godly way of living which demands accountability for ones [sic] actions as well as a nurturing of ones [sic] womanly qualities," she wrote in one post. Robyn later changed her username to "Brigids.cross" in honor of her patron saint, Saint Brigid of Kildare, whom she described as "the Patron Saint of fertility, babies, midwives, mariners, travellers, sailors, [and] fugitives," and to symbolize her aim "to offer fellowship to like minds and be a light for others in a time of darkness."[54] Here, she was tying narratives of religious salvation to a metaphor of radicalization.

Her journey to religious conversion was fostered by watching YouTube videos of Father Josiah Trenham, a pastor whom the anti-hate organization Southern Poverty Law Center describes as virulently anti-LGBTQ. Trenham has linked homosexuality to predatory behavior and claimed that tolerance for LGBTQ rights is akin to "a call for the overthrow of traditional religious and civilizational norms for family, sex and law."[55] Given the far right's homophobia and transphobia, it is not surprising that it uses traditional interpretations of religiosity to push gender norms of femininity and masculinity. Indeed, Robyn posted in Instagram Stories in September and October 2022 that "transgenderism" is a "perversion" and that "the more we let the word 'woman' get confused and muddied by the trans agenda, the less biological women will know themselves[,] . . . in the process . . . destroy[ing] womanhood."[56] These far-right figures argue that maintaining heterosexuality and the heterosexual family unit is a God-given responsibility. Any deviation results in moral decay within Western society. For instance, the Canadian influencer Faith Goldy, who is often spotted wearing her trademark cross necklace, openly identifies as a member of the Ukrainian Greek Catholic Church, having been raised in the religion. She has mentioned on several occasions the need for a return to traditional interpretations of Catholicism, arguing against progressive approaches that undermine the sanctity of family, such as tolerance of homosexuality.[57]

Of all the far-right women influencers, Ayla Stewart is the only one who identifies as Mormon. Her conversion to the Church of Latter-Day Saints occurred during adulthood, after years of her searching for a spiritual home.[58] Despite this slight deviation from the others, she aligns herself with Christianity. It's not uncommon for Mormons to consider themselves Christian; they view Mormonism as a reformation of Christianity (although it is often not recognized by Christians to be an official denomination). Like Christians, Mormons read the Bible and go to church. Ayla thus describes her experience with Christianity and Mormonism as synonymous, using the hashtag #Christian in her Instagram bio as well as #Christianity and #ChristianNation in her posts. She also recommends religious books by female Christian writers as a guiding foundation for a happy wife and mother.[59]

These far-right women are much more religious than their male counterparts, but that isn't surprising given that women in far-right movements have long been the bearers (literally) of tradition. Theological dictates regarding men's and women's roles in marriage, the family, and leadership are known as "complementarianism." That is, men and women have different but complementary roles and responsibilities according to their gender, as prescribed by the Bible. These far-right women uphold complementarianism to situate their "true," divinely ordained place.

Lauren Chen reflected this view when describing a marriage-preparation course that she and her fiancée had to complete to marry in the Catholic Church. Although her husband is Catholic, Lauren identifies as Baptist but is very open to having a Catholic husband and doesn't consider it an issue within their relationship. She stated that although she enjoyed the priest's discussion of biblical principles of marriage between a man and a woman during the course, she felt irritated by other aspects. "Where I started to get really frustrated with this class was when the talk about stewardship started," she explained. "So the issue of stewardship is a pretty big concept in Christianity, like it is, I think, in most religions, and it all has to do with taking care of something that's been entrusted to you. When it came to a talk about stewardship in a marriage class, I figured it would be about how the spouses are supposed to take care of each other and their children and, maybe more specifically, how the father or husband in the relationship is supposed to be the steward over his wife."[60] Lauren clearly indicated her belief in complementarianism here: a husband and wife are not equal but complementary, with the husband as the leader and protector of the household.

Complementarianism is not unique to the far right, and these influencers often promote it as "natural" and desirable. As Lauren continued describing what unfolded in the conversation on stewardship in the marriage-preparation course, her reaction swiftly became political. "It actually ended up being, though, a talk about how Catholics should embrace democratic socialism," she lamented. In particular, topics such as environmental consciousness and social justice triggered her far-right attitudes. "When we talk about social justice and this neo-Marxism infecting Christian churches, I think that's really one of the biggest tells that you have deviated from actual Christian theology," she complained. Yet this claim of deviation is false: theologians have shown that the demand for social justice is not new within the Christian faith (and, in fact, is as old as Jesus), and others emphasize the importance of the Christian message in changing contemporary society with progressive values.[61]

But rather than acknowledge the possibility that Christian theology has been historically interpreted through acts of social justice, Lauren described the topic of democratic socialism within the course as "an excuse to spew political propaganda." "With these people, who are trying to turn Christianity into Marxism, they're vocal, and they're not afraid to express their beliefs," she declared. "The rest of us, normal Christians, need to have enough conviction to fight back against that." Lauren assumed that most Christians are "normal" because, like her, they don't believe in promoting social justice. She argued that the focus of the conversation should be on Christ, not on "leftist politics," as if religious conviction belongs to one political ideology.

Whether by means of academic articles or religious narratives to promote the idea of gender norms based on femininity and masculinity, far-right women influencers employ a broad range of strategies in their propaganda, often including their personal reflections as a communicative tactic of networked intimacy. By targeting both secular and religious audiences, they're hoping to reach both the ears of a "recovering" feminist who is unhappy with her life situation by showing her scientific evidence that traditionalism is the antidote and the ears of a devout woman by appealing to what they see as the sacredness of her God-given duties. These far-right influencers promise women that a community of sisterhood is waiting for them.

Beyond targeting specific demographics of women, these influencers also showcase the bonds of far-right sisterhood. "Girls like to watch other girls talk, like they're there, they're having girl time,"

stated Lana Lokteff in a collab with Brittany Sellner and the British YouTuber Tara McCarthy in early 2017. "I think [these YouTube channels are] important so that other, younger girls can see, 'Hey, there's other girls that are more right-wing, and I want to be a part of that and feel like I'm a part of that conversation when I'm watching them talk.'"[62] The community of women isn't so different from such female-dominated spaces as sororities and professional networking associations.

The key difference here, though, is that these influencers repackage a racial and political identity to recruit vulnerable women into their cause. "This alt-right brand of feminization," the historian Alexandra Minna Stern writes, "is tinged with the emotional pull of white tribalism and calls to preserve Western civilization."[63] Lana made this message explicit when she stated in the same vlog, "I also think that white women are longing for a group; we don't really have a sisterhood. It's kind of been destroyed, right? Girls are longing for a group, and I think we can offer them that."

Brittany, perhaps sensing that it would be more strategic to refrain from discussing "white women" specifically, replied, "To broaden it, I think that antifeminists are also looking for a group. Everyone who bought into the feminism, you had all the celebrities you could rally around, [so] that you felt like you were accepted by everyone. . . . You felt like you belonged somewhere. But as someone who didn't subscribe to the current feminism [sic] views, you kind of feel left out."

For far-right women influencers, then, what does it mean to be a feminine figure? "One thing I find with the girls in the alt-right, there isn't certain girls you look up to like a role model, but it's almost like you have this archetype that we've created, of the ideal woman," Lana observed in this collab. She asked Brittany and Tara, "What is the ideal woman? What does it mean to be feminine [today]?"

"I really want to redefine what a strong woman is," replied Brittany, but not according to a feminist definition, which she falsely portrays as "antimen." She felt that there were few female role models she could look up to, except for the conservative commentator Anne Coulter and fellow influencer Lauren Southern, whose videos she watched before becoming politically active. "It's nice to create an environment for women who are more right wing or antifeminist, or whatever, to find like-minded individuals," she stated.

Robyn Riley had a similar experience. She found it difficult to pinpoint female role models in her life. "Women have been far more propagandized, and womanhood isn't properly demonstrated by most women today," she insisted in one of her vlogs. She instead relied on her friends and peers, citing Rebecca Hargraves and Brittany as close sources of inspiration. "It's kind of dire, finding female role models," she claimed but then enthusiastically stated, "I'm trying to be that for younger women."[64] In 2019, Robyn hosted a series called *Girl Talk* on her YouTube channel, which she described as "the podcast equivalent of a safe space for right-wing women who come together and talk about the things that are most important to us"[65] (note the assumption that right-wing women need a safe space). On the show, she invited guests to discuss topics ranging from improving fertility to dating, marriage, pregnancy, motherhood, religion, and, of course, femininity. Although these issues aren't necessarily ideological because women of all backgrounds can be interested in them, Robyn misrepresented them as areas of concern for right-wing women only.

One need not look very far to find far-right female-dominated online spaces. Whether it's the Red Pill Women subreddit or Stormfront's Ladies Only, these forums are geared toward discussions of women's experiences. But the media scholar Jessie Daniels finds that banal conversations are the norm rather than political dialogue. Women are interested in discussing "health and beauty and dating and marriage and losing weight."[66] Although some threads are explicitly racist, those threads are actually much less common.[67] What separates far-right women from other women in female-dominated spaces established to seek friendship and support is their choice to join the closed far-right community.

Mainstream women's online spaces are too left wing, according to Lauren Chen. In a vlog in mid-2020 about the subreddit community TwoXChromosomes, which is dedicated to women's issues, Lauren described it as "a de facto feminist forum" and a "feminist cesspool" where "not so much gender equality as gender ideology" was driving discussions.[68] "Gender ideology" is a concept developed by the political right that rejects the sex and gender distinction, arguing that separating sex from gender is a leftist ploy to cause societal decay and subvert the family unit. For instance, conservatives recently stoked moral panic that children are being "groomed"—a term normally associated with child sexual abuse—by gender ideology in schools.[69] The use of the term *gender ideology* functions discursively to bring together different forms of right-wing mobilization, united against progressive demands for gender equality and against tolerance for sexual diversity.[70]

And yet heterosexual gender norms still dominate mainstream society, where acceptance of conversations surrounding sexuality and women's rights remain contentious. Despite this dominant trend, Lauren believes that feminists have hijacked online forums to the point of alienating "conservative" women like herself. We "deserve a place to go to discuss lady things where they won't have Marxist, feminist propaganda shoved down their throats," she complained about TwoXChromosomes. "This is the type of environment so many female-dominated spaces cultivate; it's a very toxic one." These days, though, there are limitless options when it comes to women's online communities, including for the far right. I argue that mainstream platforms, such as the comments section on YouTube and Instagram, have by and large replaced private online forums for participating in discussions. In fact, far-right women's online communities have become exceedingly public.

One interesting aspect of these influencers is that they rarely discuss flaws in their personal lives and relationships, nearly always framing such topics in abstract terms as general reflections on the positions of young women in society today. This approach starkly contrasts with the anonymous online forums, chat rooms, and offline groups where women will admit to being in an abusive or neglectful relationship because participants feel that revealing such faults in their relationships provides a means of connecting to and eliciting sympathy from other women. Far-right women influencers, in contrast, paint an idealistic picture of married life or being engaged. I suspect that relatability has its limits in being a micro-celebrity and that far-right women feel the pressure to maintain a utopian image of the traditional heterosexual domestic life for the movement's propaganda.

These influencers frequently acknowledge, however, their past experience of not having female friends. Brittany admitted in late 2018, "I used to think that it was impossible for me to make friendships with other girls, but I used to believe this because I thought all girls have ulterior motives, or all girls just want to cause drama, etc." But, of course, after she became increasingly involved in the alt-right, this changed. "Over the course of my political activism, I've met some of the most spectacular girls in the world," she stated. "And I've made some of the most spectacular friendships in my entire life. These girls aren't at all catty or backstabbing. These girls are some of the most kind and courageous and genuine women we've ever met, and they're girls who've also taken a stand against feminism as well."[71] Brittany's message to female viewers is clear: come join us, and you'll find a "spectacular" sisterhood within the far right.

Lacey Lynn had a similar "ordeal." For her, female friendship "hasn't always been easy" and "still isn't," unlike in Brittany's case.[72] Perhaps this difference can be attributed to Brittany's political activism offline: her involvement in protests and her speaking engagements around the world have led to a strong network with other female activists, whereas Lacey was raising a young family in her early adult life and later sought friendships online.

Some far-right women influencers publicly showcase their mutual far-right friendships as a deliberate strategy of propaganda.

When Brittany hosted her wedding in the Austrian Alps, Rebecca Hargraves flew thousands of miles from the United States to attend the event, as did Robyn Riley, who was living in Brussels at the time. Both women appear in a group photo at the wedding on Brittany's Instagram page. Robyn later posted a selfie of herself and Brittany on her Instagram page with the caption, "If your [sic] looking for a woman to follow who practices what she preaches, and who is a Happy Warrior for the good left in the world, check out her social media. She's always been a great source of inspiration and motivation for me."[73] These influencers thus often promote other far-right women's visibility through the language of friendship.

Another tactic of displayed networked intimacy is the positioning of their friendships as authentic and genuine resistance against mainstream acceptance. Posting on her Instagram page an old selfie with Rebecca in mid-2020, Robyn wrote, "I met Rebecca for the first time in Austria and then we took a trip with our husbands to Budapest." "It was so incredible to actually hang out with and become friends with a woman who was like me," Robyn stated about Rebecca. "As a right wing woman, finding others like you to connect with is near impossible these days. I remember it being so spiritually energizing, to feel normal, to be around someone who had thoughts and concerns just like me. To feel relatable."[74] In this description of their selfie, Robyn's framed her friendship with Rebecca as not based solely on connection and relatability but on shared political ideology, which, she implied, creates the bond for true friendships. Yet her description of being a "right wing woman" as a hindrance to friendship and social acceptability is at odds with this frame. After all, nearly 40 percent of women voted for Trump in the 2016 election, and 47 percent of white women did so, according to the Pew Research Center.[75] That trend continued in the 2020 election.[76] Robyn's "right wing" political views, combined with her race and gender, are thus certainly far from a minority (even if she's Canadian, her commentary is mostly on U.S. politics). Rather, the intent in calling herself "right wing" was to deflect criticism and normalize her extreme far-right beliefs.

Because of the alleged potential for isolation and loneliness resulting from these political views, Robyn issued a call to action in the caption of her photo with Rebecca. "The strength and motivation I felt after that trip is exactly why they don't want us organizing. Why every time right wing people get together publicly they're slandered, doxed [i.e., having personal information revealed to the public] and have their lives ruined. They know that if we effectively organize the momentum of that will snowball into something immensely powerful."[77] Building on a perceived victimhood of right-wing people, Robyn here constructed an "us versus them" world-view that paints the political left ("they") as evil and the political right as moral and righteous.

She concluded, "Seek out those of like mind however you can, we need to find a way to come together, be it in secret or otherwise. We cannot win unless we find each other and stand shoulder to shoulder against those who wish to destroy everything we hold dear." Her final stance rang loud and clear: "I've said it before and I'll say it again, it's time to circle the wagons." One might find this type of absolutist rhetoric in a call for unity across various extremist movements seeking to mobilize adherents.

In this Instagram selfie description, Robyn very quickly and effectively shifted from discussing female friendships to enacting a call for action in just a few sentences. The framing of her journey as simultaneously personal and political can have a broad appeal to many potential recruits. In this case, Robyn was speaking directly to women to join the far right to feel a sense of validation. Thus, as I have argued throughout this book, followers of these influencers can be easily exposed to radicalizing narratives disguised as selfies and vlogs on public mainstream platforms such as Instagram and YouTube.

The way in which far-right women influencers frame their dating, relationship, and friendship dynamics within far-right politics is what makes their voices unique within the movement. For these women, it is impossible to separate personal from political content because the two are interwoven in cementing a far-right image and community. By presenting themselves as authentic and accessible to their followers—for example, by revealing a desire for or the loss of friendship—these influencers transform the language of far-right ideology into an aspirational lifestyle.

"Thinking about starting a matchmaking service" was displayed on my phone's screen. I had been scrolling through Instagram and tapped on Robyn Riley's new Story. Robyn was polling her followers to gauge their interest in such a service aimed toward heteronormative "right wing, family oriented" singles. "If there are any women of childbearing age who live in Southern California looking for a right wing man, let me know," she advertised. "I have a white dude who makes 400k a year, is 6"2 [sic] and is Christian looking for a wife. He likes guitars and guns, seems super cool lol not even joking. Dm [direct message] me if interested."[78] This announcement piqued my interest, and I wondered if this single man had directly reached out to Robyn to be a matchmaker. It also raised a question regarding the geographic distribution of her followers, particularly if many live in liberal cities and are struggling to find a partner with right-wing views. I was struck that this man lived in southern California, while Robyn lived thousands of miles away in Canada.

Robyn solicited responses by asking interested followers to email her their "sex, age, ethnicity, height, weight, net income, skills, hobbies, religious affiliation, preferences in a wife/husband, country or state [of residence]." These standard categories are found in all online dating sites, but her followers' responses would likely be less diverse than those found on mainstream platforms.

This announcement also raises the question: What happens when these single women influencers get married and inevitably start a family? At one point on her honeymoon, Brittany Sellner filmed a conversation with her newlywed husband, Martin. (She also linked the video description with their wedding photos on her Instagram page.) In a display of networked intimacy, allowing their viewers a glimpse into their honeymoon trip, the two sat under a shady umbrella at an outdoor beach café on the sunny Italian coast drinking lattes. Speaking directly to the phone camera, they discussed their decision to get married despite today's supposed social pressures against having children and families. They framed the reason for this social trend to be antitraditionalism, not acknowledging the possibility of other impeding factors that affect family planning, such as economic strain and job stability; they also identified marrying and having a family as the only correct lifestyle choice. In speaking about the struggle to have a single-income family, where the father is the sole bread winner and the mother is a stay-at-home mom, Brittany remarked, "I was doing politics full-time for a few years, but when I met Martin, and once he proposed, we talked about it, and I made the decision that when we have a family, I'm really going to step back and probably just write books." Thus, having a single-income family is not an issue for the Sellners; rather, Brittany's decision is a political choice. She continued, "Obviously I'll prioritize motherhood once we have children; our political struggle is to ensure a life and safety for our future children."[79]

The fundamental role of women in the far right is thus to weaponize motherhood for the movement. As Kathleen Blee astutely observed nearly twenty years ago of the far-right women she interviewed, being part of a social movement creates powerful bonds of community, which is considered like a family.[80] For these far-right women, their literal family is not just a household but a symbol of the movement.

As Brittany stated in an earlier vlog, "For many of us, myself included, we view the choice of having a role in politics as rather more a duty than a desire." She added, "While I'm able to have a full-time career in politics at the moment, obviously as soon as I become a mother, I'm going to have to make a choice. And obviously I've already made the choice. I choose the marriage and the family path." She did not intend to leave far-right activism entirely, however. "This doesn't mean, though, that when I become a mother, I'm going to leave this fight fully; of course not," she affirmed. "You could say that I'll still be fighting the battle, but I have changed my position on the battlefield." Her twin sister, Nicole, who appeared in this early video on Brittany's channel, agreed. "For example, helping to fight the culture war by writing books as opposed to on-the-ground reporting. Or every once in a while giving a speech or making a YouTube video," she contributed. "But of course, this wouldn't be consistent or full-time because while, right now, we only have responsibility for ourselves, in the future we'll have responsibility for children."[81] The British YouTuber Tara McCarthy also foresaw the task of homeschooling her future children as time-consuming. Thus, she noted in a collab with Lana and Brittany that when that day came, she would probably be able to make video content only part-time rather than full-time.[82] These influencers' intention to retire from full-time political activism once they have children isn't surprising given that they view being a wife and mother as the ultimate duty for a woman within the far-right cause. Yet only six weeks after giving birth to her first child in November 2021, Brittany continued to upload YouTube videos, providing reactions to current events.

Another influencer who has openly discussed her transition to motherhood is Robyn. In the announcement of her first pregnancy in September 2019, she brought up a conundrum that many influencers have probably faced or will face at one point. "There are many women, I think, who are in the political right-wing side of YouTube who would rightfully want to just sort of exit at this point [of becoming a mother] and focus on their life, their health, and their family. I completely respect, understand that because I've been considering whether or not I want to do the same thing," she admitted.[83]

But Robyn reassured her viewers that she wouldn't become obsolete. "On the other hand, I think that I should be courageous because now I really have something to offer other than my opinions and ideas, which you can get anywhere," she claimed. "We on the right wing often forget to promote what it is that we really believe in by living what we say, what we should do." This point signaled a big shift in the focus of Robyn's content from regular political commentary on current events to daily portrayals of motherhood and domestic life. Along with this substantive shift was a change in communication style as well. Robyn began slowly to transition off YouTube and instead actively promote her Instagram page, thus indicating the best fit for content creation is based on platform affordances.

"Now that I'm about to become a mom, which I'm extremely excited about, I want to start focusing on mom content, which is going to be really different for my old-time viewers," Robyn explained in the same vlog. "It's not going to be that interesting for dudes and my male audience, unless you're trying to conceive with your wife, or maybe you're a father yourself. But I've been shifting my content towards women now, and that's only going to continue." This announcement aligned with Robyn's earlier expressed goal to engage with more women followers. I wasn't the only one to notice this change in direction. When I spoke with Caleb Cain, the young man who had been radicalized on YouTube (see chapter 2), he also observed that "stuff that Robyn's doing now is a lot different."[84] Discovering that she was pregnant was the perfect time for Robyn to pursue this approach. "I'm sick of just talking about ideas. There will always be an element of that on my channel. But I want to make content about the meaning that I've created in my life," she stated in the same vlog. True to her word, she stopped posting videos on her YouTube channel and began to share daily updates of motherhood and homemaking on her Instagram account.

The next chapter looks at what happens for these influencers in the transition from being a single young woman to being married and having a family. It details the ideal tradwife, who provides advice on pregnancy, motherhood, and domestic life. I argue that this type of content is far from apolitical. On the contrary, it is extremely political because it serves a greater purpose: the pursuit of an idyllic home as the bedrock for a far-right white utopia. I contend that when this visual depiction is communicated through self-presenting frames of authenticity in the genres and practices of influencer culture, it serves an effective metapolitical purpose.

4
THE MAKING OF A TRADWIFE

oin me as I bring power back into the home while return-
ing to vibrant health and radiant living," stated Elora,
otherwise known by her pseudonym "Blonde Buttermaker," in March 2017. "Eating the way our ancestors did is a
wonderful guide to obtaining vibrant health."[1]

Never would I have expected to be learning useful culinary techniques from a woman sponsored by Red Ice TV, an alternative
media-streaming platform that was banned from YouTube in 2019
for promoting white-nationalist views. Along the way, I learned the
importance of lacto fermentation for maintaining a healthy gut, the
nutritional benefits of homemade butter, and quality purchases of
organic, local vegetables—but only from "businesses that support
our political views."[2]

Elora is different from the other far-right women influencers I
have featured so far in this book in that she is relatively older, long
married, and with a family of three children. She doesn't post vlogs
on a regular basis (and they are produced by a company), and her
content focuses almost exclusively on cooking recipes and techniques, with very little discussion of her political ideology. But

when listing the nutritional benefits of foods, Elora also stresses that such foods are important to consume based on the traditions of what she calls "northern European diets." This not-so-subtle nod explains why she is sponsored by Red Ice, which is co-owned by the husband-wife duo of Swedish white supremacist Henrik Palmgren and fellow influencer Lana Lokteff, who has openly denied the Holocaust.

As Cynthia Miller-Idriss, a sociologist of the far right, writes, food is "a particularly rich domain to embed messages about identity, tradition, culture, and obligations to families, households, and the homeland," as encapsulated in the logo for Elora's channel: "Tradition—Heritage—Nutrition." As Miller-Idriss points out, Elora's content reflects that "ideals about food, cooking, and nurturing white families have long intersected with gendered understandings of proper roles as wives and mothers within the far right."[3]

This trope of white motherhood is reflected in the opening montage for Elora's videos, which features the blond Elora looking down blissfully at her pregnant body in a field surrounded by wildflowers, and in subsequent images of her lovingly holding her baby. A quick succession of photos flash by, displaying pickled vegetables in mason jars, fresh produce and flowers placed in woven baskets, and, of course, homemade butter laid next to a pile of organic eggs. In an homage to ancestry, a collage of black-and-white photos of white European families is featured, presumably of Elora's lineage. The merging of food and family is a key element of far-right propaganda, as Miller-Idriss notes: "Food and food-related rituals have long been understood as essential to collective belonging, emotion, memory, and national identity."[4]

Robyn Riley, for instance, frequently posts on Instagram photos of food preparation and consumption in her household. "One of my newest #pregnancy related #recipes," she wrote in the description of one post in late 2019. "Wild Alaskan salmon #caviar on Avocado Toast," topped with crumbled goat cheese, lemon juice, and fresh cilantro. She also relayed the nutritional benefits. "Salmon Caviar is a superfood and that's putting it mildly. The bioavailability of Omega-3 fatty acids, folate, iron and lean protein found in roe is second to none. Making it the perfect pregnancy food for mama and baby."[5] Although seemingly apolitical content, Robyn's post, when understood in context, conveys the importance of food consumption as linked to prenatal nutrition—a gesture of her commitment to white racial reproduction. Robyn often posts Instagram Stories featuring her homemade pregnancy tea blend; organic, grass-fed products; and meal preparation of baby food, such as a puree of avocado, egg yolk, cultured butter, and sweet potato.[6] I argue that the crucial daily showcasing of foods through an intimate medium such as Instagram Stories captures these influencers' networked intimacy practices, with the potential for more interaction with followers through Direct Message, emoji reactions, poll functions, and question stickers for Q&As.

Many far-right women influencers have said that they will step back from political activism once they get married and start a family. Their focus, they claim, should instead be on domestic life and child-rearing, as depicted by Elora. But it would be incorrect to assume that pulling back from political activism means disappearing completely online. Rather, for the far right, focusing on the household is a highly political act. This is where the far right intersects with the tradwife movement.

"As a hashtag, tradlife [traditional life] dates back to at least 2015. It anchors an archive of images, videos, and other online content produced mostly by women who call themselves tradwives," writes the journalist Seyward Darby.[7] The hashtags #tradwife and #tradlife reveal one's identification not only with a certain traditional lifestyle but also with a growing online community of like-minded others that gained mainstream media attention in 2020 with the airing of a *BBC Stories* short documentary and headlines in national newspapers such as the *New York Times* and *The Guardian*.[8] Hashtags and meme sharing have long been used in digital networking to create social bonds and collective meaning within a community, while also serving as propaganda for a movement.[9]

"As a culture, tradlife is a mode of existing both online and off," Darby continues. "To be trad is to seek a wholesale return to the social norms and gender roles of the past, when life for women was supposedly better, safer, and stronger." In short, tradlife comes down to three elements: "the family unit, common sense, and self-reliance."[10] A cursory internet search of tradwives results in images and memes of 1950s-style (white) housewives cooking in well-stocked kitchens and cleaning up after their husbands and children around the house. The online community of tradwives ranges from blogs centered on homemaking to social media forums such as the subreddit community tradwife, all of them spaces for women to share tips and encourage this lifestyle. I also found that blogging and newsletters as well as more extensive use of the image-based social media platform Pinterest are more popular among tradwife influencers than within the far right in general. Tradwives use Pinterest to create and share image boards (like a digital collage) on themes such as fashion, interior decorating, food recipes, and gardening for inspiration.

Alena Kate Pettitt is a popular British tradwife who conjures up the stereotype of a 1950s housewife. She runs the blog *The Darling Academy*, where "you will find articles on good old-fashioned recipes, housekeeping, marriage and family values, including tips on how to live a simple vintage-inspired life, free from modern day pressures."[11] Articles range from cooking recipes for classic British favorites such as plum pie with custard to advice columns such as "Your Husband Should Always Come First!" Alena has also authored and self-published two books—*English Etiquette: The Motivation Behind the Manners* (2019) and *Ladies Like Us* (2016). Under the banner "Make a Home," Alena's blog also features a selection of recommended household products, such as an ironing board and a fine-china teapot (whether she makes a commission from advertising these products is unclear).

Perhaps the most well-known tradwife is twenty-eight-year-old Caitlin Ann Huber, who goes by the pseudonym "Mrs. Midwest." With more than 200,000 subscribers on her YouTube channel, she presents a modern twist on the housewife, featuring popular videos with titles such as "My Glow Up | 7 Ways I Changed My Appearance,"

"Ladylike Beauty & Grooming Tips," "How to Speak Femininely," "5 Ways to Be More Feminine TODAY," and "Ladylike Behavior & Posture Tips." Caitlin often uses buzzwords such as *vibrant, radiant, polished,* and *enhanced* to describe the ideal feminine woman. Importantly, she presents her message through self-motivation terms, encouraging her followers to "upgrade" or "level up" into being a lady as a journey of personal transformation—much like Robyn's "glow up" transformation described in chapter 2. Caitlin's YouTube channel is complemented by her well-curated Pinterest page (with 9,400 followers) and Instagram feed (with 52,000 followers).

Caitlin also maintains a personal blog with posts that include wardrobe inspirations and home decor reminiscent of beauty and lifestyle influencers' tastes. One page on her blog, titled "Shop My Life!," lists separate categories of beauty, cooking, and homemaking featuring Caitlin's favorite everyday picks.[12] Here, followers can select products ranging from cosmetic eyebrow tint ("My absolute go-to!" the description reads) to measuring cups ("Can a woman get by without her Pyrex!?") to a sewing machine ("My hubby bought me this for Christmas a few years ago, and it works a treat!"). All products include an Amazon link for purchase. Caitlin revealed in one of her YouTube video descriptions that she gets a small commission from purchases made through the links for beauty products. "Mrs. Midwest is a participant in the Amazon Services LLC Associates Program, an affiliate advertising program designed to provide a means for sites to earn advertising fees by advertising and linking to Amazon.com," reads the disclaimer. "Some of the provided links are in coordination with this program."[13] Beauty and lifestyle bloggers have long recommended products and worked with corporate sponsors, so Caitlin receiving a commission is nothing new or problematic, but the messaging here is subtle. Caitlin is selling an ideal image of a housewife, and the products listed are not just to improve one's physical appearance—and thus femininity—but also to improve one's household through cooking and cleaning supplies. She monetizes the tradwife lifestyle. Via her YouTube channel, Caitlin also sells merchandise embellished with the words *feminine family* and mugs that display the name "Mrs. Midwest," with these products featuring a white background and black cursive font for a simple, minimalist aesthetic.[14] More recently, Caitlin has gained mainstream sponsors, such as the sustainable-apparel company LilySilk, in which her Instagram Story followers can receive exclusive discount codes for future purchases at LilySilk.[15] I discuss these type of entrepreneurial practices by influencers in chapter 5, but the upshot here is that they aim to convey an aspirational image while still retaining a perception of relatability through attainable consumption.

Another tradwife, the British influencer Juliana Stewart, likewise maintains a blog called *Ladies Let's Chat*, with posts that focus on relationships, well-being, and homemaking. Juliana provides advice for women looking to overcome sex anxiety in their marriage and tips on how to "be a lady." She is also a columnist who writes articles such as "Here's Why I Decided to Become a #Tradwife," in which she defends a woman's choice to be a homemaker in response to "constant pressure to feel fulfilled by 'having it all'" with a career and family.[16] Yes, every woman should have the choice to be a homemaker, but Juliana also wrote a disturbing article comparing "a strong masculine man" and "an abusive man" that hinges on this choice: "both have similar traits." Her piece of advice to women on the dating market? "Your standards and boundaries protect you from unpleasant behavior."[17] Although she provided additional good tips on the warning signs of an abusive man, she placed the burden of responsibility on women to exercise "standards and boundaries," thus giving men a pass to perpetrate abusive behavior and legitimizing it as normal.

In addition, Juliana used her Pinterest page to promote her podcast, which had the same title. Podcasts are a popular medium for tradwives because, as Caitlin mentioned in her YouTube vlog "The 5 Keys to Fun & Productive Homemaking!," they can listen while doing menial homemaking tasks in order to "make chores fun."[18] In the beginning of the podcast series, Juliana had a few episodes featuring interviews with well-known figures in the trad community. The first episode was a conversation with Alena Kate Pettitt, while another episode featured the U.K.-based American tradwife Lillian, who goes by the pseudonym "Postmodern Mom" on YouTube. Lillian characterized her husband as someone whom "I submit to."[19] The concept of "submission" is common in the trad community, with one likely to find it in written posts in the Red Pill Wives subreddit, for example. Tradwives such as the Canadian influencer Cynthia Loewen are quick to point out that the term *submission* is frequently misunderstood as sexual obedience in a "slave and master" distinction but is instead about spirituality and faith to devote oneself to one's husband—similar to gender complementarianism discussed in chapter 3.[20] Yet I remain suspicious of the latter connotation when reading stories of domestic abuse littered across the subreddit forums.

By the time Juliana's podcast episode featuring Lillian was released, Lillian had already become a visible tradwife figure in the United Kingdom. She and her husband had previously appeared on a talk show on Channel 5 discussing their lifestyle,[21] garnering more visibility for their YouTube channel Postmodern Family, which bears the slogan "Traditional values—Modern world" and features daily home life and reaction videos. At one point, Lillian even offered her YouTube viewers the option to send a gift for their new baby using a registry link on Amazon.[22] The tradwife community is more tight-knit than one might realize. Sending gifts to a stranger isn't very common, but for this community a newborn is a symbol of the nuclear family—the bedrock of society. Similarly, when Brittany Sellner gave birth to her son in November 2021, her viewers could donate gifts registered on her wish list, and in return they would receive a personal thank you card.[23] These influencers invite their online audiences a look into and participation within the personal confines of their lives through networked intimacy. Making the content of one's domestic life public in order to promote a lifestyle is a tactic of the far-right movement.

These women effectively market their ideology under the guise of an influencer practice, such as crowdsourcing donations. Further, you can purchase branded merchandise from the Postmodern Family on Spring, bearing slogans such as "Make Britain Great Again" and face masks (worn during the COVID-19 pandemic) displaying the mantra "Give Back Our Liberty"—both phrases echoing the far right's agenda of nationalism more than a purely traditionalist cause. One can also purchase music sung and recorded by Lillian, a former opera singer, on Amazon and Apple Music, with albums called *Patriotic British Classics*, *Romantic French Art Songs*, and *Italian Classics for Romantics*. Lillian and the Postmodern Family aren't neatly classified as part of the far right, and there are clear differences at play, but the boundary between trad and far right can be blurry. Their reverence for Western "classics" and romanticism is mixed with overtones of nationalism that is more commonly found in far-right circles.

Tradlife and the far right certainly overlap on shared values such as antifeminism and traditional gender norms, and both are expressed as reactionary movements. They also similarly engage in content practices to solicit attention and build community, aiming for the perception of relatability with followers through the sharing of experiences and guiding viewers with supportive and motivational language. What isn't always clear is where the division lies.

As Caitlin Huber said in early 2020 in defense against her critics, "Traditionalism is not about bringing us back to the 1950s. It's not about extreme political views. It's simply about maintaining and celebrating traditional structures such as marriage, family, religion."[24] Tradwives often claim that they're not extremists, white supremacists, or affiliates of the far right.

"Traditional Housewives have been a part of culture for centuries, inextricably linked to and at the heartbeat of every religion, race, and nation," wrote Alena Kate Pettitt on *The Darling Academy* in 2020. "To claim [it] belongs to one specific ideology shows that you haven't done your research and have an agenda against housewives.

I am part of a community of women who are from a vast array of ethnicities, cultures, and faith beliefs."[25] After having been featured in a *BBC Stories* documentary, Alena faced much public criticism for her lifestyle. This was not the first time that she had denied association with the far right: a tradwife "is categorically not a white supremacist(!?)," she wrote in an earlier blog post.[26] At one point, she even posted a media article on her public Facebook page about an interview of me by the Swedish antiracist magazine *Expo* about tradwives, in which she accused both the journalist and me of engaging in a "smear campaign" and perpetuating an agenda.[27]

The twenty-one-year-old Canadian tradwife Cynthia Loewen likewise made a vlog debunking what she sees as myths and negative coverage of the tradwife movement in mainstream media. "I've never met a woman who is actually like the women who these people are talking about in their articles," she stated—presumably, the type of woman Cynthia had never met is one who is in the far right. According to her definition, some tradwives are women who have always wanted to be stay-at-home mothers, while others previously followed a mainstream lifestyle of career and family but were tired of balancing the two roles and chose to be homemakers instead. "The media has vilified this subset of women, and it's just a small community of people who are just looking to connect with women because a lot of women who chose to embrace a more traditional lifestyle often feel marginalized in their communities. And it's very difficult to find other people who live in very similar ways."[28]

Yet others, such as the Australian YouTuber Daisy Cousens, simply claim that feminists are jealous of tradwives because feminists are, according to the far right and tradlife proponents, unhappy.[29] Although Daisy does not identify as a tradwife or with the trad lifestyle, she defends the community. Her YouTube content is like that of other far-right influencers; she's an antifeminist who comments negatively on women's efforts in "social justice" issues and the culture wars. Her vlogs feature paraphernalia in the background that reflect her political views: a red "Make America Great Again" hat and a mug sold by the conservative commentator Steven Crowder.

Alt-right celebrity Milo Yinnapoulous's book *Dangerous* is also conspicuously placed on the bookshelf behind her. It's thus no surprise that far-right supporters would endorse the trad community for its common ideological strand.

In response to the claim that the tradwife movement isn't directly affiliated with the far right, the journalist Seyward Darby makes an astute observation: "To be sure, not every tradwife is a white supremacist, but the community's hunger for the distinct boundaries of the past makes it vulnerable to far-right messaging. Tradwives and white nationalists share core objectives (more babies), myths (America's [or the West's] moral decline), and iconography (happy heterosexual families). Such close proximity, particularly on social media, makes the exchange of ideas a straightforward prospect."[30]

The media scholar Ashley Mattheis argues that aspects of the trad scene elevate racial (i.e., white) superiority and normative gender (i.e., heterosexual) dynamics. Trad culture promotes ideals of femininity and masculinity that historically stem from white, European, upper-middle-class relations.[31] Darby agrees: "Most tradwives are white, and they embrace a dream of comfort, contentment, and affluence specific to lived white experiences."[32] The desire for this lifestyle creates the intersection between trad and far-right networks.

Ayla Stewart is a prominent figure who overlaps the tradwife and far-right communities. From recommending books on topics ranging from traditional health remedies to homemaking, Ayla was an early adopter of YouTube vlogging in 2015. She was known earlier for her blog *Mother, Lover, Goddess* at a time when "'mommy blogging' was on the rise, and Ayla jumped on the trend" in the mid-2000s, Darby writes. As "Ayla kept doing research on traditional lifestyles and gender roles, by 2010, [her] blogging tone had morphed" to attacking feminism for undermining families.[33] She later started a new blog called *A Wise and Glorious Purpose*, which she renamed *Nordic Sunrise* in 2015 and then eventually *Wife with a Purpose*, which became her trademark pseudonym.

Ayla provides advice on what she calls "traditional parenting and European cultural homeschooling" in order to "instill in your children a sense of European identity and their European ancestry." She recommends books on children's health published in the 1930s, 1940s, and 1950s—"1955 at the latest"—because earlier books contain "ancient wisdom" not tainted by modern Western medicine. Education should emphasize "European cultural identity" with folktales, stories, songs, toys, and "authentic European" foods that celebrate traditions. Doing so is important, Ayla argues, because it instills in children "character building" to "give them a sense of that great European heritage and pride through cultural traditions," which public schools lack, having been taken over by what she calls "the social justice warrior movement, that feminism, equality, this person's rights, and protest and all that." Her rallying cry is "let's preserve it, let's revive it"—"it" symbolizing white American identity.[34]

Far-right movements have long preferred homeschooling as a means to circumvent mainstream social and cultural norms. It's "a method that almost all racist groups promote if not require to prevent children from becoming 'double-minded' as they learn different racial values at home and in school," writes Kathleen Blee.[35] Both Brittany Sellner and Lauren Southern, for instance, agreed that they will homeschool their future children to avoid left-wing "indoctrination" in public education.[36] "I would be terrified if my child, for example, had to go to this crazy, leftist, liberal school," said Brittany during her pregnancy. "Then I would be terrified because every day they would be trying to brainwash and indoctrinate something that is just one hundred percent the opposite of our values, our way of life, and our vision for how the world should be, and then they would come home and be undoing all that." She mentioned the possibility of her child being exposed to the idea of gender as a fluid identity or of choosing a gender different than the one assigned to them at birth.[37] Robyn Riley likewise recently posted an Instagram Story using anti-Semitic and anti-LGBTQ slurs, asking her followers, "What are homeschool moms doing for history textbooks? I am not teaching my kids the zog [Zionist Occupied Government] globo [globalist] homo [homosexual] version of history." She added, "Can someone please make a based history textbook lol maybe I'll just use the Bible and call it a day."[38]

Far-right women hence see the opportunity to be involved in trad culture because it seemingly lacks any political ideology. Their incursion, writes Mattheis, is "a productive site for the circulation of and radicalisation to extreme ideologies because it is *not* explicitly racist and extremist. Instead, it amplifies extant racialised and gendered discriminatory beliefs intrinsic to normative culture." As a result, "what is narrated in #Trad culture as social harm (posed by feminism and modern gender roles) becomes amplified in extremist online cultures as an existential threat of (white) societal collapse."[39]

At times, it is easy to separate tradwives from far-right women based on the purpose behind their lifestyle. Although both advocate the nuclear family unit and designated gender roles, the far right has an explicit political message: to uphold and preserve Western civilization. For example, Caitlin prefers the hashtags #femininefamily and #aproncladarmy, whereas Ayla uses #nationalism, #americafirst, and #volk. Far-right women not only embrace traditional gender roles but do so with an agenda that overtly and literally reproduces a racial nationalism. Ayla's call for a "white baby challenge" detailed in the introduction of this book exemplifies this agenda more than anything else.

Immersion into these communities can be more subtle. A woman in the trad community can very easily slip into the far right (as was Ayla's experience) and vice versa. I noticed this when I saw Brittany Sellner like Caitlin's Instagram posts, who in turn liked Brittany's posts. Although simply liking someone's Instagram photos isn't enough to signal their support for the far right, it's telling that two influencers who represent seemingly disparate (as they claim) online communities—trad and far right—would follow each other on the platform. In fact, there are several mutual follows between Caitlin and the far-right women influencers featured in this book. Robyn

Riley, for instance, in March 2022 shared a selfie on an Instagram Story wearing a maternity band with the text overlay "Shout out to @mrs.midwest [i.e., Caitlin] for the amazing recommendation on a postpartum belly band. This one is fabulous."[40] Clearly, there is more overlap between these communities than tradwives would like to admit. Are these exchanges the result of an algorithmic recommendation? Caleb, the young man who was radicalized by alt-right YouTubers (chapter 2), pointed out to me that he had come across Caitlin in his viewing habits.[41]

Caitlin had deleted a Reddit account, where she actively posted in the Red Pill Women and Red Pill Wives subreddit forums, encouraging women to date masculine men and to submit to their husbands as the leader of the household. She has also liked and approved being featured in posts on Instagram pages that contain white-supremacist content and has cited the white nationalist Stefan Molyneux as a source of intellectual inspiration.[42] Perhaps most revealing, Caitlin has admitted that her political views are a bit extreme, so she deliberately masks them with feminine topics: "Because my message can be kind of intense for some people, like the things I believe, I like to pad it with skin care and how I clean my house to attract more of a female audience," she stated in early 2019.[43] The tradwife label can serve as an effective cover for more insidious political opinions. At the same time, engaging with a broader variety of topics, such as beauty and household care, helps to legitimize far-right ideology by branding it as lifestyle content through the practices of networked intimacy.

In the run-up to the 2020 U.S. election, President Donald Trump tweeted, "The 'suburban housewife' will be voting for me. They want safety & are thrilled that I ended the long running program where low income housing would invade their neighborhood."[44] This racist dog whistle pointed to the fear of an invasion of the suburbs by Black and other nonwhite Americans disproportionately represented in low-income housing. Indeed, the phenomenon known as "white flight"—the large-scale migration of white American families from urban neighborhoods that were becoming more racially diverse to homogenously white suburbs—defined housing segregation in the 1950s and 1960s and is a legacy that continues today.[45] In the nostalgic world of far-right tradwives, the image of a (white) housewife in a (white) suburb reigns supreme.

Lacey Lynn fits the stereotypical image of a far-right woman who is a tradwife. Like Ayla Stewart, Lacey crosses the trad and far-right communities. With outfits frequently consisting of a pearl necklace and collared dress, she embodies the 1950s aesthetic of a homemaker. Her Instagram feed, on the one hand, is littered with photos of homemade American meals and occasional black-and-white stills of the television sitcoms *Leave It to Beaver* and *The Donna Reed Show*.[46] Her YouTube channel, on the other hand, contains a mix of antifeminist political content and descriptions of her red pill journey, while also showcasing cooking recipes and house-cleaning tips. Lacey has claimed, for instance, that differences between races exist due to biological determinism. "There are studies done on race and IQ differences," she asserted in early 2018,[47] in effect promoting eugenics. Meanwhile, her followers can learn the method of canning pickles in another video on her channel. Lacey was at the forefront of the tradwives movement before foraying into the far right and bridges these two communities.

Lacey cites as her biggest source of inspiration a woman who has recently gained notoriety among younger audiences—Phyllis Schlafly. In the FX television series *Mrs. America* (2020), Schlafly is centered as the leader of the countermovement against ratification of the Equal Rights Amendment (ERA) during the 1970s. The ERA is a proposed (ongoing) amendment to the U.S. Constitution that would provide equal rights for all Americans regardless of their sex. In the series, Schlafly's political activism is depicted in parallel to the women's rights and feminist groups mobilizing for the pro-ERA side.

"I was enthralled by this woman," stated Lacey in one vlog focusing on Schlafly. "I wanted that smile, that confidence. The ability to shrug off insults with humility. The ability to spout off facts with confidence. I wanted to be like her." One might expect that Lacey was saying this in the context of the TV series' premiere, with its first episode introducing Schlafly to viewers, but she made these comments back in 2017. She had discovered Schlafly upon reading her obituary the previous year and soon became infatuated with her. "I began to watch her talks and debates on YouTube," Lacey continued. "When I ran out of videos, I ordered her books. And stayed up late and woke up early in order to read, and I just couldn't get enough of learning about the antifeminist movement and Phyllis Schlafly."[48]

During her fight against ratification of the ERA, Schlafly established the Eagle Forum, which is also represented on the TV series. Today, the Eagle Forum still operates as a conservative interest group that lobbies on family issues and traditional policies, and its current leader is Schlafly's daughter, Anne Schlafly Cori. Lacey mentioned that she interviewed Cori a couple of times and had initially reached out to Cori upon discovering her contact information in an article published by the far-right media outlet *Breitbart News*.[49]

As might be expected, Lacey is a member of the Eagle Forum. In September 2017, she shared photos and her reflections on attending its annual conference, the Eagle Council. Overwhelmed with emotion, Lacey gushed, "It was just the most incredible time I think I've ever had in my life," meeting other women involved in conservative politics.[50] In her vlog about Schlafly the next month, she beamed, "When I attended the Eagle Council this year, I heard from a couple of people that I'm the next Phyllis Schlafly."[51] In another vlog a few months later, she enthusiastically talked of attending a meeting with her children and interviewing speakers.[52]

When *Mrs. America* was released, Lacey quickly critiqued the show's characterization of Schlafly as leftist bias. "Let's rewrite history in a television show," she scathed, "so that current and future generations of traditionally minded women will be convinced that their entire value system is based on a lie and never existed in the first place. Or they'll be too scared to speak up when the same fate equates them when they die and someone makes a television show of them."[53] In the vlog, the viewer can see a black-and-white photo of Schlafly hanging on the wall behind Lacey as she reacts to various moments in the first episode, accusing the show's writers of being either ignorant or misrepresentative or disingenuous in their framing of Schlafly. Lacey doesn't just admire Phyllis; she literally idolizes her.

The day after Schlafly died in 2016, her book *The Conservative Case for Trump* was published posthumously. It's likely that Lacey has obsessively read this book as much as the other publications. It's not far off to suggest that far-right tradwives such as Lacey and Ayla would be fully on board with President Trump's tweet about the suburban housewife. Back in 2016, Ayla made a reaction video immediately following the announcement of Trump's election victory. Displaying her heavily pregnant body, she gushed, "That's what it's about, guys! I get to give birth under a Trump presidency. There's women right now finding out that they're pregnant, and they get to give birth under a Trump presidency. Under a new world for our children." She continued, "My children that are here are going to have more opportunities now. It's for posterity, we are trying to keep our country great, so we can hand it onto the next generation."[54] "Our" and "we" undoubtedly refer to Trump's white far-right supporters.

"I am so grateful," Ayla stated more explicitly. "My fellow white people got out to vote. Thank you for not being ashamed to be traditional, to be Christian, to be conservative, to be white." Barely containing her excitement, she concluded, "Our ancestors are the ones who built and created this beautiful country, and we want to keep it wonderful." Unsurprisingly, Ayla was the only woman invited to give a speech at the Unite the Right rally in Charlottesville the following summer, where she planned to talk about the sanctity of family. (Although her family traveled to attend the event, she withdrew at the last minute, citing security concerns.)[55]

Lacey and Ayla are close friends, often posting and commenting on each other's social media channels and doing video collabs. Both women have openly talked about their relationships to their mothers. According to Lacey, her mother was not a stay-at-home mom, so Lacey didn't have any role model to be a homemaker.[56] "Growing up in a family where my mother wasn't as present, I found validation through what they call performance orientation" by seeing other maternal figures as mother figures—what Lacey simplified as "mommy issues."[57] Ayla meanwhile described her mother as having pure resentment: "She cooked every meal, she sewed Halloween costumes and went to our school functions. . . . But she acted as though she hated it," writes Darby. "Ayla also described her mother as abusive," engaging in physical violence.[58] Lacey and Ayla's relationships to their mothers stand in stark contrast to Brittany Sellner's connection to her stay-at-home mother of eight children, who was a big inspiration to her. Brittany's mother has a master's degree, "knows three languages, is very well traveled,"[59] and is a dedicated housewife. Aside from sharing an occasional photo, the other women influencers featured here don't speak explicitly about their relationships to their mothers.

Despite the popularity of trad culture, some far-right figures such as Lana Lokteff don't necessarily ascribe to a tradwife label, although Lana "respects primordial traditionalism," or the division of labor based on biologically determined gender roles. She didn't meet her husband until she was thirty, which for the far right is considered older on the dating-age scale. Her shift toward traditionalism apparently happened gradually once she got married.

"I think you're the happiest once you have a family, and you have a husband. I got sucked into the feminist thinking in my twenties without even realizing it. And you find that you're happier when you actually settle down and have the right guy. It's a fulfillment that caught me off guard," admitted Lana in 2017. She doesn't, for instance, believe that a woman should have a certain number of kids by the time she's twenty-five because that didn't happen for her. Individual circumstances and age shouldn't be a factor. "It's never too late," but that broader latitude doesn't excuse a woman for not having children if she can: "As long as you have them, then great."[60] Thus, it is clear that Lana holds the far-right view that motherhood is a woman's fundamental duty.

With this line of thinking in mind, I was surprised to read an excerpt from Seyward Darby's interview with Lana: "Lana told me that she and Henrik had children but that they didn't talk about them in interviews. . . . In truth, they didn't have kids—not yet." I was perplexed, and Darby apparently was, too. "Why lie about having kids? To throw me off? Perhaps. Or maybe it was because Lana sensed that she would have more capital on the far right if people either believed she was already a mother or couldn't tell for sure."[61] Lana eventually had two sons, but her earlier deliberate obfuscation of the facts of her motherhood is revealing: women have to be mothers and caretakers or else be seen by the far right as illegitimate voices or, worse, as hypocrites.

Robyn Riley also doesn't like the *tradwife* label. "Ladies if you love your family, want to be a stay at home mom, enjoy cooking and domestic feminine things you don't have to call yourself trad or larp [short for 'live action role play'] that ur in the 50s," she shared in an Instagram Story in 2020. "You can just be a normal woman who lives in 2020 who likes those things." During a two-hour long livestream on her YouTube channel, she addressed questions solicited from her Instagram audience during an AMA, including one question asking for her thoughts on "feminine YouTubers." I'm curious to know if this question was referring to tradwives specifically. "I think it's quite hit or miss. Some of them I like better than others," Robyn replied after listing a few channels such as Girl Defined and Mrs. Midwest. Her main critique was how these women represent themselves. "I think it's nice when women online can be multidimensional, complex," she said. Seeing herself not only as a mother, wife, and feminine person but also as someone interested in politics, she criticized that "when we pigeonhole ourselves into a specific niche, while it can help us build a very specific kind of audience and it can make you very successful, it can kind of leave me wanting more."[62] She apparently felt uncomfortable with how tradwife influencers can come across as shallow and one dimensional. At the same time, Robyn herself ironically fits exactly within a specific niche as a microcelebrity.

"I think they're good, I think they serve a purpose," Robyn continued. "I think women are craving good role models who are feminine, who are like homemakers, who are prioritizing motherhood. It's just, I think we have a limited supply of women who are both feminine and mothers. That's what I want to see more of." She encouraged tradwife influencers to also embrace motherhood. "I just think it would be really nice to see the femininity, like good wife, tradwife, content creators also become mothers and promote that." The next month, Caitlin Huber posted an ultrasound photo on Instagram announcing that she was pregnant with a baby boy[63] and after that posted photos displaying her early pregnancy belly. Robyn "liked" the post.

Robyn was one of the first far-right women influencers I came across who explicitly rejects the *trad* descriptor. For her, the image of tradwives living in a suburban setting with a 1950s feel is outdated. Like Lacey, Robyn also shared photos on Instagram of her cooking and home life with children, but the two have very different aesthetics. Lacey prefers a bright color palate and selfies showing her dressed in pearl necklaces and circle-skirt dresses; Robyn's feed showcases earthy tones and bohemian vibes steeped within the "cottagecore" trend.[64] Lacey takes pride in making classic American dishes such as roast pork loin and casseroles from old cookbooks; Robyn, meanwhile, enjoys health-conscious superfoods such as overnight oats, organic protein-packed salads, and homemade gluten-free vegan cookies.

These preferences are no coincidence. The same time that Lacey was settling down in her new married home right after high school, Robyn was attending university pursuing a liberal arts degree. Lacey was raising two young boys in suburban Texas, while Robyn was traveling and living across Europe and Asia. Different experiences have led to vastly different tastes for these two women. Thus, they orient themselves within different milieus. As Robyn noted in

April 2020 in an Instagram post caption of an old selfie taken in the streets of Brussels where she used to live before moving back to Canada, "Of all the reasons Im [*sic*] not comfortable calling myself trad, it's mostly bc even tho I'm from the country deep down I always wanted to be a city girl."[65] Later, Robyn described herself as living in a "modern" world with habits developed as a result of contemporary society.[66] Despite this description, she had earlier moved from an urban place to a rural area in northwestern Canada: "I have retreated to the countryside to find the good life," she explained.[67]

But as Seyward Darby writes about tradlife, "What qualifies as traditional isn't precise—the only requirement is that it derive from a mythical, unspoiled version of history and celebrate clearly defined masculine and feminine archetypes."[68] For some, that myth looks like a house with a white picket fence in suburbia; for others, it's life on the rugged frontier; and sometimes it's daisy fields across pagan northern Europe. I can picture Lacey, Robyn, and Elora within each of these landscapes, respectively. These differing visual representations of a far-right utopia are equally Instaworthy in their aesthetics.

As I was writing this book, these far-right women influencers were experiencing pivotal life events that they shared with their online audiences. Brittany Sellner got married and had a baby; Lauren Chen announced her engagement to her show's producer and later had her first child; the newlywed Rebecca Hargraves announced she was pregnant and gave birth, as did Robyn Riley, who posted Instagram photos of the homebirth delivery of her two children.

In January 2020, Rebecca and Robyn launched the cohosted YouTube channel Motherland, which Robyn described as a way "to discuss everything from trying to conceive to pregnancy, family planning, childbirth education, and everything related to trying to become a mom" and geared specifically for the far-right community because the channel is "pro-natalism, pro-family, and pro-nation."[69]

As first-time mothers, the two influencers saw an opportunity to share their experiences, seek guidance, and host guest speakers such as Elora, who talked about homebirth and prenatal nutrition in one of Motherland's first videos.[70]

When I logged on to watch a livestream of Motherland with Robyn and Rebecca discussing birth and postpartum anxiety,[71] I saw commentators in the live-chat bar. Based on usernames, I noticed that nearly all were women who engaged with the ensuing conversation by offering their personal perspectives of pregnancy or by asking the hosts questions. A couple of viewers also donated to the channel during the livestream. In other livestreams, Robyn or Rebecca occasionally paused and turned off her camera to attend to a baby, while the other cohost passed the time by responding to viewers in the chat. Sometimes, they even breastfed during livestreams. Their motherhood content drew a very different audience from that of other far-right YouTube channels I had watched, in which predominately male viewers would leave comments praising Brittany's looks or saying that Rebecca's husband was a lucky man to be with her.

These far-right women influencers deliberately appeal to men and women in very different ways, as discussed in chapter 3. The former are generally drawn to content that advocates for gender norms and traditional roles, while the latter more specifically participate on issues such as motherhood and child-rearing. This enthusiasm for motherhood content is best captured by what Ashley Mattheis terms "alt-maternalism," or empowered motherhood that is combined with "anti-multiculturalist, white ethno-nationalism, and hate networks" propelled by the alt-right and far right.[72] For instance, as Robyn documented the stages of her pregnancy on Instagram, her page was flooded with supportive comments. "I love connecting with women about womanly things. I feel so blessed to have a handful of friends who are all at varying stages of pregnancy alongside me. Their insight is such a blessing onto my life and sharing it with you is my gift to young women who feel lost and confused like I once did," she reflected. "Women need that sense of community, sisterhood and genuine support when family building."[73] These women apparently provide essential motherhood not only for their families but also for the movement at large. Motherhood entitles far-right women to make social, political, and cultural claims given that their value is recognized in this role.

I expected that these influencers would focus only on the positive aspects of motherhood until I heard Rebecca's story about giving birth to her first child. During a livestream in June 2020, she described it as "highly traumatic" and expressed doubt—"I don't know if I can do this again"—which prompted Robyn to reply, "Give it a few months. I didn't have the same experience as you did, but I'm so excited to have another baby already. I can't wait. I'm so confident to do it again."[74] Rebecca's response was an expression of disbelief and skepticism. At the same time, revealing her fear of the pain of childbirth constructed her position as authentic to viewers, some of whom may have related. This act of public vulnerability displayed a deep networked intimacy that disrupted the idyllic image of motherhood held by the far right. Ironically, upon finding out she was pregnant the previous year, Rebecca had said, "If I had started at twenty-three, I could have had eight kids. But now, I'll be lucky if I can have four."[75]

As Rebecca went into the intimate details of her birth story during the livestream, she recounted that it was "gross" and "so disgusting" because of a difficult labor and complications. In fact, she said, "I resent that I was robbed a normal birth story." Yet, rather than an acknowledgment that childbirth can in fact be traumatic for many people, the biggest takeaway from this conversation was that homebirth should be the favored option given the "discomfort" and potential of malpractice in hospitals. Homebirth (with a midwife) is by far the preferred choice for these women as well as for members of the greater tradwife community, who often share their personal experiences of the event. And yet Rebecca half a year later still admitted that "every fiber in my being is telling me not to have another child." Clearly, she hadn't changed her mind in the period since giving birth, but Robyn tried to convince her that she would eventually feel differently, using far-right religious dogma as leverage. "The devil wants us to be afraid of having children," replied Robyn. "The devil doesn't want more baptized children being raised in Christian families."[76] They also discussed how part of the pressure they face is from their husbands, who want them to be pregnant.

Revitalized by her commitment to alt-maternalism, Robyn began the process of becoming a doula and increasingly focused on motherhood issues on her Instagram profile. This was especially pronounced during the COVID-19 pandemic because unvaccinated expectant mothers feeling pressured to get vaccinated or mothers having to wear masks during delivery infuriated her. A strong advocate of birthing "outside the system," she promoted living off the grid and relying on your "natural instinct." "When I am fully trained as a doula I will be offering a weekly/bi-weekly online salon via zoom for women who desire connection and community with other moms/women in the natural birth sphere and educational classes on how to have the birth they desire," she wrote in an Instagram Story in August 2022. "This can be a place for women to connect with others of like mind and empower themselves in their journey to motherhood rather than feel isolated and at the mercy of 'professionals.'" In the post, she used Instagram's poll function to survey her followers on whether they would be interested in such a salon. As she explained, she was "gauging interest level so I can set up pricing and frequency of the zoom meetings."[77] By employing influencer practices of networked intimacy, Robyn is able to present herself as accessible and authentic to her audience, interacting with them in asking them to help shape her future content creation.

When watching the Motherland channel, I noticed that the description box read that it was "a resource for pro-natalist people," but I didn't come across the term *pro-natalist* again until I watched one of

Lauren Chen's videos from April 2020. "We're going to be debunking some antinatalist propaganda," she stated at the beginning of her reaction commentary to a *Tech Insider* article on why getting pregnant in your thirties is better than in your twenties. Lauren accused the article of left-wing bias and distortion of the facts, pointing out that "low birth rates is not a good thing; it encourages real problems for countries," adding matter-of-factly, "things like social security solvency and cultural tensions brought on by mass migration, to name a few, which the U.S., Canada, and U.K. are all experiencing right now, by the way."[78] In this far-right dog whistle, Lauren left it to her viewers to interpret for themselves what "cultural tensions" were resulting from "mass migration." It is also clear that Lauren took the *Tech Insider* article out of context by equating the decision to have children later in life with antinatalism.

In this same reaction vlog, Lauren criticized the political left for spending thousands of dollars on liberal arts degrees at universities and high-cost rent in major urban cities—"Well, that's just an investment in your well-being and your future. That makes sense," she said sarcastically—but then complaining about the costs of childcare. "These people don't care about spending money. Just not when it's not on themselves," she mocked about "$20 avocado toast." In promoting the idea that the political left is selfish and entitled, she was furthering a right-wing narrative that the traditional family unit should be valued above all else. Yet an entire Story Highlights section on her Instagram page includes photos of expensive food she has eaten in restaurants—dishes ranging from tuna tartare to stuffed lobster to fried chicken and French toast.[79] These may be occasional culinary indulgences for her, but she is being hypocritical if she is participating in the same culture that she criticizes the political left for.

The main issue here isn't that the political left is neglectful of family values, as in Lauren's argument. It's that the cost of living is at an all-time high, even accounting for inflation. And university degrees are a requirement for nearly all professional jobs with stable salaries. Further, cities are hubs for industries that employ

university graduates, with few job opportunities outside metropo-
lises. Yet despite being better educated and working longer hours
than previous generations, millennials earn less income, and home
ownership remains a pipe dream for them.[80]

But the core of conservative thought places the burden on personal responsibility rather than acknowledging the society-wide
factors affecting young people's lifestyle decisions. Selfish individ-
ualism is one of the themes in the far right's mantra. And influencers such as Lauren Chen add a personalized touch: "I did everything
I could to make sure I could start my family early. I graduated with
my bachelor's when I was twenty. I dated with purpose to find a guy
who wanted kids, too," she proudly declared in 2020. "I'm only
twenty-five now, and I'm hoping to get pregnant sometime next
year. I can be a stay-at-home mom like I always wanted to be. But
still, that waiting is hard because I feel like I'm ready to have kids
right now," Lauren proclaimed to the camera.[81] Two years later, she
had her first child, but rather than be a stay-at-home mom, she ironically became more active in her political career.

Although Lauren acknowledges that nobody should be forced to
have children, the position she advocates for is a political, not just
personal, one. In her critique of the *Tech Insider* article, Lauren
smirked at one point, "Can you imagine what our ancestors would
say if they knew that some of our descendants, for whom they sac-
rificed so much to ensure that they could just come into this
world, were thinking of ending their bloodlines because of stretch
marks?"[82] She was working to provoke a sense of urgency because
she believes that duty and tradition should guide lifestyle choices.
The reality, however, is that reproduction is no longer desperately
needed for the survival of our species in modern society: the far
right ignores this fact and instead promotes narratives of "saving"
the superior white race through increased fertility.

Lauren had made this motive more explicit in an earlier video
titled "The Need to Breed," in which she claimed that it is important for (white) people to have children in order "to preserve our culture, our Western, Judeo-Christian, freedom-loving culture." She

argued that "if we as a society care about our values and our way of life, then having kids is paramount to preserving that."[83] This language of preservation is akin to the discourse of existential civilizational threat within far-right circles. Despite this fearmongering rhetoric, Lauren continues to enjoy a public, visible platform on mainstream social media sites in which her reactionary talking points are exposed to wide audiences.

If contraception is not an option for most of these women, what steps do they take for birth control, especially if sexual activity is permitted when married? Ayla's preferred method is using cycle beads to "keep track of your cycle to either achieve pregnancy or to avoid pregnancy naturally."[84] Otherwise, influencers aren't too keen to discuss birth control options other than to proclaim those options' "unnatural" effects on the body and encouragement of promiscuity, as Rebecca Hargraves pointed out in relation to hormonal birth control.[85] The Dutch influencer Eva Vlaardingerbroek (see chapter 6) went so far as to post an Instagram Story claiming that oral contraceptives are a "modern scam" "destroying an entire generation of ladies" when pregnancy "can only occur 5 days out of the month," which "can be managed totally naturally."[86] In short, for the far right, sexual desire for women is understood solely in the context of their desire to have children.

When the COVID-19 vaccine was being developed and early distribution of doses began rolling out, these far-right women influencers quickly spread conspiracy theories about its side effects. Importantly, they stressed the vaccine's alleged effects on fertility. Robyn Riley became very outspoken against taking the vaccine. In one Instagram Story post, she claimed, "The coofer jab could affect female AND male fertility. This is all a plan to reduce the population via widespread sterilization."[87] She vehemently promoted the false narrative that the vaccine is a weapon to control reproduction rates.

Even worse, she used the derogatory term *coofer*, which refers to a "stereotypical" Chinese person in Wuhan who supposedly eats bat soup and starts to violently cough, or "coof," and was first used on 4chan. The far right has since used this term for anyone infected with the coronavirus more broadly, although it retains its racist origins.

Robyn continued in her Story, "Bill Gates is speearheading [*sic*] the push for mandatory vaccin@ti0n. Friendly reminder his father is the creator of planned parenthood." Although spreading disinformation of the vaccine as the latest attempt at population control is not unusual here, I also picked up on Robyn's deliberate misspelling of *vaccination* to prevent health advisory fact-check labels from automatically popping up on her Story to redirect users to World Health Organization information. Instagram introduced this preventative tool so that inaccurate information about COVID-19 being circulated on the platform would be flagged with official expert-guided resources.[88] Robyn employed a common far-right strategy of using coded language to circumvent automated detection of her content on social media platforms (a strategy further discussed in chapter 7). In doing so, she showed how highly effective she is at exploiting the platform's capability as well as at merging distrust of science and conspiracy theories of population control related to the vaccine with far-right narratives of the urgency of family reproduction to save the white race.

Regarding women who cannot have children, far-right women influencers view adoption as perfectly acceptable. Having children is not just about continuing your bloodline, argued Lauren Southern in 2017; it is also about passing down your ideals and culture.[89] A few explicitly advocate for the adoption of white babies, many of whom, they argue, need a home.

Given that Lauren Chen is the only biracial influencer among these women, the topic of mixed-race children rarely comes up in these influencers' discussions. Lana Lokteff, Brittany Sellner, and Tara McCarthy brought it up offhandedly in one conversation in

2017. "There's a lot of mulattos; they don't feel they belong amongst whites, belong amongst blacks; they're kind of in between," stated Lana in derogatory language. "They want everyone to be like them, and they have a lot of anger towards white people,"[90] but she provided no proof for this claim of racial resentment.

Tara responded, carefully selecting her words, "I'm actually slightly mixed race," prompting a surprised look from Lana. "My grandma is half-Indian, and I see how it's fractured her identity. When you have mixed ancestry, it's very difficult for them to see other people who don't have a fractured ethnic identity because they have an intimacy with their own people that is never going to be allowed for mixed-race people. So that's being taken away from them, and it's extremely painful." Tara was alluding to tribalism: the assumption that people prefer to surround themselves with others of the same race. The logic here is that mixed-race persons will "miss out" on "intimacy" with others of their "own" kind because of the tribalist nature of society. Lana agreed: "They want everyone to be like them, and they'll feel better about themselves to belong to a group. That's another painful aspect of mixing."

That multiracial individuals want everyone to look like them, that they lose out on intimacy with others based on phenotype, and even that they hold anger toward white people are refined talking points for a white-supremacist agenda. The far right has long feared that mixed-race people will "pollute" the "pure" white race, and Lana's use of the dated slur *mulatto* signals that she possesses little regard for the history and experiences of multiracial persons.

In slightly less offensive terms, Robyn similarly cautioned on a YouTube livestream in August 2020 about the psychological problems that she believed mixed-race children will face growing up. "I'm not morally opposed to interracial marriage, but I think that people should be aware of the potential issues they could face in an interracial marriage. And that's predominately going to affect people who want to have children." "If you plan on having children, there are consequences that are worth considering when you're going to have a mixed-race child," she continued. "The sad reality is that people who are of mixed race more commonly find themselves alienated because they don't fully identify with one or the other of their parents' ethnicities. And so they feel their identity is divided, and that can produce all sorts of personality disorders; people who are mixed race tend to be more likely to have drug addiction, to commit crimes."[91] She provided no evidence for these claims.

The research provides a much more complicated picture, of course. There are no studies on how multiracial persons are more likely affected by personality disorders, but some studies explore self-esteem issues and depression,[92] conditions that are a far cry from the severity of personality disorders. Regarding drug addiction, a recent study on Black-and-white mixed-race youth found that their drug-use rates are higher than among Black youth but lower than among white youth. However, there are no significant differences between these racial groups.[93] The authors of the study further confirm that there's no universal biracial experience and that not all people experience biracial identity in similar ways. I couldn't find any information about biracial or multiracial persons committing crimes at higher rates, so Robyn must have been simply assuming that it is the case.

Despite adding that this isn't the situation for everyone and reassuring her viewers that she knows many mixed-race women who are "normal," she cautioned in the same livestream that having mixed-race children is something that parents should consider carefully because it's a "gamble." Like Tara, Robyn affirmed, "We all feel more at home in communities of people who are like us, ethnically, right? And you're kind of condemning mixed-race individuals to never really be able to experience that. To feel alone no matter where they are." Once again, the argument of tribalism was being used to advance the idea that multiracial persons are not well suited for society—a euphemism for the far right's desired white ethnostate.

Robyn's next point revealed a great deal about her audience. "I think there's a lot of hysteria worrying about mixed-race couples. The statistics show that it's a very small percentage of any population that race mixes. So if you're one of these people who's super annoyed or worried about people who are race mixing because you're worried about birth rates—if you're always online looking at these sorts of things, [starting] to feel like it's something that's a super big deal and that's threatening the future of white communities—I don't actually think that it is. It's a small number of people who engage in interracial marriages."

The number of mixed-race couples and multiracial children in the wider population is, in fact, marginal, but Robyn's manipulation of this fact is questionable: she directly addressed her viewers' racial anxieties by reassuring them that "race mixing" will not affect birth-rate demographics or pose a potential threat to white-majority communities. This reassurance starkly exposed the type of viewer who follows Robyn's channel and their concern over white birth rates.

During 2020, the Black Lives Matter (BLM) protests in the wake of Minneapolis resident George Floyd's killing went viral. In the United States and around the world, protestors took to the streets calling for action against institutional racism and police brutality. Far-right women influencers, in contrast, responded to these protests with disdain, highlighting instances of looting and violence as representative of the largely peaceful protests, especially connecting the protestors to antifa (short for "antifascists") for inciting disorder. Their social media feeds were full of videos, photos, and media headlines sensationalizing the "anarchy" unfolding on the ground, some of which was revealed to be disinformation. As I was browsing Instagram Stories, Robyn's posts of women with their children at the protests caught my eye. She had captioned one with "Using your baby to virtue signal alliance with a violent political movement is a new low for white women" and another one with "Your children are not props."[94]

Considering that Robyn's Instagram profile contains a constant stream of photos of her children with captions advocating for the joys of motherhood and aiming, in her own words, to "share and promote family life and motherhood," her stance is clearly hypocritical. As Robyn explicitly said earlier when she decided to switch the focus of her content toward motherhood (see chapter 3), "We on the right wing, we need more visual representation of happy, family-oriented, healthy, traditionally-minded people."[95] This visual representation is far-right propaganda, and Robyn is using her children as props for the movement.

Political activism doesn't need to be mobilizing out in the streets; it can also be sharing content online. Such content doesn't need to be overtly political, either, with calls to action such as voting or donating. Instead, it can be subtle and implicit. When influencers like Robyn share their lifestyle and ideological views under the banner of traditionalism, they are evoking an equally strong political message.

Far-right women often use their children as propaganda, and Robyn isn't alone in doing this. Ayla Stewart also frequently posts photos of her children on Instagram and did so previously on You-Tube, with hashtags such as #nationalism, #GodKingCountry, and #tradlife.[96] Meanwhile, Lacey Lynn promotes hashtags such as #preservehistory and #traditionalism on Instagram posts featuring her children.[97] White women have historically played an important function in "maternalist framings [that] can motivate women to participate in conservative and even extremist movements."[98] The role of women in advancing white supremacy as resistance to the civil rights movement and integration during the 1960s continues in the American far right today.[99]

White mothers with their children at the overwhelmingly peaceful BLM protests—what Robyn calls "a violent political movement"—aren't "a new low." For that low, one need only look at historical photos of mothers and their children dressed in the same Ku Klux Klan gear as the men. The sociologist Kathleen Blee observed in-person that children of KKK members are socialized into the organization from an early age, attending events such as cross burnings and assigned minor administrative tasks such as folding pamphlets.[100] Children's involvement in these activities not only benefit the internal running of the organization but also equally promote far-right propaganda of reproducing the white race.

Posting photos of playtime interactions or birthday celebrations on social media is not necessarily political. But the decision for far-right mothers to post such content publicly using hashtags such as #nationalism and #tradlife signals that banal domestic life (in all-white families) is an overt political agenda. A child's life within the nuclear family unit represents the ultimate goal of their political movement.

This constant display of domestic life and motherhood as integral to the far right can sometimes lead to ironic outcomes. "I needed to protect my family," Ayla said after deleting many of her YouTube videos featuring her children. She "retired" from public life in 2019, citing safety and security concerns for her family. Yet expressing the danger she and her family faced for exposing themselves as white supremacists is a shallow complaint considering that she made her family content publicly available as an open recruitment tool. You can't have it both ways: showcasing your homelife to the public but then decrying unwanted attention to your family, especially when that family material serves as propaganda. Ayla "reemerged" on social media in 2022, posting in an Instagram Story the reason for her departure: "There's many reasons I quit publicly speaking but the biggest is that I don't think we women should be speaking on politics," a view she justified by citing Bible verses on women's silence and submission.[101] "A woman's place" is that of a full-time mother.

Overall, children within the far right serve an operational and symbolic purpose as propaganda for the movement. I argue that under the guise of mommy vlogging, whether it consist of parenting tips on YouTube or cooking recipes on Instagram, far-right women influencers showcase their families through relatable net-worked intimacy practices to promote their ideology.

"Instances of rape and sexual assault are perpetually on the rise. It is our duty to protect ourselves and our children. There is nothing more important than taking back our responsibility," stated Elora in a YouTube vlog in February 2017 about the importance of women's self-defense.[102] Despite lack of evidence that such instances are indeed "on the rise," she also assumed that white women and their children were the perpetrators' targets. This falsehood was circulated on far-right media outlets such as *Breitbart News* and InfoWars leading up to the 2016 U.S. election and in the immediate days after Donald Trump took office, including the publication of a number of stories about Muslim male refugees spreading a rape epidemic and engaging in female genital mutilation in the United States.[103] The influence of these media outlets on the wider far right and alt-right digital news infrastructure is broad (see chapter 2).

By claiming that it's the duty of women to protect themselves and of mothers to protect their children, Elora tapped into the primal instinct of protecting one's family and kin as a means of survival against a perceived threat. The responsibility falls on women, as opposed to the perpetrators. Her solution: carry a firearm. But rather than a holster, she recommended purchasing a corset that can fit under a dress or tight-fitting clothing. Elora showed her favorite options: a hiphugger and a corset stitched with feminine lace and flower details. The products, she noted, were designed by a woman "who is trained in European tailoring." Elora modeled the holsters holding two guns (although each, she mentions, can fit three guns). "Almost like tactical lingerie," she joked.

Intrigued by this vlog, I searched for the maker of these products—Can Can Concealment—and found an available selection that includes not just corsets but also garters and sport belts designed for exercise activities. The company's images feature highly feminine apparel contrasted with firearms. Clothing meant for sexual allure and eroticism is combined with a Glock 9-millimeter pistol.

In the next chapter, I explore the universe of far-right entrepreneurism to highlight commercial products that are popular within the far right. I demonstrate that far-right women influencers are particularly attuned to selling ideology by marketing themselves and their brand as lifestyle consumption. They exploit this type of traditional economic practice as a strategy for making the movement more visible while mainstreaming it.

5

CROWDSOURCING HATE

Perhaps you have heard of a clothing company that uses only natural organic fibers produced without carcinogenic chemicals and provides a living wage to factory workers. No, it's not the popular sustainable-fashion brand Everlane headquartered in San Francisco or the London-based People Tree, which boasts several fair-trade and organic-cotton certifications. It's Lana's Llama, founded by the far-right entrepreneur Lana Lokteff, which produces so-called nontoxic clothing made of natural fabrics.

A quick browse through the website shop offers many products for professional and casual wear, such as organic-cotton blouses, hemp-silk-blend skirts, and organic-wool dresses, as well as graphic print T-shirts emblazoned with "They have to go back" on the front and a screen-printed airplane on the back. All clothing is made in the United States. You can even purchase baby clothing composed of 100 percent organic cotton, including a onesie bearing the logo of a shield-maiden. Shield-maidens are female warriors in Scandinavian folklore and here reference a speech Lana gave in 2017 at the ninth Identitarian Ideas conference in Stockholm, an annual gathering of far-right figures to discuss issues and strategies.[1]

As a millennial woman who prioritizes buying products that are ethically made and sustainable, often by online retailers, I fit within the prime demographic of the company's target audience—young-adult, professional women of childbearing age. Such products are frequently advertised on my social media feeds. I'm not an outlier in this respect. Over the past few years, we have seen the rise of the sustainable-fashion movement as consumers have become more conscious of their environmental impact and aware of working conditions for factory workers.[2] In response, fashion brands that market transparency in the supply chain have seen a dramatic increase in sales as more customers are demanding that companies share these ethics and values.

But motivation separates Lana's Llama from similar brands. Whereas most sustainable-fashion companies focus on social justice and welfare for the less privileged in developing countries, Lana's Llama engages in what Lana referred to in 2015 as an "ideological battle" for the betterment of white people in Western countries.[3] By focusing on small-scale, white producers, the company aims to uplift their livelihood and in turn promote economic practices that foster the preservation of Western culture. This aim isn't explicitly stated on the company website's "About Us" page, but it becomes clear in Lana's claims that the use of chemicals in traditional clothing manufacturing causes "gender-bending" fetal development, hormonal disruption, and fertility issues. This logic reproduces the far right's emphasis on the health and genetic superiority of the white race and on women as the "pure" bearers of the nation.

I argue that the creation of alternative commercial outlets such as Lana's Llama reflects a key aspect of far-right women influencers' approach—entrepreneurism. In this way, influencers can simultaneously sell an ideology and a lifestyle to their audiences in the form of corporate sponsors, branded merchandise, publications, and crowdsourced donations.

As with any entrepreneurial effort, an income stream allows far-right women influencers to invest in higher-quality filming gear to create more professionally produced content. The early YouTube videos they created in 2016 had amateur frames and were likely filmed using phones or laptop webcams, thus providing a sense of authenticity to viewers. Over time, these influencers switched to professional camera equipment, microphones, and teleprompters. Some were offered their own talk shows on alternative-media outlets—for example, Lauren Southern's show on *Rebel News* and Lauren Chen's show *Pseudo-intellectual with Lauren Chen* hosted by Blaze TV, a politically conservative subscription-based streaming service that viewers of her YouTube channel could sign up for using a discount code and watch related content.

Besides soliciting donations from followers, which I discuss later in this chapter, many influencers also generate revenue from advertisements and sponsors on the platform. In one of Lauren Chen's vlogs on dating in late 2019, she paused her monologue to give a message from her sponsor: a company that provides organic-cotton menstrual products.[4] In addition to using nontoxic chemicals in their products, the company upholds high welfare standards for their workers and collaborates with global partners to increase access to personal-care products and income-generating initiatives for women. Was the company aware of who Lauren is or just interested in the high number of her subscribers? I find this ad especially ironic considering that, as Lauren mentioned, her YouTube viewership is 85 percent male. Surely the company simply targeted a female YouTuber in her midtwenties with a consistent viewer rate and assumed there would be a marketable demographic for its products.

Other company sponsors of far-right women influencers have a clear ideological mission, however. Garnuu is an organic menstrual products company featuring diverse models and with a mission statement claiming that "each subscription will support feminine hygiene training and female entrepreneurship to Nepali women and girls who are vulnerable of [*sic*] trafficking."[5] The company's name is derived from the Nepali word for "rescue," *garnuu*. Its website also includes blog articles about the menstrual cycle and ovulation. Thus, the company initially seems to promote progressive values according to what communications scholar Sarah Banet-Weiser identifies as "popular feminism" within corporate advertising: seeking brand ambassadors with "a passion for empowering girls all over the world," its aim to "embrace femininity" upholds a traditional mindset about gender and sexuality.[6] Garnuu's Instagram page features a pinned post with an infographic that states, "There's a movement of a complete erasure of women and we will NEVER be part of it. We believe in women, and the uniqueness of womens' [*sic*] bodies to menstruate and create life." The post further explains, "We will never call you a bleeder, menstruator, chest feeder, or birthing person. You are a woman." A closer look upends what seems like a progressive feminist message: Garnuu clearly opposes the gender-neutral language of the LGBTQ+ community, which advocates for inclusive terms such as *pregnant people* and *birthing people* instead of *pregnant women*. To be even more explicit, Garnuu's post affirms, "Periods are for women only. Pregnancy is for women only. We're taking our periods back. This is a GIRLS ONLY club!"[7] Garnuu's branding strategy deliberately hijacks the discourse of empowerment and femininity to claim ownership over an intimate condition and restrict it solely to womanhood. It presents this far-right message through the page's aesthetic of product placement and humorous meme posts to normalize a traditionalist mindset regarding gender. In addition to menstrual products, the company sells clothing and stickers with slogans such as "freedom fighter," "woman not menstruator," and "#protectfemininity Girls Only can have babies and menstruate." Through effective marketing strategies, companies like Garnuu are able to present conservative ideology within a familiar and relatable aesthetic for mass appeal.

Another interesting sponsor I came across was through Robyn Riley's YouTube channel—My Patriot Supply. When I clicked on a link in the description box, I was directed to a website for emergency survival kits. With a focus on customer "self-reliance" and "emergency preparedness," My Patriot Supply embodies "not just food, it's freedom." Products range from dehydrated food in NASA-grade bags with a twenty-five-year shelf life to survival essentials such as drinking-water germicidal tablets, blood clot powder, water filters, and air purifiers. Food kits are available to "customize your food storage plan" with the number of servings in the hundreds. Scrolling through the company's site, I discovered that the advertised "Ultimate Preparedness Kit—Survival Made Simple," which includes a four-week food supply, water-filtration system, fire starter, cutlery, camping stove, and solar-recharging kit was sold out at a retail price of $600. Products are geared toward "helping Americans achieve independence" in a crisis, whether "economic collapse, global conflict, major natural disasters, epidemics or viral outbreaks." During the height of the COVID-19 pandemic, My Patriot Supply experienced shipping delays due to heightened order demand.

The sociologist Cynthia Miller-Idriss, who has studied the far-right cultural scene for years, writes that "food is central to the far right in many other ways, including within crossover communities like extreme preppers and survivalists who are preparing for apocalyptic end times." She notes that one can often find "online guides to homesteading, techniques for growing and catching food," and "off-grid living,"[8] the latter appealing to far-right survivalists such as the members of the militia group the Oath Keepers and the Russian-origin (but now transnational) Anastasia ecovillages. Even Alex Jones, the well-known conspiracy theorist and owner of the website InfoWars, has an online store that sells goods for emergency preparedness. Robyn revealed in early 2021 that she purchased a water-filtration system from the InfoWars store.[9]

Yet the My Patriot Supply food kits are a stark contrast to Robyn's tastes. In one Instagram Story post in late 2020, she featured "some of my fav prepper pantry items," including coconut milk, dried shiitake mushrooms, and an organic selection of canned peeled tomatoes, strawberry jam, and chickpeas.[10] Her health-conscious staples could not be more different from the high-carb, high-fat, and nonorganic offerings from My Patriot Supply. She even stated in a vlog that her home "doesn't have any freeze-dried food" and that she has stocked up on "oats, jams, nut butter, jerky, baby foods, raw honey, and fats like coconut oil and ghee" instead.[11] Indeed, Robyn's holistic approach to health has garnered interest from other smaller businesses that sell wellness products, so viewers can access discount codes offered to her followers on Instagram Stories for grass-fed beef liver supplements and organic herbal products such as adaptogenic tonic and immunity boosters.[12] She has also posted on her Instagram page household gift recommendations available to purchase through Amazon, revealing to her followers that posted links are affiliate links in which she receives a small commission.

Instead of reflecting Robyn's dietary recommendations, My Patriot Supply's sponsorship was strategically tied to her vlog topic: protests against police brutality in the summer of 2020. Voicing fear and anxiety about white people being targeted by BLM protestors and the "radical left," Robyn characterized the riots as "people burning down small businesses" and "gangs beating up defenseless, innocent white people"—rhetoric not dissimilar to that of an impending (racial) civil war.[13] As Robyn's sponsor, My Patriot Supply was capitalizing on the fear of societal instability to sell its extreme-prepper products to her YouTube viewers.

In the same vlog, Robyn described herself "as a person who is not antiwhite, as a person who is not someone who propagates the idea that white people should feel guilty for what happened four hundred years ago." I assume she was referring to slavery, an institution that held Black Americans in bondage from 1619 to 1865. Importantly, Black Americans were enslaved for longer than they have been free in the history of the United States, a fact that Robyn ignores. She continued, "For someone who's a nationalist, very proud of my heritage, of my ancestors, [and] as a woman who has a little white boy who's growing up in this world, it's been extremely unsettling." Here, Robyn twisted the aims of a protest movement demanding the recognition of Black lives against police brutality into a false narrative of white victimhood. "[If] you live in the West, it's on your doorstep," she alerted her viewers. Hearing this dog whistle, I'm not surprised that Robyn's audience is the same demographic that purchases products from My Patriot Supply out of fear of an imminent race war. In fact, her viewers can receive a discount code for emergency food-supply kits.

Robyn is not the only far-right woman influencer sponsored by My Patriot Supply. In the Canadian influencer Faith Goldy's livestream on the topic of a government ban on assault-style firearms in mid-2020, an advertisement displayed across the screen indicated where viewers could get a discount code.[14] Commenters in the live-chat box, meanwhile, were also sharing the hyperlink for the discount page. In early 2022, My Patriot Supply again popped up as a sponsor for Brittany Sellner, with discounts accessible through preparewithbsellner.com. "Given the overall global instability that we've witnessed over the course of the past two years, there has really never been a smarter time to be a prepper," advised Brittany, "to have at least a small supply of long-lasting food stored away at home for you and your family in the event of an emergency."[15] This sponsorship was featured on Brittany's video supporting antilockdown protests—protests that she participated in, as displayed on her Instagram page.[16] Clearly, far-right women influencers are connected to a wide network of like-minded sponsors aiming to reach their specific audience demographic through spreading alarmist content.

Soon after the transition from the Trump administration to the Biden administration, these influencers felt despair concerning the state of U.S. politics. When Trump left office, the alt-right fragmented, no longer united by a leader (see chapter 1). This mentality quickly shifted to prepper and survivalist mode, which had been building during the COVID-19 pandemic. On January 26, 2021, Robyn and Rebecca discussed on their cohosted channel Motherland the steps that families could take in anticipation of things getting worse, from stocking up on pantry staples to gaining knowledge about hunting and fishing, foraging, and preserving food in order to create a self-sufficient homestead. Another tip they gave is to buy cigarettes and alcohol as potential barter-and-trade goods. Rebecca recounted her experience of prepping: "In 2015, I bought one year of freeze-dried food. I bought water-purifying tablets; I bought seeds." Such purchases are the norm in a prepper lifestyle, but Rebecca's other acquisitions are not. "We bought tons and tons of weapons," she said. "A general rule of thumb for people that own weapons is try to have a thousand rounds for each gun that you have. So we have a thousand or two thousand or something for our AR-15, and that's enough for home defense." She didn't reveal how many guns her family owns—apparently "tons"—but she described her husband as "a firearms expert." Robyn said she considered such prepping essential to prevent "starving to death or being shot on our doorstep by communist neighbors," and laughed at her "joke."[17]

By participating in a common social media influencer practice of getting corporate sponsorship for income generation, far-right women engage in branding tactics that fulfill their self-image as well as their viewers' consumer desires. Whether sponsors ideologically align with the influencers' viewpoints or not, sales apparently trump ideology: these influencers represent market potential and high visibility.

Selling branded merchandise is a cornerstone of the far-right scene because it helps build a sense of collective identity. In the past, Lauren Chen sold her own merchandise, which included adult and children's apparel, stationery, mugs, and phone and laptop cases. Robyn likewise sells T-shirts, sweatshirts, and mugs emblazoned with slogans such as "Ride the Tiger" (an idiom derived from fascist philosopher Julius Evola that individuals should take self-responsibility) and "New Nostalgic" (to counter modernity). Links to Robyn's merchandise are listed in the description box of all of her YouTube videos.

Rebecca Hargraves sells merchandise based on a weekly YouTube podcast called *Matt & Blonde* (previously *Beauty & the Beta*), which she cohosts with Matt Christiansen, a livestream gamer turned political commentator. Most of their apparel features the show's logo of the two of them with an American flag in the background, surrounded by microphones and the barrel of a rifle. Other slogans include the show's inside jokes and Trump quotes such as "Great. Terrific. Tremendous. Frankly the Best."

Clothing and fashion are a consistent staple within the far-right scene as a means of identifying in-group members and giving exposure. Importantly, clothing "integrates humorous iconography, jokes, and insider codes that lend a sense of secrecy and amusement to the consumption process," writes Cynthia Miller-Idriss.[18] At first glance, much of the apparel these women offer seems banal or lacks any political meaning. It's only through context that one can recognize the symbolism attached to clothing that promotes the message of Western civilization or white identity politics. Fashion further provides designers with a means of circumventing the legal consequences of wearing banned symbols through creative coded messages.

I asked Cynthia Miller-Idriss what she thinks is the key defining trend in far-right fashion circles. "The past several years have seen a dramatic shift in the aesthetics of far-right extremism," she told me, "as far-right style has become decidedly mainstream, all but abandoning the shaved heads and combat boots that so clearly signified the racist skinhead look for a generation of neo-Nazis in the 1980s and 1990s."[19]

She explained, "Europeans became aware of this phenomenon in the late 2000s, as high-quality, mainstream-style brands emerged that sold products laced with coded far-right messages and symbols." In comparison, "Americans were caught off guard a bit later by the pressed khakis and white polo shirts worn by dozens of young men in 2017 in Charlottesville, Virginia, as they carried flaming torches and chanted 'Jews will not replace us.'"

The change in contemporary far-right fashion and appearance is significant. "These aesthetic shifts are meaningful because they disrupt the associations that the public has about what racist or extremist people look like," Miller-Idriss told me. "But they also reflected strategic efforts on the part of the far right to appear more mainstream in order to make the public more receptive to their ideas." It is important to recognize these rebranding efforts because they are highly effective at presenting the far right in a manner that is acceptable to a mainstream audience.

What's different in the case of far-right women influencers is that none of the suppliers for Lauren, Robyn, and Rebecca are linked to the far right, as one might expect. These companies tailor to small-scale businesses and entrepreneurs by offering production services for made-to-order products. I contend that this relationship illustrates the feasibility for far-right influencers—who can label themselves content creators or independent artists—to sell merchandise that appears to have no ideological message but uses coded symbols in order to bypass scrutiny and accusations of hate speech.

Spring (previously Teespring), the T-shirt company that produces apparel for Robyn and tradwife influencer Caitlin Huber (Mrs. Midwest), has faced public criticism several times for selling T-shirts emblazoned with swastikas, violent white-supremacist slogans, and even clothing praising Dylann Roof, the terrorist of the Charleston church shooting in 2015.[20] The site continues to offer controversial products, not least T-shirts emblazoned with the slogan "It's ok to be white," a phrase popularized by the alt-right, in particular by Lauren Southern.[21] But far-right women influencers' more careful navigation around any potentially offensive words in their product designs allows them to sell merchandise while still legitimizing far-right ideas to an audience with insider knowledge.

Like clothing merchandise, music from White Power rock to metal, punk, and folk genres has always been prominent within far-right circles.[22] It's an effective medium for bringing together a community through artistic expression. The far-right music scene has long been confined to the fringe, viewed as a subcultural milieu. Although it remains so, new opportunities for music production mean greater potential audience reach.

An ideal example is the far-right influencer who goes by the pseudonym "PhilosophiCat." Her YouTube channel consists of vlogs that discuss the writings of the Italian fascist philosopher Julius Evola, who is an intellectual inspiration for the contemporary far right.[23] She breaks down for her audience Evola's archetypes for women and men[24] and modern society's failures to adhere to these gendered roles. She appeared on Lana's podcast *Radio 3Fourteen* on Red Ice TV in 2017 and on Robyn's channel in a collab discussing these issues in-depth in mid-2019.[25] PhilosophiCat not only has an interest in metapolitics but also provides vocals for the paganist neofolk band Überfolk. The band's album *Music for Nations* features singles such as "My Ancestors," "A Prayer for My People," and "Song for Sweden (Europa!)," the latter including the lyric "I want to live in the land of yesterday." This music harks back to an idyllic Nordic past built by the Vikings that gave rise to what the musicians consider the cultural and political dominance of Scandinavia.

These overt references to paganism and Norse folklore may seem well intentioned. As the musicologist Benjamin Teitelbaum writes after spending years with self-described nationalist musicians throughout Scandinavia, "Contemporary nationalists treat folk music as a music 'of the people,' one that is inherently native either in its musical structure or via the population coalescing around it." In other words, the folk music created by bands such as Überfolk plays a significant role in perpetuating a nostalgic portrait of the Nordic region through sound and imagery. Even the Swedish far-right politician Mattias Karlsson admitted, "Folk music is seen as connected to nature, there is a sound in Swedish folk music that developed in some form of symbiosis with the Swedish landscape."[26]

The Nordic region has always been an object of fascination for the far right. They perceive it as a historical utopia of white, racial purity. Since the "refugee crisis" of 2015, however, Sweden has accepted more refugees per capita than any other country in Europe, so much so that far-right actors in Sweden, Europe, and even the

United States have portrayed the country as under threat by a Muslim invasion, depicting the migrants as "rapefugees" and the neighborhoods where they live as "no-go zones." This imagined chaos, violence, and societal decay are what the anthropologist Cathrine Thorleifsson describes as the far right's vision of "the Swedish dystopia."[27]

Some of the far-right women influencers have promoted the narrative of Sweden facing a societal collapse. In March 2017, Lauren Chen made a vlog dedicated to the topic of Sweden accepting refugees as "a warning of what can happen when we make the wrong decisions." Citing sensationalized far-right media headlines of migrant "no-go zones" and "Muslim rape gangs" from *Breitbart, Russia Today,* and the British tabloid the *Daily Star,* Lauren feared that Swedish people are "losing their culture and becoming a minority within their own country."[28] Lauren Southern similarly argued in mid-2017 that these migrants don't "understand European culture or European values" and that they pose an economic and security threat in addition to a cultural one.[29] Rebecca Hargraves claimed that male migrants engaging in mass rape and crimes in Sweden will destroy "native" Swedish culture by "allowing Islam into Western societies."[30]

PhilosophiCat's music contributes to the ideal representation of the Nordic landscape as a pristine white utopia that is unblighted by immigration and Islam. "The idea that women should be respected, that is a uniquely European idea—that's part of our culture," she told Lana on a podcast,[31] a description well situated within far-right ideology (see chapter 1). PhilosophiCat has northern European ancestry and grew up in a homogenous white community of many Scandinavian descendants in Minnesota. Her music reflects a combination of her political views and racial identity. For instance, the most important issue to her is "the continuation of our race" and "our survival by any means necessary" because "white people living outside of Europe" have been "cut off from our culture and our heritage."[32] Her music clearly expresses the reclaiming of white European culture and heritage for white Americans, referring to the theory that white people will become a minority in Western countries by means of a white-genocide conspiracy orchestrated by the political left and nonwhite immigrants. This myth is a far-right tactic of fearmongering to gain enough adherents to establish a white ethnostate across Europe and the United States.

Overall, for far-right women influencers, the entrepreneurial activity of selling branded merchandise such as clothing and music creates an opportunity for name recognition as well as financial streams. It also cements a process of collective identity building for the movement through consumption.

Brittany Sellner prefers to stick to a more traditional form of income revenue for far-right women—publishing. In late 2018, she launched her book *What Makes Us Girls*, which she described as a "self-help book targeted towards girls" who "have rejected third wave feminism but still struggle to navigate everyday issues such as purposelessness, inauthenticity, rejection, and lack of self-worth."[33] There's nothing explicitly political about this book. On the contrary, its pages describe very personal details. She mentioned in the announcement how she was reclusive and introverted as a young girl, with not many female friends, but that over the past few years she had developed strong friendships with other (far-right) women, as discussed in chapter 3. The common thread she attributed to these new friendships is that they all include the rejection of feminism. But, she stated, most of her friends still struggle to navigate everyday issues in society, so she decided to compile her wisdom and advice in a book, aiming to share this knowledge and inspire girls like herself.

Women in far-right movements have historically published books to further the cause. Some notable examples include *The Surrendered Wife* by Laura Doyle, *The Proper Care and Feeding of Husbands* by Laura C. Schlessinger, and *Fascinating Womanhood* by Helen Andelin, which Ayla Stewart said, crying tears of joy, "completely changed my life" in her rebuttal to modern feminism.[34] Brittany noted on her book's launch day that it is filling a gap: "There aren't really any others like it for conservative-minded girls. Of course, you have a few similar books way back when, like the '50s and '60s, but you don't have anything like it for the modern day."[35] Her book essentially speaks to the modern far-right woman.

The biggest difference between Brittany's book and books published in the past is that her book is widely available to a global audience through sellers such as Amazon and Barnes & Noble. Upon its launch, Brittany was even sending signed copies to domestic and international locations. Meanwhile, on Amazon you can still find a copy of Lauren Southern's book *Barbarians: How Baby Boomers, Immigrants, and Islam Screwed My Generation*, published by the Canadian far-right media outlet *Rebel News* in 2016. The cover displays an endorsement by the conservative pundit Ann Coulter that reads, "Buy this book before liberals ban it."

In 2020, Lauren published another book that she described in a vlog as based on "how the media spins things, lie about people, how the press can get stories wrong, ruin lives." It is her response to what she sees as the media's representation of politics and portrayal of her. But unlike *Barbarians*, which targets young-adult readers, this publication is a children's book: *Henry the Sheepdog & the Wolf of Mossville*. Lauren warned her viewers that "conservative" parents need to take an active role in parenting. "If you don't raise your child, someone else will do it for you. And it'll probably be the state, it'll probably be the education system, it'll probably be celebrities." The book is not partisan, Lauren asserted; it simply teaches kids about critical thinking.[36] A few months later she released a second children's book, *The ABC's of Morality*, which she promoted in an Instagram Story as a gift idea for "last minute Christmas shopping."[37] Both books have potentially wide distribution through Amazon.

Also in 2020, Brittany shared on Instagram that she had a new book coming out soon, which she called "a political non-fiction." "It's undoubtedly the most personal book I've ever written—or ever will write," she confessed. Later, she explained in a YouTube video: "I'm working on a book about my political experiences since 2016. So obviously it includes a lot of my husband, Martin. And it's kind of just a book for closure, in a way, to set the record straight about everything that's happened from 2016 to 2020 because there's so many lies about us."[38] These "lies" concern the couple's involvement and leadership in propagandizing the alt-right and Identitarian movements. In April 2021, the book was self-published under the title *Patriots Not Welcome* and again has mainstream distribution through Amazon.

Only a month after Brittany's book announcement, Robyn Riley revealed on her Instagram page that she was beginning to write an ebook on "birth prep and guidance into motherhood,"[39] following the success of her YouTube channel Motherland, cohosted with Rebecca Hargraves. During one livestream, Robyn discussed the prolonged research she conducted for the book: "I learned an immense amount about the process of trying to conceive, I learned about fertility, I learned about diet, supplementation, exercise," she said. "Different techniques about how to have an easy labor, newborn essentials, things that you want to do during the newborn phase to make your life easier, postpartum in general." The purpose of the ebook, Robyn stated, is to educate her friends and followers: "I want to be able to share what I learned with the community of women that I've built over this past nine to ten months of documenting this process."[40] Robyn engaged with followers throughout the process, such as when she crowdsourced suggested topics using the poll function on Instagram Stories in a display of networked intimacy.[41] In the past, far-right women would solicit feedback from their friends, family, and mentors when writing books. Today, I argue, far-right women can look beyond their immediate circles and gather suggestions and advice from an interactive, global audience along the way, made possible by the publicness and networked intimacy of mainstream platforms.

Sometimes, publication can take shape beyond books into short reads. While browsing Lauren Chen's Instagram feed, I discovered that she is a contributor to *Evie Magazine*. The magazine's website design has a clean, minimalist, pink-and-white aesthetic, and the magazine itself is reminiscent of many fashion and influencer blogs aimed toward professional, millennial women.

Founded in 2019, *Evie*'s slogan is "Seek Truth. Find Beauty," and its mission statement says,

> Millions of women across America have been forgotten by the publishing world. They're tired of having to go to trashy or politically biased sites and magazines just to get quality reads on health, beauty, and more. For years, these publications have focused on proving how women are great by showing how they can be just like men.
>
> Not us. We focus on women and celebrate what makes us so wonderfully unique. Because men can't be us. And the ones who know that are the ones who love us the most. With that in mind, we'd like you to meet *Evie*.[42]

The magazine claims that it "affirms your femininity, encourages virtue, and offers a more truthful perspective than the biased agenda of other publications." The section categories in the drop-down menu are standard: health, beauty, fashion, relationships, career, and culture. Certain topics, such as networking and self-improvement under the career section, are tailored to a young professional woman reader. Articles provide tips ranging from how to negotiate for a higher salary to what podcasts on productivity readers should listen to.

The magazine diverges from standard women's magazine fare in articles such as "It's Okay to Aspire to Motherhood Over a Career," which is written as an attack on feminism, claiming that patriarchy is a false notion and advocating for motherhood as a "sacred duty."[43] This isn't framing motherhood as a choice—it's framing motherhood as a necessity. A further browse of articles in the culture section reveals much more about *Evie*'s political orientation, with topics that target left-wing politicians and embrace celebrities that uphold traditional family and faith values and with commentary on pop culture and entertainment news that reinforces heteronormative gender norms. The magazine tells the "truth" and thus provides an interesting contrast to the "biased agenda" of other publications, *Evie* claims.

Evie's Instagram page is a collage of pastel colors and features the description "Empowering Women to Seek Truth & Find Beauty."[44] Most posts feature headlines and lead images from the magazine's articles with a variety of ideological and nonideological content, ranging from "It's a Retro Summer: The Cutest Pieces to Get the Season Started" to "It Seems Like Society Is Almost Rooting for Young Married Couples to Fail" and, of more concern, "Overturning Roe v Wade Will Improve Women's Sex Lives and the Quality of Men They Date in the Long Run." Interlaced with these posts are features on traditionalist Instagram celebrities: young, attractive women and heterosexual couples who promote marriage and motherhood. A recurring theme in these posts is the reconstruction of the image of female empowerment not as a successful career but as the embrace of domestic duties.

Evie looks aesthetically similar to other women-oriented digital magazines. Its interface closely resembles that of the alternative-media magazine *Bustle*, which also targets millennial and Gen Z readers but holds a socially progressive and inclusive outlook. *Evie*, like *Bustle*, encourages its readers to buy products from local, small businesses and features people of color, including interracial couples (although it clearly omits same-sex partners). Unlike the blog feel of *Bustle*, though, *Evie* tries to retain some elements of the traditional magazine structure by featuring issues with covers of women figures that is common for print editions.

I didn't expect the women photographed for *Evie* to be wearing low-cut tops and miniskirts or articles discussing sex, both of which are usually omitted in far-right outlets. When we think about calls for traditionalism and conservatism, most of us probably assume that women in this movement promote modest dress and shy away from clickbait article headlines such as "5 Health Benefits of Orgasms (They're Not Just for Fun)," which was published in *Evie*.[45] The ability to speak to the interests and concerns of young women today, presented through a familiar aesthetic, is what makes the contemporary far right's propaganda outreach especially powerful.

Evie was gaining a larger readership as I was writing this book. When scrolling through Instagram, I saw that one of Robyn Riley's Stories featured a screenshot of the *Evie* article "You Don't Need a Perfect Man. You Need a Man with Potential," displaying her byline.[46] A year had passed since one of the far-right women influencers I had been following had penned an op-ed for *Evie*. Robyn, who had briefly studied journalism in college, was invited to write the article. Its intended audience, according to Robyn in a vlog commenting on the article, was not just "conservative, trad women," but a wider demographic including "a recovering feminist who's in her early 30s" as well as "a young, trad Cath [Catholic] woman who desperately wants to start having babies." Robyn hoped that she would be able to write articles for *Evie* again. "It's the one medium online that I have yet to break into," she said.[47] Only a few months later, she announced in an Instagram Story that *Evie* had hired her to be a regular freelance writer, "meaning I have a new avenue to make money from home and discuss the things that I am passionate about."[48]

The publishing industry has been a consistent avenue for the far-right to communicate its message and build in-group identity, but now the scale of distribution and readership for far-right literature is vaster than ever before. Not only are far-right women aiming to reach broad audiences, but they also do so through contemporary aesthetics and frames for a legitimizing effect, often through genres such as self-help and wellness to normalize their message.

By far, the women themselves are the most crucial form of entrepreneurism as influencers. They capitalize on their looks and youth to construct themselves as the most visible women on the far-right frontlines. Building audiences on platforms such as YouTube and Instagram, which are visually oriented, is possible due to what the media scholar Alice Marwick describes as "Instafame": "an online attention economy in which page views and clicks are synonymous with success and thus online status."[49] The concept of the "attention economy" is key here. As the sociologist Zeynep Tufekci notes, "*Attention* is a key resource for social movements" because the latter depend on it to frame their goals, convince the public of their causes, recruit, neutralize the opposition, create solidarity, and mobilize supporters.[50] If we think about the far right as a social movement, then these women influencers play an integral role in furthering its aims within the online attention economy.

Far-right women influencers solicit attention by curating a microcelebrity profile that strategically reveals personal information while also coming across as a source of inspiration for their followers. They maintain a delicate balance of accessibility, authenticity, and aspiration. "Microcelebrity is linked to the increasingly pervasive notion of 'self-branding,' a self-presentation strategy that requires viewing oneself as a consumer product and selling this image to others," writes Marwick.[51] Building upon Rebecca Lewis's research on reactionary-right YouTubers, these women influencers are "selling" the far right through their own "political self-branding," in which "they live their politics as an aspirational brand."[52] Whether that brand is achieved by selling merchandise featuring their catchphrases or simply by posting selfies of behind-the-scenes action, these seemingly banal activities serve a very important purpose: far-right propaganda.

These influencers thus practice a type of "relational labor," which, the media scholar Nancy Baym writes, entails ongoing audience engagement over time to build social relationships. However, unlike sole emotional labor, relational labor usually involves connections tied to earning money.[53] Perhaps one of the best indicators of such connections within the online attention economy is that supporters can choose to donate money directly to these influencers. Payment processors such as PayPal, Patreon (or the alt-tech equivalent Hatreon), Donorbox, CashApp, SubscribeStar, and the alt-tech site Locals and MakerSupport (a far-right crowdfunding site that was taken down in 2018)[54] are popular avenues for crowdsourcing donations if these influencers haven't been banned from them. Otherwise, direct donation on their websites is possible.

Cryptocurrencies such as Bitcoin and Ether (Ethereum's currency) present a secure means to gather donations without the risk of bans. Lauren Southern made a "101 explainer" vlog about cryptocurrency in 2017, encouraging her viewers to consider learning more about safely protecting their finances. The only awful alternative, she noted, is to use websites that would tax their transactions, with such taxes going toward "importing migrants" and their housing or "government-funded gay pride parades."[55] Lauren Chen also made a vlog debunking the idea that cryptocurrencies are a scam; the video, incidentally, was sponsored by a retirement account company with a branch dedicated to crypto accounts, and it featured a conversation with the company's president.[56] Soon after Trump left office and the prepper mentality set in, more far-right women influencers such Robyn and Rebecca became interested in cryptocurrency options as a means of financial investment for their families.[57] Robyn even posted in an Instagram Story a QR code of her Bitcoin wallet, asking her followers, "If you enjoy the content I provide across various platforms please consider making a one time donation in Bitcoin so show your support! My family deeply appreciate your generosity!"[58] Soliciting donations from her audience was thus framed not just as supporting her but also as supporting her family in an act of networked intimacy. She directly tied the monetization of her content to the far right's broader goal of sustaining the nuclear family unit.

It's difficult to trace transactions through sites such as PayPal and Patreon, but I thought tracking Bitcoin could give me a glimpse into the amount of donations these women receive on a regular basis. Using a blockchain-explorer website, I input the Bitcoin accounts (addresses) provided by these influencers on their social media channels to get an overview of transactions. Lauren Chen received only a couple hundred dollars each in Bitcoin and Ether, but Robyn reached nearly $1,300 in Bitcoin funding. These minor amounts are to be expected. After all, as Lana Lokteff once said, "I hear some people say, 'Oh some of these girls are in it for the money.' What money? There's really not much money. Maybe there's a couple girls who rake in some money, but generally they'll make more money at some other job." She joked, "Or [they could] marry a rich guy; just go marry a rich guy, have a bunch of babies." [59] Thus, I initially didn't presume that these influencers would be receiving much money.

Digging further, though, I discovered that both Rebecca and Faith had received more than $23,000 each in Bitcoin donations. Lana earned nearly $38,000 from Red Ice (plus almost $5,000 from Ethereum transactions). But I was most stunned to see that Lauren Southern had received more than $100,000 in Bitcoin donations. Granted, this total came in over a three-year period, but she had collected dozens of transactions even before releasing her vlog on cryptocurrency. By March 2023, the received transactions had totaled more than $212,000, while the total volume of sent and received transactions was more than $425,000. [60]

If these influencers are receiving large Bitcoin donations, then the overall amount they receive in donations, including from payment processors using traditional currencies, must be even more impressive. It would be a challenge to gather the relevant bank transactions and financial documents, but I wouldn't be surprised if these influencers are receiving hefty sums—if not from donors, then from patrons.

When I was researching these women, a recurring issue popped into my head: Are these influencers merely talking heads supported by a strategic far-right leadership? Do they write their own scripts for their vlogs, or do they have ghostwriters? As Lauren Southern revealed recently, some far-right celebrities, including her, do have their own writers or editors. [61] If these influencers can't be financially independent based solely on crowdsourced donations and ad revenues, the notion that they have (likely male) patrons doesn't seem unlikely. After all, Lauren Southern's travels around the world to film documentaries with a camera crew as well as her and Brittany's trip to Moscow, which I discuss in the next chapter, bring up the question of how these excursions were funded. Finding answers to these questions was beyond my capacity, but analyzing far-right influencers' financial activities could be an avenue for future research.

As noted earlier, besides crowdfunding, activities such as publishing books and articles, producing music, selling merchandise, and generating advertising revenue and sponsors reflect what the media scholars Brooke Erin Duffy and Urszula Pruchniewska have analyzed as "female entrepreneurship in the digital age." They observe that women who obtain income in the digital creative industries often conform to notions of femininity, identified through three social media tactics: "soft self-promotion," or branding that is deemed "organic" or "subtle"; "interactive intimacy," or relation-building practices; and "compulsory visibility," or putting their private lives on public display. These three tactics have emerged in response to the "masculine-coded nature of entrepreneurship and its markers of success" and place women in positions of feminine self-presentation to succeed within online ventures.[62] Thus, far-right women influencers are not necessarily unique in drawing upon feminine representations as a means of succeeding in digital entrepreneurialism, but they are importantly exploiting these entrepreneurial strategies for ideological practices and with the intent to advance a far-right political agenda.

The attention economy that these far-right women enjoy on social media has become increasingly global as platforms offer users around the world the ability to make instant connections. In the next chapter, I explore the global aspects of the far-right movement through these women influencers.

6

FROM PROTESTS TO PARLIAMENTS

To think that myself, a young Christian woman from Canada, who has never been part of any terrorist organization—I've never endorsed any terrorist organization, I've no criminal record whatsoever—I'm sitting in a room with the Kent police being asked how I feel about running over Muslims with trucks, was just absolutely absurd."[1]

This is how Lauren Southern described her experience of being arrested and detained for six hours at the U.K. border after traveling there from continental Europe in 2018. She was detained along with Brittany Pettibone and Brittany's then boyfriend, Martin Sellner; the couple were imprisoned for three days and then deported due to their extremist political activism. Meanwhile, Lauren was detained under the United Kingdom's Schedule 7 Terrorism Act, which she described as not giving her "even . . . the right to remain silent." Following this incident with U.K. border control, she had difficulty securing a visa that summer to visit New Zealand and Australia, where she participated in a speaking tour with the Canadian white nationalist Stefan Molyneux and was featured in an infamous photo wearing an "It's okay to be white" T-shirt. Lauren's tour was funded by an Australian company that had also supported Milo Yiannopolous and Jordan Peterson.[2]

But in 2018 Lauren wasn't describing the incident via a webcam in a bedroom, nor was she livestreaming from outside the police station. She was speaking within the chambers of the European Parliament, with a recording uploaded onto her YouTube channel.

Seated on the panel with Lauren was the former far-right U.K. Independence Party (UKIP) member of the European Parliament Janice Atkinson, who invited Lauren to discuss the issue of "free speech" in the wake of this event. Lauren continued, "They asked me how I felt about right-wing terrorism, which I once again told them, you can watch any of my social media, you can look at any of my videos online, not once have I endorsed terrorism."[3]

That a YouTube influencer who first began broadcasting from her bedroom discussions about antifeminism was defending herself against accusations of supporting right-wing terrorism in the European Parliament shows the extent to which the far right has become a mainstream phenomenon.

Cas Mudde, a pioneer political scientist in the study of the European far right, argues in *The Far Right Today* (2019) that we're currently witnessing the so-called fourth wave of the far right: its mainstreaming and normalization.[4] This mainstreaming is symbolized by the posting of Lauren's Instagram photo of having coffee with Janice Atkinson and Nigel Farage, former UKIP leader and lead Brexit spokesman, the same day as giving her talk.[5] Only a few days earlier, she had shared a photo of herself giving a speech for the youth wing of the Belgian far-right political party Vlaams Belang.[6]

Mudde observes that just a few decades ago the far right was seen as being on the fringe of the political margins, with ideas and behaviors considered too toxic to be legitimate. Today, the far right occupies the political mainstream: more far-right political parties have been voted into national governments or have entered into coalitions with center parties that accommodate far-right agendas in their legislation. Mudde attributes this shift to the "refugee crisis" of 2015 in Europe. That same year, for instance, UKIP secured nearly

4 million votes in the general election, a little more than 12 percent of the vote. The alleged threat from Muslim male refugees and sensationalist media headlines about the growth of the Islamic State of Iraq and Syria (ISIS) created a perfect storm to heighten public anxiety. UKIP campaigned on the platform that it was the only political party to vocalize these insecurities to voters.

Recent years have witnessed a wave across Europe of far-right parties entering into public office at the national and regional levels. Whereas the Europe of Nations and Freedom group of far-right political parties within the European Parliament constituted less than 5 percent of seats in 2015, in 2019 its successor, the Identity and Democracy group, held nearly 10 percent of seats.[7] Over time, these far-right parties have created alliances and cooperated on legislative issues in order to advance nationalism, Euroscepticism, and anti-immigration within the European Union.[8] Meanwhile, one need only look at the political climate within the United States since Trump's presidency to note the rise of popular far-right politicians in the Republican Party, such as Matt Gaetz, Josh Hawley, Marjorie Taylor Greene, Lauren Boebert, and Ron DeSantis.

Not only is the far right mainstream, but it is also *global*. From Brazil to India, Israel to Australia, the far right is operating and, importantly, succeeding on an international scale. This success can take shape in the form of political parties but also at the grassroots level. As we have seen, the contemporary far right successfully functions as an online-based movement. Communicating through vlogs and chat rooms means that anyone from anywhere in the world can join with just a few clicks. As Lauren told Brittany at one point, putting her hand on her shoulder, "I had lots of girls come up to me [in Australia and New Zealand], telling me they loved our videos. And that you inspire them."[9] Both were smiling, clearly touched by the support from adoring fans around the world.

Lauren's claim that she doesn't endorse terrorism is true. She doesn't *explicitly* endorse terrorism, but she does promote right-wing extremists' ideas concerning anti-immigration, antiliberalism, and antifeminism that circulate within the broader far-right ecosystem.

Such promotion is "a point of pride and a strategy," writes the journalist Seyward Darby. "When alt-right proponents wanted to suggest that they had strength in numbers, they could point to all the people agreeing with them on the internet. When they wanted to distance themselves from someone—a murderer, say—they could suggest the person wasn't really alt-right. They'd never met him, or chatted with him, or seen him at a conference. They washed their hands of responsibility for the online ecosystem that nurtured violence."[10] Because the alt-right was a leaderless and ideologically diffuse movement, its adherents had the advantage of being able to latch onto existing parties or groups but then claim they were not affiliated if that relationship turned out to be unbeneficial. At the same time, such parties and groups could build connections with the alt-right but then not endorse the alt-right's activities that had violent consequences. The relationship was a win-win for both.

Like all the far-right women influencers, Lauren Southern merely represents the tip of the iceberg of extreme racism, anti-Semitism, Islamophobia, and violent misogyny. She is presented as the friendly face of the far right or, as Lauren calls herself, a "journalist" and "activist" –terminology that reflects the far right's mainstreaming. As the historian Alexandra Minna Stern cautions, "The power of these alt-right women to push the Overton window and move alt-right discourse into the mainstream should not be underestimated."[11]

Lauren returned to the European Parliament to speak about immigration in early 2019. "What an absolute pleasure it is to be here in the European Union Parliament [sic] talking about my work once again." She continued, "I must admit that I'm surprised to be speaking here once again. If I'd been told two years ago that I would be invited to the belly of the Marxist beast, the European Union, twice, I don't think I would be alone in being surprised."[12] Yet we shouldn't be surprised when considering how far-right ideas have shifted into the mainstream.

This time Lauren's speech wasn't about defending her actions to the security services or calling out the political establishment. She was calm and collected. "For the last twelve months, being older and perhaps a little wiser, I backed away a bit from the in-your-face troll-style politics." Instead, she chose to pivot toward "the pursuit of understanding." What does this mean, exactly? Lauren was promoting her new documentary, *Borderless*, which she described as an honest and fair portrayal of "immigration, culture, and the upheaval that happens when the balance between these things is upset."

In traveling around the world as a political activist, Lauren effectively combines professional pursuits with personal reflections. As she was filming *Borderless*, which traces migrant journeys and their impact on local communities in the ongoing refugee crisis in Europe, she was regularly posting glamor shots of herself posing in front of ancient European relics and behind-the-scenes footage at Champ de Mars Park near the Eiffel Tower in Paris, thus inviting her audience a peek into her deliberately crafted, desirable lifestyle.

Her previous documentary, *Farmlands*, had focused on the "genocide" of white farmers in South Africa. While in South Africa, she posted selfies in the desert brush, quoting the writer Rudyard Kipling: "All we have of freedom—all we use or know—This our fathers bought for us, long and long ago."[13] In alluding to the poet who morally justified colonialism as the "white man's burden," Lauren was suggesting that white South Africans have a moral claim to the land.

Soon after *Farmlands* was released in 2018, it received widespread attention. "So many eyes on this issue. People were just enthralled with what we discovered in South Africa," Lauren later reflected in 2022 on its release. "It's getting reported on everywhere, everyone starts talking about this issue, millions of views—Tucker Carlson, Donald Trump tweets about white farmers in South Africa, the Australian government come[s] out and says they're considering taking them in as refugees."[14] In August 2018, she posted a screenshot of a tweet by Donald Trump articulating concern for South African land and farm seizures and the alleged killing of white farmers reported by then–*Fox News* anchor Tucker Carlson.[15] It's no coincidence that in the summer of the documentary's release, the U.S. president was calling for the State Department's investigation into attacks on white South Africans' farms. In influencing U.S. foreign policy through cultural outputs, the far right has never been simultaneously more mainstream and more global in reach.

In mid-2020, Lauren revealed how she would be going forward with choosing the topic for her next documentary. "I really want to invite you guys to be a part of the documentary-making process as well, helping me narrow down and decide which documentary I'm going to make. Seeing how the creation, filming, and editing occurs behind the scenes. Plus, this will really help finance the creation of these documentaries themselves."[16]

She sold her decision to take this approach in the following way: "Hell, documentaries are stressful . . . they are hard work. But it's doing something meaningful. It's not just taking shots from a comfortable studio or a living room. It's really exploring what's going on, on the ground. And that's what makes it worthwhile," inviting her audience to take part in something genuine and authentic. "I really do hope some of you consider joining me on that mission," she concluded and told her viewers that they could follow the progress of her work on the fundraising platform SubscribeStar.[17] Here, subscribers who contribute a monthly donation ranging from $5 to $250 could engage in livestreams, ask questions, and post comments. By allowing her fans to influence how content would be framed in the documentary-making process—through reliance on crowdfunding—Lauren framed their participation as vital for the movement.

Six months later, Lauren announced the release of her new documentary about BLM protestor violence, *Crossfire*. But this time, viewers wouldn't be able to access it on her YouTube channel. "I loved hosting *Farmlands* here. I loved hosting *Borderless* on YouTube," she explained. "The reason I used YouTube in the first place, despite all the problems, is because people got to see the hype. They got to see the millions of views; they could translate it; it was on a mainstream platform, so people that I normally wouldn't be able to reach could maybe get it in the recommended bar and watch it." But "those days are gone," she claimed.[18]

"While *Borderless* and *Farmlands* dealt with very extreme themes, *Crossfire* has managed to exceed that," Lauren stated, leaning into the camera. "It's even more controversial than *Farmlands* and *Borderless* combined." She was strategically marketing the film by emphasizing its controversial nature, describing scenes of violence in addition to political opinions expressed by figures banned on mainstream social media platforms. Because of *Crossfire*'s content, Lauren believed that uploading it on YouTube would be a poor decision because it would either be taken down very quickly, be made inaccessible, not receive any ad sponsorship, or be age restricted. This tactic of perceived stigmatization built up anticipation in her audience. Instead, she said, viewers could access *Crossfire* through its own dedicated website. Although the film was available to watch without purchase, Lauren made a last-minute appeal to her viewers to donate whatever amount they could and to help promote the film through sharing on their social media networks. "Let's try to get that traction that unfortunately Silicon Valley has largely taken away from dissident projects," she urged in a final call to action.

Far-right women influencers not only influence the echelons of state diplomacy and legislative chambers but are also deeply involved with on-the-ground mobilization and protest events.

"It's crazy because so many people think this is some weird mission of just a few people that have these opinions, that these borders need to be secure, just a few fascista," streamed Lauren Southern onsite from the French Alps in April 2018. "No, it's normal people here that are saying, 'We don't want illegal immigrants in France.'" She continued, "I just got here, and we've seen bikers go by that live in the area, and they're cheering, saying, 'Love you guys.'"

"Actually, there were some locals just hiking up the mountain yesterday, and the activists had to haul up all of this water and stuff, and they [the locals] helped," responded Brittany. "They just grabbed the stuff and helped carry it up. It's been really awesome to see the reactions from the locals." She quickly added, "Of course, the media will paint it as something else. That's why you have so many independent journalists here as well."[19]

The two were livestreaming during the Defend Europe mission, a campaign organized by the youth-led Identitarian movement in 2018 to stop refugees from crossing into Europe. As noted in chapter 1, the Identitarians can be considered the European equivalent of the U.S. based alt-right. When Brittany Pettibone and Martin Sellner, well-known leader of the Austrian branch, got married, there was much celebration within the far right because the couple symbolized the merging of these two movements.

The camera was shaky, and the picture is poor quality, a fact acknowledged by Lauren, who clarified that the internet connection was unstable but that she was trying her best. She panned the camera to the crowd that had congregated in the area, mountains looming in the background, and stopped for a moment to check comments in the chat box of the livestream and to thank her praising fans from the United Kingdom, Germany, Australia, Denmark, and other countries around the world.

Lauren was then joined by Brittany's then fiancée, Martin. Switching to a journalistic line of questioning, they discussed the campaign's operations and strategies, including collaboration with their French and Italian counterparts. They joked about the age group of activists present:

"Everyone here is under thirty, right?" Lauren asked.

"Yeah," Martin smiled back, causing the two to start laughing.

"It's a bunch of young people coming out, with their own money that they've fundraised from the public. Not state money. Doing the job that the state [is] in place to do. That is wrong," affirmed Lauren.

After talking with Martin about political and media reactions as well as the threat posed by antifascists to the Defend Europe mission, Lauren ended the interview by promising that she would share more footage as the campaign unfolded, including a surprise for her viewers. At that moment, the police arrived, although the interaction with them remained conflict free, and they just patrolled the area. Lauren ended the video when they had to quickly move to another location and waved goodbye with Brittany, who also shared news that a special announcement was coming soon on her YouTube channel.

Later, Brittany made a video responding to media criticism that the Defend Europe mission was a failure, arguing that this assessment was false. To prove her claim, she cited the actions of Matteo Salvini, the former deputy prime minister of Italy and a politician for the far-right Lega party. Under Salvini's post as interior minister, Italy shut down one of Europe's largest migrant centers and ports for rescue ships. Salvini also collaborated with Viktor Orbán, the far-right prime minister of Hungary, to form an antimigration bloc.[20] She made clear that far-right goals are becoming legitimized and institutionalized through major government actors throughout the world, not just in the United States.

Brittany and Lauren had participated in the Defend Europe campaign the previous year, too, but the video content produced from that trip had a very different tone.

"Hey guys, I'm with Lauren, and we're in Cyprus right now," said Brittany to the camera on that occasion in August 2017.[21] The two were sitting next to each other on a bed in what looks to be a holiday Airbnb rental—a likely supposition given that the extremism researcher Julia Ebner attended a UK branch Identitarian meeting undercover at an Airbnb location in London.[22]

"We wanted to make another casual video that we got the idea from because of an Instagram post that Lauren made of a picture of her and me," Brittany continued. The post she was referring to has the caption "It's hard making female friends these days in a world of feminism and cattiness ~ but @brittpettibone is one of the sweetest down to earth ladies I've had the pleasure of befriending."[23] They discussed this topic during an ongoing campaign to stop refugees at Europe's border in August 2017.

"I was reading the comments on this post, and there were so many girls who were reading it and quoting it, being like, 'This is me, I can totally relate,'" said Lauren in the vlog.

The two discussed the struggle of trying to connect with other "girls" and make deep friendships, of finding someone who is loyal and understanding, not just a superficial acquaintance. Although friendship is an innately apolitical topic, they agreed that the main reason for their lack of true friendships was the spread of notions of "female empowerment," which they felt had created social dominance. "Feminism is leading women into a trap in both their friendships and their relationships," they falsely concluded. In reality, not just women are having this problem. One-third of millennials report feeling lonely, much of it attributed to social media use in which individuals are constantly comparing themselves to online images.[24] Considering feminism to be the sole cause for failing to create friendships limits the issue's wide field.

After this informal ten-minute chat, Brittany and Lauren concluded by encouraging viewers to follow updates of the Defend Europe mission and to look out for new video content coming soon. I argue that the mix of networked intimacy and political activism streamed on YouTube is bedrock propaganda of the modern far right. These influencers position themselves as relatable and authentic to their audience, while also showcasing an aspirational lifestyle.

The Defend Europe missions were not the first time that Lauren had done a livestream on the ground. She also filmed on-site during the notorious Free Speech Week organized by a conservative student association at the University of California, Berkeley, in October 2017.[25] Prominent far-right and conservative commentators such as Milo Yiannopolous, David Horowitz, and Lucian Wintrich were confirmed to speak, and it was rumored that Ann Coulter and Steve Bannon would make appearances, but the event was canceled at the last minute due to poor organization.[26] Nonetheless, many alt-right and far-right supporters had already booked travel to attend, so they organized a protest in response to the cancellation. Brittany and Martin revealed that they had rented an Airbnb for the trip and spent time filming videos of themselves interviewing other far-right individuals.[27] Free Speech Week at Berkeley was not just a protest event but also a gathering of influential far-right actors from around the country and across the Atlantic.

This was evident when Lauren livestreamed the protest, joined by several far-right figures at various points, such as Cassandra Fairbanks (who organized the infamous DeploraBall after Trump's election) and the British antifeminist YouTuber Carl Benjamin, known by his pseudonym "Sargon of Akkad." As Lauren made her way from the campus entrance down Telegraph Avenue—home of the progressive counterculture student movement of the 1960s—she was confronted by counterprotestors, which was to be expected given Berkeley's strong left-wing student activism. But more often than not she received praise from adoring fans and requests for selfies.[28] In fact, Lauren is so popular with university students that at one point the Republican student association at Cal Poly San Luis Obispo invited her to give a talk, which she entitled "The Return of the Traditional Woman: How Marxism Ruined Gender Relations."[29]

University spaces are a hotbed for far-right recruitment. As Julia Ebner observed from talking to Identitarian recruiters, the movement is highly selective of new recruits, who must be young, trendy, and well educated.[30] Fresh faces such as Lauren and Brittany provide legitimacy through an aesthetic that is appealing to mainstream audiences. Gone are the days of swastika tattoos and skinheads, which have been replaced with polo shirts, hipster haircuts, and attractive people. Cynthia Miller-Idriss writes that such appearances are part of a deliberate top-down decision to shift public perception, making it harder to recognize the far right and interpret their extreme ideas (see chapter 5).[31]

There's no better place for the contemporary far right to find new supporters—other than online—than among the well-dressed and articulate young people on university campuses. This strategy stems from a long history of the so-called culture wars. The term *culture wars* refers to cultural conflicts between social groups regarding values and beliefs on issues pertaining to morality, such as homosexuality and abortion. The arena for culture wars was originally the student counterculture movements across American university campuses in the 1960s.[32] Protesting against the Vietnam War while promoting the civil rights and gay liberation movements, students created a subculture based on sexual liberation and psychoactive drug experimentation. The University of California's Berkeley campus became a national symbol for the counterculture movement when it spearheaded the free-speech movement in a mass act of civil disobedience (the Free Speech Movement Café on campus still remains a popular hangout). It's no wonder, then, that far-right dissenters strategically selected Berkeley as the location for the Free Speech Week event.

Since the 1960s, conservative and far-right circles have viewed university campuses as an ideological battleground of ideas. Campuses have been spaces to recruit young talent in the hope of cultivating them as future political leaders. These young people are provided opportunities to network at large conferences and be guided by mentors to further their careers.[33] Student associations are also encouraged to put on events and activities with the aim of provocation. One year, for instance, the Berkeley College Republicans hosted the controversial Increase Diversity Bake Sale, selling baked goods priced according to buyers' race and gender. The purpose of the bake sale was to protest affirmative action (a policy that considers an individual's racial, sexual, or religious background) in the university's admissions decisions regarding new applicants.[34]

In 2012, the national student organization Turning Point USA was established with the intent of promoting conservative principles. Both the Anti-Defamation League, a Jewish civil rights organization, and the Southern Poverty Law Center, an antihate organization, have criticized Turning Point for its affiliation with far-right activists.[35] Its sister branch, Turning Point UK, was founded in 2018. Turning Point sparked controversy when it launched the Professor Watchlist in 2019, calling for student members to report university professors who "discriminate against conservative students and advance leftist propaganda in the classroom"; the organization's aim was to "expose and document" these incidents.[36] In this move of the campus culture wars, the Professor Watchlist webpage maintains a running list of faculty members whom students have reported. Both Turning Point branches have been endorsed by prominent politicians, including Donald Trump, who spoke at the Turning Point USA annual summit in July 2019.[37]

When following far-right women influencers on Instagram, I received a suggestion to follow Turning Point's account.[38] A quick browse through its posts reveals young, attractive people advertising guns and clothing as well as tabling events with tagged geolocations at universities across the United States. Infographics and memes are interspersed among these posts warning of the dangers of socialism and the "radical left." Turning Point has recruited a large number of conservative influencers, called "ambassadors," who assist with the organization's branding and outreach on Instagram to fight the online culture war.[39] Although Turning Point's social media content isn't that extreme, where do we draw the line between conservatism and the far right? Until this point, I was following far-right women influencers on Instagram who openly advocate for a pro-white Western civilization and fear an impending Islamic and migrant invasion. But now I was being recommended more mainstream conservative accounts to follow.

Do these women influencers support Turning Point? That's what I assumed until I watched Lauren Southern speak out in 2018 against the organization's hypocrisy on being against identity politics while still using identity politics in its favor. She pointed out that Turning Point USA has "always taken part in identity politics" and criticized its Latino Leadership summit, Young Women's Leadership summit, and Young Black Leadership summit, "all" of which are "based on identity." The problem, stated Lauren, is that Turning Point would never hire a white or European representative for the group or use hashtags such as #whiteawakening. "Groups like Turning Point USA and people in the mainstream right pretending they don't partake in identity politics when they so obviously do."

Lauren would prefer Turning Point take an overtly pro-white nationalist stance in the name of inclusion.[40]

Despite her criticism, Lauren did think that "it's a good thing that some different views are being brought to the mainstream" by Turning Point. These "different views" include pro–gun rights, pro-fossil fuels, antiabortion, and opposition to the BLM movement. A few years later, Lauren Chen shared on her Instagram page an official poster that she would be speaking at Turning Point USA's largest student event of the year, America Fest, in 2022 and then shared selfies during the event.[41] She became a Turning Point ambassador as I was writing this book, demonstrating that, if anything, the boundary between mainstream conservatism and the far right is becoming ever more blurred. Ideas and actors from the far right are traveling into mainstream conservatism, or mainstream conservativism is adopting the far right in a shared agenda. Student politics and the culture wars are a battleground for the far right, providing opportunities for overlap with the broader conservative ecosystem.

The far right is also becoming globally more strategic than ever before. "In Europe, you have the advantage of taking to the streets. In America, you have conquered social media," Martin Sellner told Brittany in October 2017. The couple were sitting in the sunny backyard of Brittany's family home in Idaho, having just come back from Free Speech Week at Berkeley. Although the video is titled "Right-Wing Movements: America Versus Europe," the title is a sanitizing label for what was actually a comparison of Identitarian and alt-right movements.[42]

"What do you think is the best way that each movement can help one another?" asked Brittany.

Martin highlighted that actors in each region have their own nationalist priorities and know their local context best, but that collaboration can come from learning strategies and tactics from one another. "Meme warfare, of reconquering YouTube with this huge variety from satire to pranks to political commentary, interviews, is very effective," he observed. The Identitarian movement is lagging behind in this area, he noted, but activism on the streets is where Americans can learn from Europeans.

"Now people are catching up and copying what you're doing," he smiled at Brittany.

"Ah, I see," she replied, grinning back.

"Not you personally."

"Yeah, yeah, oh sure, Martin," Brittany teased.

The ensuing conversation switched from serious topics such as the militant structure of rallies and demonstrations to an exchange of inside jokes.

"You're a Nazi 'cause of your haircut, Martin," mocked Brittany.

"The glasses are balancing it out," he replied, "because someone with these glasses can't be extremist; they're too hipster."

This playful exchange reflected the couple's display of networked intimacy for their viewers, who felt as if they were invited into the private space of Brittany and Martin's relationship. The couple have made other vlogs together that directly link to their political activism, such as when they responded to the incident of being banned and deported from the United Kingdom, when Martin faced imprisonment in 2018 over hate speech promoted by the Identitarians, and later when they heard the court verdict acquitting him.[43]

Martin was banned from visiting Brittany in the United States in March 2019 after authorities found out that the Christchurch right-wing terrorist who murdered fifty-one people had donated $1,500 to Martin the previous year.[44] A couple of months later, however, the two were reunited at "a secret, undisclosed location outside the Schengen zone," casually discussing their wedding plans on a vlog.[45]

Brittany has similarly faced police investigations because of her affiliation with Martin but also after interviewing the Australian neo-Nazi Blair Cottrell, who likewise received donations from the Christchurch terrorist.[46] After they were married, Brittany moved to Austria and began setting up their new home, but she described

the process as difficult for the couple given a year of criminal investigations and court dates, and Martin complained that it "damaged
our reputation" and "our movement."[47] Brittany eventually made
private all the videos featuring Martin on her YouTube channel.

Within these vlogs, there is a constant denial of affiliation with
right-wing terrorism and a condemnation of violence. Yet Martin
and Brittany repeatedly echo the "Great Replacement" theory
throughout their videos. Martin lamented that police and government treated them unfairly "just because we're talking about issues
like demographics, birthrates, and the Great Replacement."[48]

"If the Great Replacement is a conspiracy theory, why is it then
that the UN itself says otherwise?" asked Brittany in one vlog, citing a UN recommendation of "replacement migration" to offset low
fertility in some countries.[49] The UN's suggestion of replacement
migration, however, isn't the same thing as what the far right calls
the "Great Replacement." The UN's report on the topic, published
many years earlier, in 2001, explored eight low-fertility countries
(France, Germany, Italy, Japan, South Korea, Russia, the United Kingdom, and the United States) and only suggested, without specific
guidelines for implementation, international migration to offset
population decline and ageing.[50] The release of the UN's report
was controversial and heavily criticized by experts, but, importantly, the motive behind replacement migration was addressing
economic growth and a decline in labor productivity—not racial
reproduction.[51]

The Great Replacement, in contrast, is a conspiracy theory that
white European populations are being intentionally replaced by
nonwhite migrants, specifically Muslims, to create a new political
order.[52] The political left and mainstream media, which the far right
commonly call the "global elite" or "globalists" (an anti-Semitic
slur), are viewed as leading this process. The Great Replacement theory was first developed by the French intellectual Renaud Camus,
whose writings the extreme right have adopted to promote the
closely related white genocide conspiracy theory; according to the
latter, white populations are being replaced by mass immigration,

racial integration, low fertility, abortion, and organized violence, a plot overseen by a global Jewish elite. The Great Replacement theory inspired the Christchurch terrorist as well as the copycat attacks by the El Paso and Buffalo shooters.[53] These metapolitical narratives strongly resonate among the far right, who view ethnic and racial minorities as a threat to Western (i.e., white) civilization.

In one of Brittany's vlogs about "what makes a great woman" in October 2019, displayed in the bookshelf behind her is the book *Ethnos and Society* by the Russian philosopher Aleksandr Dugin, arguing for the preservation of ethnic communities by upholding traditionalism and fighting against modern society and degeneracy.[54] Published by the white-nationalist publisher Arktos, it has been banned by major online retailers such as Amazon.

The year before Brittany made this vlog, in mid-2018, she and Lauren traveled to Moscow to meet Dugin in person. In a four-part video series, they interviewed him about his philosophical beliefs and metapolitics.[55] It's a long discussion with topics that span from the millennial generation to the future of conservatism, the critique of liberalism and feminism, the evil of modernity, and the revival of religion. This exclusive interview represents how women influencers like Brittany and Lauren act as a bridge in building intellectual connections between the far right in Europe and the far right in North America.[56]

Their conversations with Dugin can be found on Lauren's channel, but Brittany also uploaded a video of her interview with the far-right Russian female activist Maria Katasonova during their trip.[57] A twenty-seven-year-old journalist and influencer, Maria is the face of Russian nationalism and gained notoriety for leading the Women for Marine campaign when Marine Le Pen, leader of the French far-right National Rally party, visited Moscow in 2017.[58] Sitting next to each other on a couch, Brittany and Maria discussed Western feminism as being so detrimental to biologically "natural" gender norms that it will ultimately lead to "demographic collapse." The video is titled "What Most Russian Women Think of Feminism," but it features no exploration of the growing feminist and women's rights movement in the country and considers feminism only as a West-ern import to Russia.[59]

In contrast to their formal interviews with Dugin and Katason-ova, a more informal video of their Moscow visit can be found on Brittany's channel. For this video, she and Lauren changed out of the dresses they wore for the interviews and into jeans and shirts. "Hey guys, so we are in the final stages of our trip here in Russia. And we thought it would make for an interesting video to share a couple of the crazy stories that have occurred to us while being [here]," stated Brittany.[60] Lauren sat cross-legged next to her on the bed of their hotel room, and the two couldn't stop smiling and laughing as they gave a few anecdotes of their time spent in Moscow. Although this video didn't garner nearly the same high number of views as the other videos filmed in Russia, the casual nature of their discussion provided a light-hearted balance to the formal content. Once again, we see the behind-the-scenes networked intimacy of these influenc-ers' professional careers. A few years later, Lauren even shared an Instagram Story video of the two of them, stumbling with tears of laughter while wearing fur hats and holding vodka bottles. It's cap-tioned "SubscribeStar Only Content LMAOOO," implying that only her closest fans would understand the history and friendship of her political activism.[61]

The interview with Aleksandr Dugin was not the first time that Brittany spoke with a well-known far-right figure in person. The most popular video on her channel is an interview with the former English Defence League leader Tommy Robinson (real name Stephen Yaxley-Lennon). Brittany posted this video, titled "The Tommy Rob-inson Interview That Got Me Banned from the U.K.," on March 14, 2018, shortly after being detained and deported with Martin at Lon-don's Luton Airport.[62] The main reason Brittany cited for her deportation was that she had planned to interview Tommy during her trip to the United Kingdom. The uploaded interview was filmed in Vienna and conducted immediately following British authorities' refusal to let Brittany enter the country. Much of the interview focused on Tommy's experiences with law enforcement and imprisonment after he "expos[ed] Islam." Brittany had also interviewed Tommy a year earlier, and their discussion focused on what they saw as the prospect of Muslims invading Europe and replacing the "native" population.[63]

Far-right women such as Brittany not only produce and circulate far-right ideas within the movement but also promote leading (male) far-right figures as part of their activism. These influencers provide exposure to more extreme voices—who often have been banned from platforms—and internationalize their audience. I argue that far-right women influencers, compared to their male counterparts, are less likely to be banned from mainstream social media platforms despite reinforcing the same ideological talking points. Because of the "softer" framings of their content, these influencers enjoy greater mainstream visibility and legitimacy.

With Brittany Sellner's relationship to Martin, she symbolizes the merging of the North American alt-right and European Identitarian movements. Her YouTube channel features interviews with European far-right women, showcasing them for an American audience. Naomi Seibt was largely unknown to the public until she began appearing in German newspapers in 2019,[64] which described her as the "anti-Greta," a reference to the progressive climate-change activist Greta Thunberg. Naomi was soon promoted by conservative circles as their antidote to climate-change activism and for a period was funded by the U.S. conservative think tank the Heartland Institute, speaking at its functions and making media appearances in which she advocated a so-called climate realism (a euphemism for climate-change denial) approach. In the past few years, Naomi has transformed from an amateur YouTuber to spokesperson for climate-change denial within international circles. It's evident that the far right quickly tapped Naomi as their Gen Z representative.

I first came across Naomi when she was invited onto Brittany's channel for an interview in 2019. Brittany opened up the interview by stating that she had decided to stop conducting interviews on her channel nine months earlier but made an exception for Naomi, whom she described as "impressive" for her political activism at a young age (Naomi was nineteen at the time). The interview was structured in a get-to-know format; Naomi described herself as politically "libertarian" and as largely inspired by the Canadian white nationalist Stefan Molyneux to become more vocal in her views. In particular, she pointed to the 2015 "refugee crisis" as a watershed moment in her political awakening—at fifteen years old—followed by increasing participation in "the political sphere online."[65]

Like other far-right women influencers, Naomi is critical of feminism, of "uncontrolled" immigration by those who are "not so compatible with liberal Western ideals," and of the mainstream media for their supposedly biased coverage. Throughout the interview, you can sense that Brittany held a sisterly affection toward Naomi and was proud of Naomi's willingness to voice her political opinions. At one point, the two discussed how difficult it can be for young women to build and maintain friendships after being ostracized by previous friends but how they both now have support from a community of like-minded others and feel liberated to be themselves.

This sisterhood reminded me of another relationship: Ayla Stewart and Lana Lokteff. "Ayla later described Lana as 'a bit of a mentor,' someone who was 'public and professional,'" writes the journalist Seyward Darby. When Ayla appeared on Lana's podcast *Radio 3Fourteen* on Red Ice TV, the "conversation validated Ayla's choices and offered her a worldview that celebrated them."[66] Indeed, Lana regularly promotes and provides visibility to other far-right women on her podcast.[67] I saw a similar moment unfolding between Naomi and Brittany. Brittany has interviewed other German and Austrian far-right women as well, and they discuss specific issues such as the #120dB campaign—the far right's #MeToo equivalent (with the motto "women defend yourselves")—as well as their personal experiences as far-right women activists in Europe.[68] As in her interview of Naomi, Brittany expresses a sisterhood with these European women.

Brittany also conducted a one-on-one interview with the popular French activist Thaïs d'Escufon in August 2021. Discussing the jump-start of her political career, Thaïs mentioned growing up in a "right-wing Catholic family" (in fact, a surviving family of bourgeois French nobility) and being exposed to nationalist values at a young age. Attending university exposed her to the world outside of her sheltered upbringing, in particular the area around the campus that "houses lots of Islamists, lots of immigrants." Thaïs felt uncomfortable taking public transport to her lectures, where she was surrounded by "immigrant men . . . like Arabs, African type." Compelled to prevent her "country collapsing," Thaïs joined the local Identitarian movement branch through a friend's recommendation. "This is where I belong, this is a real community," she stated of joining the group. "I wanted to make a real difference." For Thaïs, this meant drawing attention to "problems linked to mass immigration," especially "the sexual harassment, sexual assaults, and rapes" of white women as well as the growing "Islamization" of Europe and the "rise of anti-native French sentiment."[69]

When Brittany asked if there are a lot of right-wing women in France, Thaïs responded, "There is a trend of more and more right-wing women getting involved in politics because they are faced with new problems such as sexual harassment and rape by migrants." The media's willingness to give more visibility to women than to men, she claimed, allows right-wing women to be publicly recognized. Yet, she noted, "the media likes [sic] to portray me as being part of a strategy, which consists of giving a more presentable face of the radical right-wing ideas."

"It was exactly the same for me. They would refer to me as a Barbie," Brittany interrupted. "As if you're a puppet in a way, and you're not making your own decisions, and you don't actually hold these opinions, but, exactly, you're being used." She continued satirically, "It's all a big strategy; you couldn't possibly have a mind of your own."

Thaïs responded by laughing. "This is exactly the portrait they made of me. But still, even if they depict me as the Barbie, etc., people understand that we are not the demons and just normal people. And I was clearly not a strategy." Yet, as I show throughout this book, women like Brittany and Thaïs indeed represent a far-right metapolitical strategy to give its ideology a more presentable public face.

Until the French government proscribed the Identitarian movement in 2021, Thaïs served as an official spokesperson for the group and more recently has actively produced social media content on her individual channels as an independent influencer. Thaïs was banned from Twitter in 2020 and from TikTok in 2021 and regularly faced suspension of her Instagram account before it was permanently deleted in 2022 (although in 2023 she created a new Instagram account), so she remains the most active on Telegram. She launched her own YouTube channel in 2021 and now has more than 166,000 subscribers. Her videos feature English titles even though she speaks in French (with English subtitles available), reflecting an attempt to internationalize her content. Like the North American far-right women, Thaïs speaks directly to the camera but also has high-quality video and audio production.

On Instagram, she has been particularly adept at showcasing behind-the-scenes content of filming and editing YouTube videos to give her followers a sneak peek of upcoming releases. Like companies that host promotions or special events to market their brands, Thaïs would use Story features such as the countdown sticker so that her followers could subscribe to the countdown event—that is, the video release—and then be sent a reminder when the time elapsed so that they could check out her YouTube channel.[70] This type of self-branding is closely tied to networked intimacy techniques of engagement. Like Lauren Southern, Thaïs decided to produce professional documentaries; in 2022, she filmed her first documentary in the war zone between Armenia and Azerbaijan. Although known mainly within the French far-right scene, Thaïs is only twenty-three years old and has already amassed a popular global following. A figure like her represents the next generation picking up tips and learning from millennial far-right women influencers and capitalizing on hot-topic issues such as white privilege and the culture wars to advance a far-right agenda.

Finally, another activist I came across in a selfie posted on Brittany's Instagram page[71] is the twenty-six-year-old Dutch influencer Eva Vlaardingerbroek, a former politician who worked as a trainee for the far-right Forum for Democracy (FvD) party in the European Parliament in Brussels. She holds a master's degree in philosophy of law and pursued a PhD in the Netherlands before dropping out to focus on politics full-time. Eva became a rising star among the Dutch far right for delivering a speech critical of feminism in 2019, but the next year she ended her membership in FvD following internal party divisions—not least complicated by her romantic relationship with its leader, Thierry Baudet, a few years earlier. At the time she exited FvD, she was dating Julien Rochedy, a French politician of the far-right National Rally party and later moved to Sweden to become the host of a YouTube program called *Let's Talk About It*, run by the Sweden Democrats, a party with roots in neo-Nazism.[72] She returned to the Netherlands at the end of 2021 to take up a position at a law firm to fight government mandates such as mask wearing and vaccination against COVID-19.

U.S. audiences may be familiar with Eva because she began regularly appearing as a guest commentator on Tucker Carlson's show on *Fox News*, discussing the "skyrocketing crime epidemic" in Sweden, which she linked to mass immigration and demographic change.[73] She tweeted segments from her *Fox News* interviews stating that "people coming from these radically different cultures, first and foremost Africa and the Middle East[,] . . . have very little respect for Swedish culture, very little respect for the West in general" and dog-whistled the Great Replacement by blaming "liberal left-wing elites" for orchestrating this chaos. "This is all part of their plan to destroy our social fabric, and to destroy our identity and our society," she claimed. Eva tweeted her praise for the reelection of Hungary's far-right leader Viktor Orbán, who "doesn't cater to the globalists, doesn't cater to the [EU] bureaucrats," but "caters to a Hungary that is strong, that is proud, that's Christian, and celebrates its own national identity, that protects its borders, and also supports families."[74] Eva later met Orban in person while speaking at CPAC Hungary in 2023.

In 2022, Eva announced on her Instagram page that she had gotten engaged to the American PragerU podcaster Will Witt. Through her relationship to Witt and increasing exposure within the right-wing media ecosystem, she began regularly traveling to the United States to participate in events such as the Conservative Political Action Conference (CPAC) and began to embody a truly global commentator, frequently appearing on far-right and conservative media outlets in the United States, Canada, the United Kingdom, and Germany. When Brittany Sellner interviewed Eva in November 2022, she asked about her growing prominence in the far-right movement. Eva replied, "What I was able to do, what I didn't do before, was spread [awareness] internationally." Brittany was full of compliments for Eva: "You're doing an amazing job. I'm so happy that you are so active now, particularly internationally. I knew this would happen when I first saw your work. I was like, yeah, she's going to grow really big." Eva smiled back, flattered: "Oh wow, that means a lot from you." Brittany continued, "'Cause you're so intelligent as well and well spoken. And you know a lot about the issues; you're not just talking about the same talking points that everybody says. You've really done your homework and research. I think that you've done wonderful work and are a huge asset to us."[75]

Eva is extremely active on Instagram (with the highest number of followers of all the far-right women influencers), where her selfies are featured alongside clips of speeches and TV appearances. She models for small businesses that provide beauty services, capitalizing on her attractive looks. Like Thaïs, Eva extensively uses Stories to engage with her followers through networked intimacy, posting behind-the-scenes selfies before or after recording a TV interview or short clips of media appearances with embedded links to full videos. Eva's rise in popularity represents the face of an increasingly transnational metapolitical far-right scene in which fame is linked to a strong online presence within the attention economy.

Whether through casual chats or formal interviews, far-right women influencers play an important role in solidifying the far right's global connections. They discuss nationalist ideology, travel disruptions, strategies for far-right collaboration, conspiracy theories, and marriage plans. By producing professional documentaries as well as intimate conversations for their viewers, these women appeal to a broad online audience. Both the places they visit and their followers are spread across the world, from North America to Europe to Australia, which adds to the far right's international dimension. In looking ahead, the next chapter details various approaches to countering and challenging head on the threat of radicalization, recruitment, and propaganda posed by this fast-spreading far-right culture.

7

COUNTERING THE FAR RIGHT

To be honest, though, I don't doubt that I'm soon to be banned. Not because I'm an extremist but because the establishment considers me and many other people like me to be a threat. I guess it's just too bad, though, because they don't have one hope in the entire world of stopping us. If they ban us from online, I'll just write books. If they ban my books, then I'll take to the streets and continue all my peaceful activism there."[1]

Brittany Pettibone (soon Sellner) said this on her YouTube channel back in 2018. Five years later, not much has changed, although now she encourages her viewers to follow her on Telegram, BitChute, and Parler. "I think it might be a good idea to subscribe to me on alternative platforms at the moment just because there's wave after wave of censorship; it just keeps coming. You'll never know when I'll be next," she warned in July 2020.[2] Yet as of early 2023, Brittany's YouTube channel is still active and has more than 174,000 subscribers. The same goes for Rebecca Hargraves, who back in 2017 said, "I'm subjected to the whims of YouTube, and I don't expect my channel to be alive for much longer. I pretty much wake up every day to see if it's still there."[3] In January 2021, Rebecca interviewed Black Pigeon

Speaks, an extreme-right commentator, to whom she said, "I really need to rebrand, but what's the point 'cause I'm going to be banned in like four seconds."[4] In 2023, she had 126,000 subscribers. Rebecca has continued to feature politically extreme guests on her channel, such as Paul Ray Ramsey, Owen Benjamin, Devon Stack, Gavin McInnes, Lauren Witzke, and Jared Taylor. It does not seem that things will change anytime soon for these influencers—and herein lies the problem.

That the modern far right is largely an online community remains the biggest challenge toward countering the movement. Major tech companies have taken "hard" approaches in the form of content moderation to address the far-right presence on their platforms. The media scholar Robyn Caplan defines content moderation as "a set of practices" that includes "banning or removal of content or accounts, demonetization (on platforms like YouTube), de-ranking, or the inclusion of tags or warnings against problematic content."[5] I call these practices the "Four D's of content moderation": *deplatforming, demonetization, deranking,* and *detection*. There are also "soft" approaches, often called *counternarrative* efforts or, less commonly, *counterinfluencers*. In this chapter, I elaborate on the effectiveness of hard and soft online methods in challenging the far right but also look at offline strategies as a complementary approach. Both online and offline steps are necessary if we're to successfully counter the far right.

"It's like it's being run by Stalin over there. They're trying to erase people," complained Lauren Chen about Big Tech companies such as Twitter in mid-2020.[6] In this case, Lauren was reacting to the bans of the Canadian far-right figure Gavin McInnes and the British tabloid columnist Katie Hopkins from YouTube and Twitter, respectively, in June 2020. (McInnes was banned from Twitter, Facebook, and Instagram in 2018.)

Lauren is a strong vocal critic of online *deplatforming*, which is when social media companies shut down accounts and users. In this particular case, she suspected that content Gavin posted on his Parler account led to YouTube's decision for suspension. "It's not only now that you have to be user terms-of-service friendly on a platform itself. Just you as a person need to comply with the very biased enforcement of these social media rules," she claimed. The far right frequently criticizes Big Tech companies for enforcing "biased" terms of service motivated by what they see as a leftist agenda. "They're just looking for any excuse" to deplatform someone, Lauren grumbled. "And sometimes it's not even a specific thing that you've done; [you're] kicked off just for a general dislike of [your] content."

McInnes is the founder of the Proud Boys, a men's rights far-right "hate group," according to the Southern Poverty Law Center.[7] The Proud Boys were central to the U.S. Capitol insurrection on January 6, 2021, leading to their designation as a terrorist entity by the Canadian government.[8] Meanwhile, Katie Hopkins has described migrants as "cockroaches" and called for a "final solution" (code for the Holocaust) following the Manchester Arena terrorist attack by an Islamist extremist in the United Kingdom in 2017, comments that led to her being banned from Twitter.[9] Her frequent employment of dog whistles and her spread of conspiratorial content had long violated (pre-Musk) Twitter's policies of conduct. With these details in mind, we can clearly see that Lauren's framing of McInnes and Hopkins as "conservative voices" being censored was intended to make these figures appear more legitimate for their ideas. Tech companies, meanwhile, are seen as false arbiters of truth, suppressing free speech. "Right now, all the power rests with these social media companies," Lauren stated in the same vlog. "This should concern everybody who actually cares about democracy."[10] This wasn't the first time Lauren had criticized Big Tech. Earlier, she had noted that "we've been blacklisted on some platforms," so she asked her viewers to share, like, and subscribe to the channel. "We're not dependent on places like YouTube or Facebook, which frankly at this point by now [we] know they don't like us."[11] Despite the far right's public outcry against Big Tech's conservative censorship, research shows that such claims are unfounded and often false.[12] Rather, these false bias narratives are a type of political disinformation meant to delegitimize platforms.

Some may argue that deplatforming is targeting the symptom, not the cause. I asked Megan Squire, a computer scientist and deputy director for data analytics at the Southern Poverty Law Center who looks at how extremist groups organize online. She replied, "Deplatforming affects the ability of hate groups and terrorists to achieve their three main goals when using social media: 1) Propaganda, 2) Organization, and 3) Trolling/Harassment." She said that to achieve the first goal, propaganda and recruitment, "hate groups and terrorists need to be on mainstream social media to (a) normalize their ideas, and (b) expose them to as many people as possible."[13] Platforms such as Twitter and YouTube offer visibility to a large audience, while making it possible for these influencers to appear as if they have acceptable ideas on mainstream platforms.

Concerning the second goal, planning and organization, Squire warned that "allowing a seamless pivot from recruitment to organizing on the same platform is dangerous." This is especially important for "platforms that have both a propaganda side—via public posts—*and* an organization side—via private chats." She cited some examples: Facebook's Pages (propaganda) versus its Groups and Messenger (organization); Twitter's timeline (propaganda) versus its Direct Message (organization); and the messaging app Telegram's Channels (propaganda) versus its Chats (organization). With respect to far-right women influencers, Instagram can be situated as a platform that offers this dual function with Feed/Story/Reel (propaganda) and Direct Message (organization).

Finally, the third goal, harassment and trolling, what Squire calls "a 'major' fun activity," can be affected by deplatforming. Removing these users reduces their toxic behavior targeting "either 'normies' or people in some ethnic/religious/etc. group that they don't like."

I asked, "If these far-right users are kicked off social media, won't it be harder to track them if they migrate to other platforms?"

"Not necessarily," Squire told me. "This worry usually comes from folks that don't actually know how to track these groups on those other platforms, or from folks who worry that people like me will be doing extra work to track bad actors all around the Internet." In fact, the migration to other platforms can have the opposite effect. "It might make my job harder initially because I will have to learn a new platform, but there are a few things that almost always offset this cost, namely that the 'alt' platforms are often *easier* to systematically collect data from"—compared to accessing and scraping data from the major tech companies—and that usually these users "are not as adept at using 'alt' platforms, either, so they make mistakes." Thus, researchers and law enforcement still have the means to track users on alternative platforms—and might be doing so already. Far-right users are rarely present on just one platform alone.

Last, Squire explained the so-called petri-dish effect, which is similar to the echo-chamber analogy, wherein users get radicalized at an exponential rate because they're engaging only with content that resonates with their political views. A commonly held assumption is that echo chambers will force far-right users to become more extreme. The media scholar Richard Rogers studied far-right celebrities who have been banned on Twitter and migrated to Telegram as their primary platform and found that although their posting activity remains steady, these actors actually become *milder* in their language, and their audiences have thinned.[14] Although this finding may seem counterintuitive, part of this change can be attributed to the fact that these far-right actors no longer face daily online interaction with the "enemy" and thus confront little opposition to rile up their audiences. Squire reminds us, "This reasoning [the echo-chamber effect] forgets that by the time someone gets deplatformed, they're already engaging in toxic behaviors"—and continue to do so, just no longer on a mainstream social media platform. In short, deplatforming can be an effective strategy that places the priorities of victims over that of perpetrators while significantly limiting the influencers' reach.

Exposure is the most important factor in radicalization and recruitment, as chapter 2 explored. Rather than "preaching to the choir" on alt-tech platforms, far-right influencers are amplifying their views to a wide audience on mainstream social media platforms. When Rebecca Hargraves asked Lana Lokteff on a YouTube livestream in July 2021 why Red Ice's channel was banned from YouTube, Lana said, "We were experiencing massive growth, and we had videos that would get a million views towards the end. So we were reaching a lot of people."[15] Cutting off that exposure on YouTube didn't necessarily cease Red Ice's operations, but it did affect the attention its videos were receiving on a mainstream platform. What complicates deplatforming efforts is that content *sponsored* by Red Ice on YouTube still remained on YouTube even after Red Ice itself was deplatformed—for example, the Blonde Buttermaker's channel. Thus, efforts to target the far right online must take into account how affiliated content can circumvent regulation.

Suspension is simply temporary deplatforming. Influencers don't commonly experience this, but it does happen—for example, when Brittany's Instagram account was suspended for three months. According to Brittany, Instagram censored photos of her husband, Martin Sellner, and consequently suspended her account for displaying facial photos of him.[16] But regulation is difficult when cross-posting occurs on many platforms. Although Brittany no longer shares photos of her husband's face on Instagram, and in photos of the two of them she usually covers his face with an Austrian flag emoji, she will share the exact same photo of them, undoctored, on her Telegram channel. Thus, platform-specific responses are only somewhat effective in a digital environment where these influencers have a presence across several platforms. Alt-tech platforms also often serve as effective backup libraries. Robyn Riley shared an Instagram Story in July 2020 that she was now using DLive as a backup channel for livestreaming, fearing that YouTube might soon ban her account.[17] Others, such as Rebecca and Brittany, have long used BitChute and Odysee as a means of backing up their YouTube videos.

Not only does content originate on one platform and then get shared on others, but connections are being formed across platforms as well. For example, during a YouTube livestream in 2018, Ayla Stewart responded in the chat box to a friend whom she also knew on Gab.[18] Given that the far right is adept at using new platforms, some may wonder if these influencers are gaining an audience on TikTok, which is one of the most popular social media platforms to have recently emerged. Since its founding in 2018, the Chinese-owned social media app has seen a spike in users, mostly teenagers, who prefer its format of a short-form mobile video accompanied by trending music. Platforms such as TikTok present an opportunity for influencers to reach a wider (and younger) audience. Studies show that far-right actors have already exploited TikTok to spread hate and propaganda to viewers.[19] But I doubt that TikTok will be replacing YouTube or Instagram anytime soon for these millennial influencers. The app's design of short-length videos isn't conducive to a vlog format of sustained interaction, and users are encouraged to constantly watch streaming viral content in their default home feed. In switching to TikTok, these influencers would likely only retain viewers already familiar with them rather than reach new viewers. For instance, Lauren Chen has a TikTok account but infrequently posts, and Lauren Southern has a TikTok account with significantly less followers than on her other social media channels. Yet because TikTok has become YouTube's biggest competitor in terms of demographic reach, it remains to be seen whether the far right will effectively adapt to this new medium or, more likely, encourage younger influencers to use it. Nonetheless, U.S. colleges are increasingly banning the app over campus Wi-Fi networks—a key issue since students are a prime demographic for far-right recruitment (see chapter 6).[20]

One strategy YouTube has heavily employed is *demonetization*, wherein channel creators are no longer able to monetize their videos from advertisements. Monetization is especially important for

YouTubers who earn income from viewers watching their videos. In early 2017, YouTube worked with advertisers to implement changes that meant advertisements would no longer be randomly assigned to channels with a high number of subscribers but instead directed toward specific content or creators. These changes resulted in new tougher restrictions on hate speech as well as advertisers' greater control over ad placement.[21]

Lauren Southern was one of the YouTubers affected by these policies for inciting hateful content in her videos. In response to repeated demonetization efforts, she announced in 2017 that she was done with political commentary and that perhaps "a change in approach" was needed for her viewers. "So I've decided to become a beauty guru," she gushed before smiling sarcastically and launching an electronic dance music soundtrack. Visuals in hot pink popped up on the screen, while Lauren made pouty faces reminiscent of beauty bloggers.[22]

The video then progressed into a mock makeup tutorial. After applying foundation to her face and using a makeup sponge to spread the foundation, Lauren said, "And you're just going to want to take that foundation and cover up all of your face's imperfections. Just like your history teachers have covered up all of Islam's crimes throughout history." She continued to apply foundation while the screen was overlaid with words in pink cursive writing: *slavery, jihad*, and *pedophilia*. "And you really want to make sure you get those dark circles under your eyes because no one wants to be reminded of ugly things like slavery and the massive expansion of the caliphate throughout Europe."

This video is a prime example of creative means to circumvent regulation. Lauren knew very well how to navigate YouTube's algorithm that detects hate speech and did so this time by hiding behind a seemingly innocent beauty vlog. She continued the rest of the makeup routine by applying eyebrow pencil (be sure to use "nice and sharp strokes—just as sharp as the knives Allah instructs us to use on the throats of disbelievers"), eyeshadow, and eyeliner ("just close that eye, just like you would to every single terrorist attack that happens in the Middle East and Europe everyday"). As Lauren was putting on the eyeliner, a clip played out in the corner of the video frame showing Mayor Sadiq Khan of London commenting on the London Bridge terrorist attack that same year. Taken out of context, Khan says, "It's part and parcel of living in a great global city. You've got to be prepared for these things, be vigilant." Lauren's most recent, demonetized video had commented on the terrorist attack as "a sickness within Islam" that had been caused by "mass migration" (despite no evidence at the time that the perpetrators were migrants).[23]

In the finishing touches, Lauren applied mascara ("The last thing you want is your eyelashes clumping together. You want to keep them nice and separate, just like men and women in a mosque") and blush ("It's a nice pink shade that screams 'I care more about social approval than calling out the reality of mass female genital mutilation, stonings, rapes, and oppression of women in the Islamic world'"). To complete the look with lip color, Lauren started to move the lip color pencil away from her mouth—"If you mess up, and you accidently go off, you can fix that after; it's not a big deal"—and began drawing on her cheek.

"You're just going to want to apply that nice and gently," she said while writing "FUCK" on her right cheek. "Perfect," she said, examining herself in the mirror. "Looking good," she continued and proceeded to write "ISLAM" on the other cheek. She drew away from the camera, looking at herself in the mirror. "Awesome, all right, that looks great. Now, you're complete, you're done!"

"You've got this cute, ad-friendly makeup look," she smiled. "Honestly, I wear this look almost every single day, I just love it so much." In a final shout out to her viewers, she said, "Anyways, I just wanted to thank you guys so much for watching, and make sure to hit like, subscribe, and share. And submit or die."

This video reflects how the far right is always one step ahead of tech companies when it comes to exploiting loopholes. By using a nonoffensive title and thumbnail for the video—"Ad Friendly Makeup Tutorial"—Lauren did not technically violate any of the platform's terms of service but nevertheless spewed Islamophobic hate through visual content and speech.

Rebecca was another of the influencers affected by YouTube's demonetization efforts in early 2017. She warned other YouTubers that they need to be careful about decreasing ad revenue for their content. For many of these content creators, she noted, ad revenues and donations are their primary source of income given that they're not able to hold full-time jobs because of the controversial views they promote on their channels. Rebecca suggested that one solution is for YouTubers to promote each other's content on their channels to increase visibility in an organic way. Because of the effects of demonetization, she considered alternative platforms such as Minds and the increasing likelihood of transitioning off Twitter (from which she was later banned that year),[24] Facebook, and YouTube in the future. She also appealed to her viewers to provide suggestions for other platforms and to continue to support influencers with donations through PayPal, Patreon, and Bitcoin.[25]

But even payment processors have taken steps to deplatform and thus simultaneously demonetize these influencers. Importantly, deplatforming doesn't have to be limited to content creation on social media platforms. Brittany mentioned on her website that she had been banned by PayPal, Patreon, and Donorbox, so supporters would need instead to donate directly on her site. Lauren Southern, meanwhile, began legal proceedings to sue Patreon following her ban in 2017 (although followers could still donate using PayPal).[26] Digital-currency platforms are taking action, too. Rebecca revealed in an Instagram post on October 30, 2020, that she had been banned from Coinbase, an online platform where you can buy, sell, and manage cryptocurrency transactions through a financial portfolio. The screenshot of the email Rebecca posted states that she violated the Coinbase terms of service. Rebecca was outraged, writing in the description, "next will be bank accounts."[27]

Rebecca discovered in 2017 that YouTube had removed and held some of the comments on her videos for review as well as auto-unsubscribed her viewers and prevented them from receiving notifications when new content was published on her channel.[28] She was alarmed, but not as much as when her videos started getting demonetized without notice around the same time.

YouTube was undertaking a broader category of actionable measures within content moderation that aren't as drastic as deplatforming and demonetization: *deranking*. Rather than banning Rebecca's account, here YouTube was narrowing its regulatory efforts to a singular piece of content, such as a post or video. This type of moderation usually takes two forms: removing the content outright or affixing a warning label such as "Disclaimer: This post contains false information." YouTube has a strikes policy to respond to violations, where videos or posts are removed, and sometimes access to features or ability to post is restricted. It has also introduced measures of restricted access, such as requiring account sign-up for viewing videos. Meanwhile, Twitter employs a related tool called "shadowbanning," or removing the algorithmic visibility of a user's content on social media without the user's knowledge. With shadowbanning, users on a platform and sometimes the followers of an account are not able to view such content.

One of the biggest advantages of YouTube for content creators is its algorithmic ranking of content: when videos are ranked for visibility in search results. But the process of ranking is opaque and subject to perceptions of bias, such as when Lauren Chen told her viewers that "YouTube now deranks our content" and asked them to share videos from her channel.[29] Another time, she complained that "YouTube has put us in the algorithm gulag."[30] One time I was searching for a video that I had previously watched on Lauren Southern's YouTube channel only to find that it was no longer listed in her gallery of videos. Had Lauren decided to remove it? I fortunately had saved the hyperlink and clicked on it, expecting to see "video unavailable" or "video has been removed" on the web page. I found instead that the video was still available for viewing, but under the title a small text box read, "Unlisted." YouTube videos with an "unlisted" designation means that they do not appear in search results, subscriber feeds, and suggestions. However, anyone with the URL can view and share the video. In short, unlisted videos fall in between public and private. Whether Lauren or YouTube made changes to the video's settings is unclear. However, unlisting could be a potentially effective tool for platforms to moderate content deemed harmful by restricting visibility without facing accusations of total censorship. Research on YouTube has described this tool as "demotion," or the manipulation of search ranking and recommendation mechanisms to prevent problematic content from gaining too much engagement before it infringes community guidelines.[31]

The media scholar Bharath Ganesh describes the "ungovernability" of online spaces where the far right is present. He characterizes this presence as "a swarm" with three central components: "its decentralized structure, its ability to quickly navigate and migrate across websites, and its use of coded language to flout law and regulation."[32] All three elements combined means that regulating the far right online is exceedingly difficult, even if tech companies, governments, and civil society collaborate to find solutions. This is especially true regarding the third component—coded language—which falls within a legal gray zone. Most tech companies consider only explicit calls for violence or terrorism made by a user as a violation of rules, which is distinguished from hate speech (itself a vague term). Because of this narrow interpretation, many far-right users use coded language as a loophole to avoid *detection*.

The same principle of coded language applies to spreading disinformation, as when Robyn deliberately misspelled "vaccination" as "vaccin@ti0n" to prevent an automatic fact-check pop-up on her Instagram Story (see chapter 4) or, more recently used the letter *v* followed by the axe emoji.[33] This coding adheres to a longer history of Instagram users employing "thinly veiled alternative spellings" of hashtags, using many hashtags to disrupt the classification of images in order to circumvent the policing of hashtags, and increasingly relying on the privacy of Direct Messages and self-deleting Stories, which decreases the chances of flagging by users. Further, Instagram's "algorithms can be foiled by low resolution images and *other visual elements* that distort the digital footprint" but that can be clearly detected by human viewers (such as Robyn's spelling "vaccin@ti0n"). Over time, observe the media scholars Tama Leaver, Tim Highfield, and Crystal Abidin, "the development of communities also leads to norms within these groups, ideas of acceptable practice and conduct, which might work against what other users view as appropriate, or even against Instagram's own guidelines."[34] For far-right users, frequent use of coded language is now entrenched as a norm widely practiced on the platform.

These practices of circumvention, argue the media scholars Brooke Erin Duffy and Colten Meisner, are common among social media content creators in order to avoid automated detection of content: "Using platforms' community guidelines as benchmarks, creators engage[] in circumvention to resist algorithmic *detection*, while still acknowledging the necessity of algorithmic visibility in their success on social media." Main avenues for achieving this evasion are to use "linguistic signals that would send coded messages to viewers 'in the know,' while simultaneously avoiding content policing" and to "circumvent platform policing by limiting the presence of text-based content" under the assumption that text is more regularly moderated than visuals.[35]

Today, major tech companies have adopted some automated detection of content using artificial intelligence and machine learning rather than human moderators, which has allowed for more content to be removed more quickly. However, many of these efforts have targeted Islamist content—in fact, the blueprint of many content-moderation tools was based on the intent to detect ISIS accounts.[36] The use of humor, irony, and jokes with obscure references, including coded language, makes it easier for far-right users to evade automated detection.[37] There is a further issue of large-scale content-moderation systems that fail to appropriately detect or that inconsistently flag content and can sometimes generate false positives.[38] For instance, when in one Instagram Story Robyn shared a photo of her new vacuum, an automated banner popped up with a link to information about the COVID-19 vaccine. Robyn wrote in a textbox overlaid on the post, "Dang the algorithm is paranoid it thinks any word that starts with v is a dog whistle for jabs lmaooo."[39] Although it's possible that Instagram's algorithm had mistaken the word *vacuum* for *vaccine* given their linguistic similarity, in reality we don't fully understand how the false positive was generated for this post.

Human content moderators still have an important role to play. They sift through material that has been identified and flagged by other users on the platform in a process known as crowdsourcing. Often, though, these content moderators do what Sarah Roberts identifies as "invisible" labor—working long, exploitative hours, with almost no mental health counseling despite viewing consistently disturbing material.[40] The main problem, though, is the lack of transparency concerning human content moderators employed by platforms to assess material within the decision-making process. The guidelines for assessment are sometimes outright confusing and contradictory. This is especially problematic for far-right material, which is often not illegal per se ("lawful but awful") but is regularly flagged as offensive by users. A compounding issue is that humans are prone to bias in their judgment of both those who produced the material and the material itself.[41]

The biggest question to ask, however, is: If social media platforms operate on a profit model, why would they be motivated to change? This is a serious issue worthy of consideration if we are to rely on tech companies to provide solutions to the spread of misinformation, disinformation, and hate-infused ideologies.

Content moderation consists not only of the tools platforms and institutions use but of what Tarleton Gillespie describes as a "moderation apparatus" composed of "the policies of content moderation, the sociotechnical mechanisms for its enforcement, the business expectations it must serve, the justifications articulated to support it."[42] Other scholars, such as Robert Gorwa, conceptualize these relationships as a "platform governance triangle" that includes the state, corporations, and nongovernmental organizations, all of whom have competing agendas for online regulation.[43]

Government and law enforcement responses are varied. European countries have much stricter policies regarding regulation, whereas the U.S. government partners with tech companies more commonly because most major tech companies fall under U.S. law that limits government intervention, especially with respect to freedom of speech under the First Amendment. Legal regulations take shape either to limit user behavior directly or to limit social media companies. The latter type of law holds tech companies accountable for content published on their platforms.[44]

This issue has been highly controversial in the past couple of years because of Section 230 of the Communications Decency Act of 1996, which provides immunity for intermediaries that provide access to the Internet regarding the content published by users on the site; that is, intermediaries are not "publishers" in the legal sense. In other words, social media companies cannot be held liable for material produced by users. In addition, Section 230 provides a second aspect of immunity: if an intermediary does intervene or regulate users' content, it does not lose its safe-harbor protection. Content that an intermediary does remove will not automatically turn them into a "publisher" or require a standard of policing.[45] Yet twenty-seven years ago, when Section 230 was passed, few could have foreseen the pivotal role that social media platforms would play in shaping public discourse today. Importantly, Section 230 requires tech companies to remove criminal material that infringes on copyright and engages in sex trafficking, so many have called for the inclusion of hate speech and terrorist content in the definition of criminal material.

Late in his term, President Trump passed an executive order calling out social media companies for censorship, stating that if companies want protections under Section 230, they can no longer act like publishers making editorial decisions on content—note the difference from "publisher" in the legal sense.[46] However, experts quickly pointed out that the executive order is illegal, and Section 230 doesn't prevent tech companies from moderating content deemed false or offensive.[47] Regardless, the executive order received much praise from right-wing commentators: "Trump finally has taken a step to kind of address social media censorship, which I think is amazing, and, frankly, it's about dang time," Lauren Chen gushed three days after Trump issued the order.[48] She pointed to two specific areas of the executive order that affect YouTube: First, "algorithms to suppress content or users based on indications of political alignment or viewpoint" (which Lauren described as "the highlight of Trump's presidency, this is protecting democracy") and, second, "acts that limit the ability of users with particular viewpoints to earn money on the platform compared with other users similarly situated" (i.e., demonetization). According to Lauren, social media companies shouldn't be able to make editorial decisions on their platforms. All in all, though, tech companies have done little to respond to a federal directive that isn't legally enforceable.

To be clear, there's no evidence to support the claim that Big Tech disproportionally targets conservative let alone far-right voices. There's just a general *perception* that social media companies are censoring users based on political ideology.[49] Yet far-right women influencers are adamant that their views are under attack. "It's become abundantly clear through YouTube's partnering with the ADL [Anti-Defamation League] to remove conservative content that is not in violation of their terms of service that Google has launched a full-scale attack on the right," stated Rebecca in August 2017. This claim was made despite the fact that the YouTube–ADL partnership focused exclusively on curbing extremists and terrorists' online activity, including anti-Semitic and white-supremacist accounts. Rebecca framed the process as an "attack" on "conservatives," not on the far right: "We know that YouTube is trying to silence conservatives, particularly people who talk about race."[50]

Far-right figures consistently argue that Big Tech companies such as Google-owned YouTube have a left-wing bias and work with leftist civil society organizations to silence supposedly "conservative" voices. Rebecca accused YouTube of "engaging in ridiculous levels of delusion about gender, human nature, race, sexism, and a multitude of other remaining, darling issues of the regressive left." The end goal for YouTube and all Big Tech companies, she stressed, is a left-wing cultural dominance. "They want to selectively choose who can be influential, so it reinforces their vision of a Marxist utopia," she stated matter-of-factly.[51] The far right thus sees Big Tech as a "powerful enemy" intent on allegedly suppressing their presence.

Similarly, Lauren Chen told Robyn Riley in a collab, "On the show, we've talked a lot of about online social media censorship. So we're talking about platforms like Twitter, YouTube, Facebook, even generally Google searches, how they target mainly right-wing or conservative opinions for deplatforming." She continued, "So if you're a conservative Twitter user, you have a way bigger chance of being banned from the platform for something that you've said than if you're a liberal; even if you're not actually breaking terms of service, they're going to be a lot more critical of anything you post. If you're a YouTuber, like we both are, there's a way bigger chance of a video being put into restricted mode or even just being taken down even if it's nothing that's breaking the terms of service and even if it's nothing that's nearly as bad as someone perhaps on the left would be saying."[52] Remember, Lauren includes extremist figures such as Gavin McInnes and Katie Hopkins under the label *conservative*.

Lauren warned that there is a real danger posed by censorship. "The reason why I've spent so much time talking about online social media censorship is because how can the right or conservatives in general expect to spread our views and influence change in society when we can't even talk about our viewpoints on the platforms where most of the people in our society are? It's at a point now where if we don't do something, then our principles won't really mean much when there's absolutely none of us left." She perceives Big Tech as systematically engaging in a witch hunt to purge conservatives.

Yet Duffy and Meisner note in their study of social media content creators that "users' understandings of algorithms and other governance mechanisms are neither even nor consistent. Indeed, users possess markedly different algorithmic literacies, including those linked to demographic variables, economic incentives, existing knowledge structures, and affective orientations." In short, content creators interpret and perceive, which in turn affects their engagement online.[53] Duffy and Meisner's study is also notably focused on historically marginalized identities, such as people of color and LGBTQ+ persons, and they find that platform governance is embedded in social inequality—a sharp contrast to white far-right influencers' position of social privilege. If anything, media reporting shows that companies such as Facebook have actually gone out of their way to allow far-right figures to proliferate on their platforms, even bending the rules to accommodate them.[54] The greatest irony is that far-right influencers have relied on Big Tech platforms to recruit and radicalize supporters and that, despite their complaints, very little has changed regarding their use of that approach. The far right continues to benefit from social media tools such as algorithms to attract and retain followers. However, proposed legislation in the United States, such as the Algorithmic Accountability Act, is seeking to hold companies accountable by introducing mechanisms that facilitate transparency and oversight of algorithms, including impact assessments of bias in automated-decision systems.[55] This promising area of online regulation holds platforms liable for the algorithms used in their operations rather than for content published by users.

Finally, far-right figures frequently use free speech as a defense. From a legal standpoint, though, the claim that they are exercising free speech according to the First Amendment of the U.S. Constitution and that this right is being restricted is false. The First Amendment doesn't guarantee freedom of speech in all areas of public life. Instead, it prevents the U.S. government from making laws that abridge freedom of speech; the First Amendment applies only to the power of the state, not to private entities such as companies. So, in fact, tech companies don't have a legal requirement to allow unlimited free speech on their platforms.

From an ethical standpoint, it can be argued that as the basis of a healthy democracy, anyone should be allowed to voice their opinions on social media. In many ways, the contemporary public sphere has moved from offline to online. However, it is important to bear in mind that social media platforms are designed in such a way that algorithms deliver personalized content to users in order to generate profits from advertising. Each of us has different, curated social media feeds that only reinforce our preexisting preferences. Free speech has become targeted speech to an audience enclosed in an echo chamber of like-minded views, even on mainstream platforms. This is why legislation such as the Algorithmic Accountability Act is a promising step forward to redress these outcomes.

A related clarification is that freedom of speech doesn't guarantee freedom from responsibility for the consequences of that speech. Victims of hate speech and abusive language (whether discrimination on the basis of race, ethnicity, religion, sexuality, or some other characteristic) suffer when we allow perpetrators to write and say whatever they want without restriction. Our focus should instead be on prioritizing human dignity and respect through a human rights framework of inclusivity.

Along with the "hard" or repressive approaches of content moderation, or what I call the Four D's (deplatforming, demonetization, deranking, detection), alternative "soft" approaches—commonly known as "counternarratives" and what I call "counterinfluencers"—can be implemented to counter the far right. It is helpful to think of these approaches as supplementary tools rather than comprehensive solutions. A popular soft approach called *counternarratives* involves government, private-sector, and civil society organizations overseeing programs that promote positive narratives through campaigns in order to counter and challenge extremist propaganda. "The assumption underlying counter-messaging programs is that offering an alternative set of facts or interpretations, debunking myths and exposing lies will alter people's attitudes and, eventually, impact behaviors," writes the media scholar Kate Coyer.[56] Much counternarrative activity takes place online, often through a combination of tech software and human intervention.

Within this counternarrative "industry," one of the biggest players is the Google unit Jigsaw, a so-called technology incubator that takes action ranging from "countering violent extremism to thwarting online censorship to mitigating the threats associated with digital attacks."[57] Jigsaw partners with the start-up company Moonshot (previously Moonshot CVE, or Countering Violent Extremism), headquartered in London and Washington, D.C.. I asked Vidhya Ramalingam, cofounder of Moonshot, about the work it does. "Moonshot is a social enterprise specializing in countering violent extremism," she told me. "We design new methodologies and technologies to enhance the capacity of our partners to respond effectively to violent extremism as well as broader online harms, both online and offline."

How does Moonshot operate? "Our team of analysts, developers, and project managers use fresh thinking and decades of experience from different sectors to respond to some of the world's toughest problems with effective, scalable solutions," Ramalingam responded. "Our work ranges from software development and digital capacity building to leading global counter-messaging campaigns."[58]

To learn more, I spoke with Clark Hogan-Taylor, who is now director of Tech Partnerships at Moonshot, who told me about their day-to-day operations. "There's now more far-right work; probably 40 to 50 percent of what we do is countering the far right," he said.[59] Whereas Moonshot's previous projects focused mostly on countering Islamist content, that focus now makes up only about 30 percent of the company's work, while the remainder aims at a miscellaneous mix of problems, including incel violence. Much of that shift is attributed in part to a greater far-right presence online and in part to how authorities are now recognizing far-right activity as a serious threat.

Moonshot has pioneered the "Redirect Method" in its counternarrative campaigns. According to Hogan-Taylor, the Redirect Method consists of a continuously updated database of keywords with indicators of extremist ideology, sometimes country specific but often global in scope. Content is then produced and distributed using Google's advertising technology to target users exposed to extremist content online, which either debunks the extremist content or "redirects" users to another webpage. As Hogan-Taylor described the process, "You can create an ecosystem on Google ads" using far-right vocabulary familiar to a user but without trying to further entrench their views. Over time, he said, Moonshot has experimented the most with figuring out the best demographic to target in their campaigns. He described the Redirect Method as "incredibly flexible," more like "a principle" to redirect a user rather than a static model that depends solely on advertisements, for instance.

Although the Redirect Method sounds like a promising approach, there is little research or evidence on the effectiveness of counternarrative campaigns in deradicalization, even though they have received much attention and praise (and funding). In fact, studies criticize that counternarrative campaigns may not be as effective as promised. "This is partly due to issues in the evaluation of counter-narrative approaches, which lack data about audiences beyond metrics (often provided by the online platforms from which they are disseminated), as well as [in] the targeting of specific communities; some identify groups that are 'at risk,' while others are targeted more generally," writes Bharath Ganesh.[60] Quantitative metrics such as impressions and views or tests on audiences that are not the target demographic sometimes have counterproductive effects and raise serious concerns about a counternarrative approach. In short, counternarratives are "not easy to measure or quantify" for effectiveness.[61] Further research shows that especially on YouTube the use of counternarratives with the algorithm can backfire by contributing to polarization.[62]

To get a balanced view, I asked Hogan-Taylor how Moonshot measures impact. "You can do it in a few different ways. You can go big and relative, or you can go small and precise," he explained. "The more campaigns we run, the more we get an idea of what's a good click-through rate." For example, "How long do people watch countercontent on average?" According to Hogan-Taylor, if a user watches more than a minute of a countercontent video, that's very good. Most users will watch a video for only seventeen seconds or so. This test is one way of measuring a broad and relative indicator based on experience. "That's not impact, but it's toward impact," he clarified. It is an especially good way of assessing the success of campaigns if you're comparing them, he assured me.

Or, he said, "you can go smaller and more precise because you can collect the volume of Facebook posts or Tweets made by a cohort of people. You can code them for the amount of racism and hate speech, incitements to violence." The next step, he explained, is "you can treat them, and you can then measure the equivalent, say, one month after, two months after. And you can code those tweets, and you can do statistical significance—'Did we have an effect?' " In analyzing these findings, Moonshot can see what worked and what didn't and then try to apply the successful techniques in a campaign.

Another approach that Moonshot has increasingly moved toward, Hogan-Taylor mentioned, is, "rather than sending people to other platforms," you redirect them to a website with content that you have created. This is useful because you have control over the website's data, such as interactions on the site and the detection of users revisiting the site.

Counternarratives should be considered as a supplementary and multipronged approach in challenging the far right. The Redirect Method is not a perfect tool, but it is better than not taking advantage of social media infrastructure to target at-risk users. On a reassuring note, Moonshot works with grassroots organizations, Hogan-Taylor told me. It designs campaigns with stakeholders who have in-depth knowledge of local context. Online communities might be global, but people understand and connect issues to their local experiences.

Another trending concept to emerge recently within the broader field of counternarratives is "attitudinal inoculation," which is used to build resilience against extremist propaganda when individuals are incrementally exposed to it. Although the number of studies is small, there is some slight promise of favorable results. Individuals exposed to inoculation messaging were found to be more resistant to the persuasion of extremist propaganda.[63] However, we should be cautiously optimistic when assessing the effectiveness of attitudinal inoculation given marginal evidence of its robustness.

Finally, some may argue that the best soft approach toward preventing and countering radicalization lies in strengthening digital and media literacy, so that individuals can spot the signs of disinformation and extremism. But this can be a misguided approach. It assumes that young people lack digital literacy when in fact they are the most digitally literate of all age groups. Research shows that older people are actually the most prone to sharing disinformation on social media.[64] Growing up in a world where the internet is ubiquitous, young people today are better able than older users to identify advertising and targeted content. However, this does not mean that they are immune to extremist narratives and disinformation, and they can still be psychologically susceptible to ads and targeted content.

The problem with the call for digital literacy, as Huw Davies, a scholar in digital education, observes, is that it completely neglects the pivotal role played by the manipulation of the technology infrastructure, as in photoshopped images, deep fakes, mis/disinformation, pseudoscience and junk news, bots, ads with undisclosed funders, algorithms, and so on. "No digital literacy programme is ever likely to work unless it produces reflexive critical thinkers, motivated to challenge their own thinking," writes Davies.[65] But digital literacy is fundamentally at odds with the technology infrastructure of online platforms. As the media scholar danah boyd notes, a digital-literacy approach places the burden of responsibility on the individual rather than on the tech company or platform or even society at large to self-investigate and make wise decisions in an information landscape that is vast, fragmented, driven by manipulation, and very confusing when users are looking for answers to questions. Encouraging young people to develop media-making skills, seen as a solution to counter disinformation, is moreover not the same as investing in critical thinking, boyd points out.[66] Further, far-right actors and communities themselves practice media-literacy practices as a new strategy for recruitment and propaganda,[67] as in how influencers' parse academic articles as "evidence" for their claims and reject sources they consider to be noncredible (see chapter 3).

Counternarratives, attitudinal inoculation, and the building of digital- and media-literacy skills are thus not without their flaws. Although these types of soft interventions can facilitate improvement, it is crucial to also consider their drawbacks. A major oversight of these approaches is they don't address a key feature of online interaction—culture. But strategically employing counter-influencers offers potential to focus on aspects of digital culture that are key in engagement.

Hard approaches are rightfully criticized for neglecting the powerful bonds among members of the far right, which has cemented a collective identity and desire for belonging. An examination of far-right women influencers' Instagram feeds shows mainly apolitical content on their profiles, usually as selfies and food blogging (although the captions they add can be political sometimes). Perhaps this is a tactic to avoid getting banned on the platform, but it's most likely a way for them to be seen as authentic and relatable to fans and new viewers—a strategy of retention.

An often overlooked but fundamental component of this scenario is influencer culture. In some cases, mainstream platforms have rewarded these far-right women influencers. When scrolling through Lauren Southern's Instagram account, I came across a post of her in May 2018 holding a YouTube award plaque for surpassing 100,000 subscribers on her channel.[68] (Today, she has seven times that amount.) YouTube gives Creator Awards to recognize popular channels based on subscriber count, with tiers at 100,000 subscribers (Silver Creator Award), one million subscribers (Gold Creator Award), and, finally, 10 million subscribers (Diamond Creator Award). According to the eligibility rules, these awards are given at "You-Tube's discretion" (although it's likely an automated system) to channels "subject to review before awards are issued."[69] Part of the evaluation includes the platform's community guidelines regarding hateful content that "promotes or condones violence against individuals or groups based on race or ethnic origin, religion, disability, gender, age, nationality, veteran status, caste, sexual orientation, or gender identity, or content that incites hatred on the basis of these core characteristics."[70]

Yet when Lauren described "enclaves" of migrants in France or the supposed "sickness within Islam,"[71] wasn't she violating the platform's hate speech policy? She received the YouTube award even though she had made an earlier video about having been banned from Patreon because she took "part in" what the company calls "activities that are likely to cause loss of life"—a clear red flag that YouTube should have seen.[72] Far-right influencers' ability to garner a high number of subscribers for their content and be awarded for it by the platform despite the content they produce should be of concern. Lauren may even be given the next-tier award in the future.

It is even more revealing when YouTube was used as a platform to jump-start these influencers' political activism. "It's nice to have a reminder of where this all started. I truly appreciate each and every one of you who have grown with me and followed my chaotic adventures," Lauren wrote in the Instagram post on receiving her award in 2018. "Here's to us." YouTube isn't simply a website where Lauren posts vlogs about political topics. It's a space where like-minded users and viewers can form a community as they engage in a shared commitment to nationalism, traditionalism, misogyny, homophobia, Islamophobia, and racism.

Among methods to counter the far right, the potential of *counterinfluencers* may have promise. The YouTuber known as ContraPoints (real name Natalie Wynn) is a good example. In vlogs that have garnered millions of views, ContraPoints breaks down issues such as incels, gender, and the strategies that the far right uses to appear legitimate.[73] In a vlog titled "Decrypting the Alt-Right: How to Recognize a F@scist," for example, ContraPoints explained in September 2017 in response to the Unite the Right rally footage at Charlottesville earlier that year what fascists believe (i.e., their ideology); the dog whistles they commonly use (i.e., "Western culture," "white genocide" and the Great Replacement, and "white ethnostate"); the motivations and rhetoric that the contemporary far right uses to appeal to young people today; and how viewers can recognize far-right propaganda that is "subtle" and "indirect" rather than overt neo-Nazi slogans and logos.[74] Through simultaneously entertaining and educational content, ContraPoints debunks far-right myths and provides useful information on how to spot propaganda—using important elements of humor, satire, and parody to undermine the far right's credibility.[75] The name "BreadTube" is used to describe a loose coalition of progressive YouTubers such as ContraPoints whose content debunks far-right talking points. BreadTube creators will often engage in algorithmic hijacking or focus on the same topics discussed by far-right influencers in order to shift algorithm recommendations to viewers away from far-right channels.

Similarly, Instagram influencers such as Eiselle Ty provide colorful and eye-catching infographics that give educational background on terms such as *white privilege*, *cultural appropriation*, *cancel culture*, and *systemic racism* in easily digestible formats to scroll and swipe through. For instance, a post defining *white privilege* states it as "an institutional (rather than personal) set of benefits granted to those of us who, by race, resemble the people who dominate the powerful positions in our institutions." Slides in the post explain why recognizing white privilege may be difficult for those born with access to power and resources and how their access is viewed as "normal."[76] The explanation of white privilege in direct, clear, non-judgmental, but informative language provides legitimacy and accessibility for the post to reach many viewers.

On TikTok, other popular influencers include Abbie Richards, who debunks disinformation and conspiracy theories, and FrauLöwen-herz, who decodes far-right symbols and creates catchy content on topics related to gender, sexuality, and race and on political ideologies such as nativism.[77] FrauLöwenherz, who is a German graduate student of American studies and a freelance journalist, has produced a series of sixty-second TikTok videos called *Decoding the Right*, which looks at Nazi codes and symbols, dog whistles, numerical codes, the origin of the name "Kekistan," and far-right fashion. She also uses her platform to create content connected to her identity as a queer woman, debunking narratives of sexism and misogyny and explaining concepts such as "intersectional feminism," pro-life and anti-abortion viewpoints, and transgender rights. FrauLöwenherz even sells merchandise that is pro-feminist and pro-LGBTQ+ and offers speaking engagements for workshops.

Tech companies, governments, and nonprofit organizations—such as the nonprofit Life After Hate (which helps people leave hate groups)—should consider partnering with YouTube, Insta-gram, and TikTok counterinfluencers. Such counterinfluencers are usually the most up to date on current topics and can effectively frame their language for young audiences. They are also especially adept at knowing how to circumvent the automated flagging of content—which the far right does—by hijacking hashtags and conversations for search engine optimization and delivering content that is inclusively oriented. Counterinfluencers understand platform affordances and create content that is relatable and accessible. In fact, the Biden administration has turned to TikTok influencers to help communicate and amplify legislation and issues, recognizing the greater potential they have to reach younger audiences.[78]

But arrangements between influencers and programs countering extremism should proceed with caution, given the blowback that
government-sponsored programs have received when using influencers (mostly to counter Islamist extremism) in a manner that can
come off as disingenuous and top down.[79] The academic Benjamin
Lee, based at the Centre for Research and Evidence on Security
Threats in the United Kingdom, writes that "chief among the concerns has been the ability of counter messaging providers to deliver
convincing and authoritative counter messages," concerns that
point to a general distrust in the system. In studying what he terms
"informal counter messaging actors" (e.g., counterinfluencers)
who lack the support of large institutions such as government or
government-backed organizations, Lee found that they can be seen
as more credible than formally recruited countermessengers. Interestingly, he discovered that many informal countermessengers
have already been approached by larger organizations with mixed
results; although some enjoy collaborating with organizations due
to greater access to resources, there's "a strong desire to retain some
measure of control over content" in order to avoid risking their
credibility by association. Thus, he recommends, influencers should
be given autonomy and the space to develop individual creativity.
There's a further question of effectiveness when countermessaging
specifically targets those who are at risk of radicalization versus
those who are already radicalized. In most cases, he argues, countermessaging by informal actors seems to have the greatest effect
when aimed toward a broad general audience.[80]

I asked Lee how formal organizations can work informally with
countermessaging actors in such a way to maintain their credibility.
He told me, "Teaming up with a better-resourced formal organisa-
tion can help expand the reach of these messages." But, he warned,
"both parties need to be careful that any relationship won't com-
promise either[] [one's] integrity in the eyes of audiences. Negotiating these relationships means being clear and open about goals and
methods as well as accepting that in some cases a relationship may
actually damage the interests of both."[81]

Despite potential risk, Lee still sees the value of informal coun-termessaging actors as long as these conditions are met. "In my opinion, informal actors are likely to hold greater stores of symbolic capital and other resources that can help them reach various extremist audiences, and their messages resonate when they do," he continued. "This might be an approach, shared experience, common language, image, or style that audiences are likely to understand and respond to." In short, counterinfluencers might be an effective means of challenging the far right if they are supported in the right way. But given the potential pitfalls, such as skeptical audiences who may view them as "propagandists," they should be used in combi-nation with other approaches.

Of course, counterinfluencers aren't the only ones who can engage in informal countermessaging; "in many cases, the most effective counter-messages are likely to come from individuals' social environments, including friends and family," writes Kate Coyer.[82] In the radicalization stories of far-right women influencers discussed in chapter 2, it is striking that many of them discuss the impact of how past friends and family members were resistant to their being red-pilled. They described it as an alienating experience, so we cannot underestimate the power of immediate social bonds to affect someone's ideological questioning and direction.

A combination of hard and soft online approaches in countering the far right uses most but not all of the tools in the toolbox. Tack-ling offline dynamics is also key. Before moving on to the discussion of offline approaches, however, I want to stress a final point regard-ing the effectiveness of hard and soft online techniques. As we have seen, far-right women influencers have by and large managed to survive on mainstream social media platforms, despite some tech company efforts toward content moderation as well as the applica-tion of limited counternarrative and counterinfluencer strategies to challenge the influencers' reach. Does this mean that countering these far-right women influencers online requires different tech-niques? Not necessarily. In fact, the solution is straightforward: recognize the type of content produced by far-right women as propaganda and systematically apply preexisting policies on hate speech and disinformation to that content. If a content-oriented approach fails, a second option is an actor-network-oriented approach—that is, target their involvement or engagement with known far-right or criminal organizations. This two-pronged solution is effective. The greatest obstacle that tech companies and associated countermessaging industries face is not the lack of tools but a failure to recognize these far-right women as dangerous and thereby not applying community guideline standards to the content these women produce.

Finally, there are many online resources for countering far-right propaganda, such as the Center for Countering Digital Hate; the Coalition for a Safer Web; Change the Terms; the Global Internet Forum to Counter Terrorism; the Global Project Against Hate and Extremism; the Santa Clara Principles on Transparency and Accountability in Content Moderation; Sleeping Giants; and Stop Hate for Profit.

Beyond online methods, or "in the real world," some fundamental but difficult issues in society must be addressed to effectively counter the far right.

"I think the most important thing is for states and scholars to recognise and explore in-depth the reasons why men and women become involved in movements like the alt-right or groups on the far right," stated Elizabeth Pearson, a lecturer in the Conflict, Violence and Terrorism Research Centre at Royal Holloway, University of London, who specializes in gender and extremism. One such issue to explore is how men and women might differ or be the same in different far-right groups, she elaborated.[83]

I asked Pearson what she thinks this means for designing a government counterextremism strategy focused on the roles of women in far-right movements. "We need to better understand that women promote and support alt-right ideas that can appear regressive, but are empowering to them, and important within far right movements—[such as] that women should not work, that motherhood matters. Maternalism *is* empowering to some women," she tells me. This means not discrediting the potential for some far-right women to feel worthy and valued, despite their lower status relative to men in far-right movements. Another consideration for governments, Pearson said, is that they "shouldn't homogenize the far-right, and they will need different and tailored responses for different groups." This means recognizing that women are viewed as having different roles within different types of far-right organizations.

Take the fact that women who are drawn to the far right come from a range of socioeconomic backgrounds, although most influencers described in this book are middle class. In this case, there isn't an easy prescription to address social deprivation or economic grievances. Many also live or have lived in predominately urban areas characterized by racial and cultural diversity, so a lack of exposure to difference isn't necessarily the issue. Instead, the one element that unites far-right women (and tradwives) is antifeminism. As demonstrated in these influencers' life stories, several had initially identified with feminism at a young age but over time came to adopt a more traditional, conservative perspective on gender. It was during their transition that most of them experienced social backlash from family and friends and subsequent alienation for their views.

Certainly, criticisms can be directed toward feminism today. After all, progressive movements must engage in internal critique to reform toward a more inclusive agenda. One can consider a woman's choice to be a homemaker just as valid as the choice of any another lifestyle. The problem, however, is that this argument by the far right and tradwives is "propped up by the twin pillars of disillusionment and antipathy," writes the journalist Seyward Darby.[84] For these far-right women, the issue isn't solely about individual choice—rather, they are propping up a movement. They look to the past to map their future. They believe that everything was simply better "in the good old days," ignoring the vast social and racial inequalities that drove progressive political activism throughout the twentieth century.

When these women revert to traditional gender norms as a reactionary movement against feminism, they reflect a generational amnesia. The term *generational amnesia* is often used in discussions concerning climate change; it refers to the idea that "knowledge extinction occurs because younger generations are not aware of past biological conditions."[85] For example, consider a species of fish that becomes extinct over a period of one hundred years. The first generation notices the baseline level of abundance of the fish, and then when they retire, they notice that the level is lower. The next generation, though, considers the new low level of fish to be normal, unaware of the baseline level used by the previous generation. The cycle continues with each successive generation starting at a lower baseline until eventually the species of fish is extinct. However, no single generation witnesses all the levels of change from abundance to extinction. By the last generation, the extinction is no longer seen as a major loss. In other words, generational amnesia is "the tendency of each generation to disregard what has come before and benchmark its own experience of nature as normal."[86]

The concept of generational amnesia can also be applied to social phenomena such as feminism. Gen Z and millennial far-right women have forgotten or likely take for granted the achievements of the feminist movement in past generations. From the women's suffrage movement in the early twentieth century to women entering the workforce in droves during World War II to the historic *Roe v. Wade* U.S. Supreme Court case on abortion (before its overturning in 2022), the modern woman has opportunities that were made possible by the previous generations' efforts. But the baseline has adjusted with each new generation, so that the right to vote or be employed in the labor market is seen as normal.

Far-right women take advantage of this generational amnesia regarding feminism. "What can Western women do to start providing value to men again?" asked Rebecca Hargraves in early 2018. Her advice was to avoid going to college, which will ostensibly repair gender relations and start to build a more functional society. Arguing that a majority of women don't have the intellectual capacity or skill set for public life but are instead happier being mothers not confined to their careers, she called upon women to "learn to cook," "control emotional outbursts," "learn to listen," and "read" instead of "allowing a bunch of Marxists to shape the way young women think."[87] Her comments ironically make it clear that now more than ever education plays an especially pivotal function in acknowledging the gains of feminism and particularly in redressing generational amnesia.

Another irony is these far-right women influencers would not be in their positions of influence today were it not for the achievements of past feminists and for the education they themselves received. Nearly all of the influencers attended university, and one even obtained a master's degree. The cultural capital they received from education gives them leverage as articulate, intellectual thought leaders in the far right. These influencers also receive crowd-sourced donations from viewers and revenue from advertisers, which wouldn't be possible if earlier generations of women hadn't demanded the right to wages, access to personal bank accounts, and opportunities to invest. Despite urging their viewers to follow a traditional lifestyle in which the husband is the family's breadwinner, these influencers also remind them time and again that monetization is an important source of income for them and their families. Paradoxically, on the feminist-driven International Women's Day, these influencers shared photos on Instagram commemorating the holiday.

Far-right women revere a nostalgia that life was better "back in the day," but this nostalgic picture is far from the reality of life in the past. As the acclaimed feminist Betty Friedan wrote in *The Feminine Mystique* in 1963, the mythical image of a happy housewife in the 1950s and 1960s resulted from (male-dominated) advertisers and corporations that sold magazines and household products.[88] One need only look at the infamous Chase & Sanborn coffee advertisement targeting housewives, which illustrates a man spanking his wife for not buying fresh coffee grounds, or at an advertisement published in the *Canadian Medical Association Journal* for Mornidine—a drug for morning sickness during pregnancy—urging housewives to take it so that they can once again cook breakfast for their husbands without feeling nauseous.[89] In real life, Friedan found widespread unhappiness among housewives, who felt limited in other pursuits and in the expectation of "career" fulfilment as a housewife-mother.

Although seemingly obvious, how our political leaders talk about gender matters, too. As Elizabeth Pearson pointed out to me, "Women and men are responding not just to the rhetoric of groups but [to] the rhetoric of states." Politicians as role models and government policies about gender have an impact on how the far right mobilizes, and state leaders should be aware of this indirect effect.

Finally, the elephants in the room need to be addressed: hate and bigotry. They stem in part from ignorance but also in part from the amplification of misguided anxieties that people have about their status in society. It is easy to create scapegoats when you feel as if the privileged position you once had or hold now (as an in-group) is being threatened, whether this is simply a perception of loss or not. People drawn to the far right are looking to reclaim what they see as their lost power, to have a voice. But being given a platform shouldn't come at the expense of dehumanizing others. Instead, we should be shifting our focus to who is *actually* benefiting in society and who is not. Countering the far right needs to take this into account by offering a realistic narrative to young people that addresses the necessary support provided by social structures: educational awareness, employment and social mobility opportunities, income equality, and potential for home ownership, just to name a few. All these factors shape happiness and quality of life.

At the end of the day, these far-right women influencers serve as propagandists. Underneath their personal stories of disavowing feminism and feeling the pain of losing friends and family after being red-pilled, they are promoting the ideological agenda of an exclusionary movement. Far-right actors and organizations have long used emotional appeals to build a sense of belonging and community. Although we must acknowledge that far-right ideology and, to a smaller extent, a trad lifestyle will always appeal to a fragment of the population, it is our social responsibility to ensure that this fragment stays small and that these ideas do not grow and spread. This means recognizing the warning signs of personal grievances becoming weaponized into political movements.

CONCLUSION
"I've Taken the Real-Life Pill"

Although Lauren Southern announced her "retirement" from public life in 2019, she resurfaced on Instagram after less than a year. She revealed that she had gotten married, rediscovered her faith, and given birth to a baby boy. She wrote that life is full of challenges, and despite the highs of traveling and reporting on issues around the world, nothing was more rewarding than the family that surrounded her every day.[1] Six months later, she announced in a video titled "Why I Left, and Why I'm Back" on her YouTube channel that she had returned to political activism.[2]

"It's been just over one year since I stepped away from social media," Lauren stated in the vlog while showing a screenshot of her blog post "A New Chapter." She revealed how during that time she got married and had a baby—information her followers on Instagram already knew. She later shared on Instagram that she had settled down in Australia because her husband and son are Australian.[3]

In the "Why I Left" video, Lauren stated that she had taken the time to do what she described as recentering herself, rediscovering her faith, and finding meaning. Her monologue quickly turned to a reflection. "Family was not the only reason I took a step back, although it's the main one," she admitted. "The world I was a part of, especially earlier on in my YouTube career, was a very unhealthy one." Did Lauren finally recognize the harms she perpetrated as a far-right influencer? "This whole mess, this whole disaster that I was a part of, is something that I began realizing in people around me, and I started to see within myself as well. I was actively assisting in creating this culture of entertainment and hot-take politics."

If this was the case, why was Lauren coming back to public life? Her explanation: for "nuance or genuine, thoughtful content" that gives two sides of every story. In 2018, Lauren had started making documentaries aiming to explore in-depth issues that she cared about. Now she returned to public life to continue making documentaries with what she considered an open mind. "I also don't see the possibility for growth when I'm restricted by the expectations of an online right-wing tribe that I hold certain beliefs or that I'm not a part of them anymore," Lauren continued, "because I also have questions and criticisms within the right as well. There are some issues there. I want to just genuinely look at the world, even if it bursts my bubble of what my preconceived notions may have been." Was this Lauren's redemption story? It was hard not to be suspicious of her intentions given that her previous documentaries and vlogs contained an explicit political agenda and explicitly bigoted comments.

"If anything, I'd say I've taken the real-life pill. I think people are multidimensional, complex beings, and they are worthy of trying to understand," said Lauren.

How did other far-right influencers respond to Lauren's return? "I've nothing against Lauren personally. I have enjoyed her content in the past," said Robyn Riley the day after Lauren made her announcement. But this earlier enjoyment didn't make Lauren immune from Robyn's criticism. "The *Borderless* documentary I was really disappointed with because I felt like there was way too much attention placed on 'humanizing' the migrants and playing up the victim narrative of the migrants when the story of what's happening in Europe is about Europeans," Robyn explained. "There is a replacement of that population [of Europeans] occurring. There have been rapes, there have been murders that have gone without justice." In short, Robyn felt that Lauren should have used her platform to promote far-right ideology more effectively. "We wanted someone with notoriety, with a large reach, to tell that story for the silent victims—who are Europeans in this situation."[4]

Many viewed Lauren's (brief) transition out of the far-right scene following *Borderless* as a betrayal given that she promoted the film as a balanced and nuanced professional documentary (even though that's far from the case), which made her seem inauthentic to a far-right audience who preferred her partisan commentary and hot takes in vlogs. Robyn thus remained skeptical of Lauren's agenda outlined in the comeback video. "If it's an authentic video, if she's not being paid by someone to make this content—which I think is a possibility—I think she really does want to tell both sides of the story. I think she wants to be objective." But Robyn wasn't satisfied with this direction. "If Lauren thinks she can be objective, she's naive in thinking that. *Idealistic*, maybe, is a more charitable word."

Other far-right figures, such as the Groyper founder Nick Fuentes, were even more cynical. "I don't buy it. I think you like to be an e-celebrity, which is fine, so do I," he told Lauren during a livestream. "I think you like to be on the camera. I think you like the life. But you come back and say, 'I want to tell stories with nuance.' Also, nuance is bullshit—we're in a war. And this like 'We need to hear both sides, everyone needs to tell both sides.' No, we don't."[5]

Despite her proclaimed commitment to objectivity, Lauren was soon appearing on right-wing media outlets such as the television broadcaster Sky News and writing for the *Spectator* magazine in Australia, providing political commentary with the same old talking points.[6] She also cohosted a new podcast series with fellow Australian far-right YouTuber Randall Evans (which is available to stream on mainstream platforms such as Apple Podcasts and Spotify).[7]

She also started regularly posting reactionary vlogs on her YouTube channel again. Although most of them had the same type of vlog format, on July 11, 2022, Lauren, now twenty-seven years old, also uploaded what is perhaps the most distinctive video on her channel to date: a nearly three-hour-long video titled "The WHOLE Truth," in which she broke down her entire political career since 2015. "I'm so nervous because I never talk about this stuff on camera," she laughed. "This video is probably going to severely hurt my career. Severely. There'll probably be a bunch of people who cut me off, maybe people that pursue me legally. It's not going to be good. But I have sat for so long wanting to make this video, and it bothers me all the time, every day, when I don't. So I just have to."[8] Framed as an act of moral courage, her video is an exposé of the drama that unfolded behind the scenes of the alt-right while it was at its peak.

Lauren described her first political career break and exposure to high-level conservative politics: "So many eyes on me, so many opportunities I thought I would never get in my life, and I was desperate to make it work. If I got this opportunity and made it work, that would change my life forever." She justified her early political activism as genuine: "I believed this was a civilizational battle for the heart of the West, for goodness, for righteousness, for conservatism, family, Christianity. That was all something that I truly, truly believed in the core of my heart and soul."

Explaining the successful rise of the alt-right, Lauren reflected that "no one was talking about this stuff at the time," at least online. Before the alt-right, "there wasn't this massive sphere of political creators and streamers and all these little media companies that had become online entities [on YouTube]. And they weren't talking about these controversial, hot-button issues like feminism going wild in universities at the time." As I discussed early on in this book, the political resonance of the alt-right is also a story about social media and its consumption within everyday life. Far-right figures saw and grabbed an opportunity to merge their political ideology with personal branding in the online attention economy.

Lauren further divulged the drama and conflict within the far-right political scene, including blackmail, threats, betrayal, and rumors. "We have a lot of cultlike dynamics of our own, where people can get excommunicated, where we don't really look into things that deeply if the saints of our movement say it," she critiqued. According to her description, the far-right milieu is engrossed in the spectacle of celebrity and fandom. She was now largely pessimistic about the world in which she rose to fame: "The fact [is] that so much of this 2016 alternative-right, dissident-right movement was so coded in selfishness, narcissism, cult of personality, and none of it was about helping people. It was about how well latching onto this person's struggle [will] potentially boost my career."

For viewers who didn't know what people she was referring to, she stated explicitly, "I'm talking about the people at the top." The leading figures Lauren criticized in the video are Ezra Levant, Milo Yiannopoulos, Tommy Robinson, Faith Goldy, and Paul Joseph Watson. She exposed these individuals' atrocious behavior either toward her personally or toward others who were victimized. "A lot of money, influence, power, and faith people are putting in people is getting squandered away. Squandered away due to ego. . . . It's really important to highlight just how messed up the culture was in this political movement," Lauren explained.

Although the vlog is focused mostly on the drama that unfolded within the alt-right, Lauren also reflected on her personal experience of becoming a celebrity in the movement, detailing her big breaks and increasing exposure in the scene, including travels and tours. But she became increasingly fed up with the drama of the alt-right. "I'm sick, I'm tired of politics. I cannot stand all the backstabbing. I cannot stand the behavior, the selfishness, all of it," she clarified. Her frustration with far-right activist culture led to getting married and wanting to start a family in Australia. However, there was another obstacle that few people knew about and that she was revealing to her viewers for the first time.

"Because of everything I'd done in politics, because of all the activism I'd done—South Africa, *Borderless*, all of it—I'd been put on a list called VACCU [the Visa Applicant Character Consideration Unit list]," she revealed. "It is typically a list [of] criminals and terrorists that can't travel to other countries because they've got a record that won't allow them to enter other countries. And I'd been put on that list due to political activism. And it meant that I couldn't get a visa to go to Australia." She asserted that to be able to see her child and family, she was advised to quit politics altogether. Rather than make a slow transition, Lauren took a hasty exit by publishing the fare-well letter on her website in 2019, stopping all social media, and shutting down her subscription site instantly. "Otherwise, my visa was going to be rejected, and I was never going to be able to enter the country," she explained. After her public departure, she was granted a visa but on the stipulation that future, similar political engagement violating character-assessment standards could result in visa refusal or cancellation. "I wanted quitting to be on my own terms," Lauren said sadly and continued in tears, "I definitely feel like the end of my political career was stolen from me.... I didn't think that when it came to career, when it came to how this would affect my family, my friends, I didn't think it would be so extreme or ever get to this point."

But in 2020, her situation had changed. "Fast forward to 2020. I'm a mom now; life's changed a lot. I'm in Australia, and I finally got news that I was on a more substantial visa, one that was not going to be compromised by this VACCU stuff. I got to this point where I was like, 'I can talk to you guys again. I can do what I love. I can speak about the world and the issues that I cared about.' ... I wanted to come back. I made that video, 'Why I Left, and Why I'm Back,' where I wasn't entirely honest. Told you the truth but left out most of it, my fault."

The new Lauren in 2022 positioned herself throughout the video as someone with a moral conscience who cares about the people sur-rounding her and about rising above pettiness. "I believed every-one was as passionate and genuine as I was about wanting to change things, about wanting to save the West." Despite her ideals, she apol-ogized for her complacency in promoting a toxic culture. "My 'loyalty' to this movement, not wanting to expose these people that so many people look up to, not wanting to talk about the truth of conservatism because we've got the [political] left to go after, we've got all this insane progressivism to go after, we can't be in-fighting. What happened is that by ignoring the problems in my own side to try to protect it, I just allowed a lot of toxicity to cor-rode it from the inside." But Lauren also detached herself from responsibility within the movement: "It collapsed anyways and deservingly so. I can't sit here and pretend like the larger half of what happened to the dissident right wasn't entirely their own fault . . . the selfishness, the ego, the cult of personality. Believing people just because they were big and famous and leaders of the movement . . . that was the downfall of the dissident right."

In contrast, Lauren repeatedly appealed to her viewers and the "left behind" as the ones who were victimized, positioning herself as authentic and accountable to her audience by "being the voice for people." She admitted, "I'll be honest with you all. Half of this is for selfish reasons. I just want to tell my side of the story. I just finally want people to hear my side 'cause I've stayed silent for so long. And then the other half is genuinely for you. You deserve to hear all of this. You deserve to hear the truth of what was going on behind the scenes." She remained optimistic. "All I can do is hope that maybe out of its ashes, we can create something more genuine. You guys," she stated, pointing directly to the camera, "the actual people who this is about, can make something more genuine."

In closing, Lauren offered somber thoughts. "These people and these figures you watch, they aren't perfect people. I'm not a per-fect person. And you never want to disappoint your audience," she said in tears. "You never want them to look at you and think, 'I believed in you, I believed you were, like, this hero.' . . . But I think that was the mistake from the start . . . trying to be heroes instead of just being people that are confused and broken in this world as well and trying to make sense of it all and just being hon-est." As a microcelebrity, Lauren herself was highly effective at being an influencer. Her engagement with her audience, more so than that of other leading far-right figures, made her image more relatable. She was a prime example of networked intimacy. Her final remarks reiterated her commitment to her fans: "I love you all, I care for you, I've cared for you the whole time. I've never been a fraud or lying. I've never wanted to hurt any of you. I really, really believed in this all. And I'm sorry that I probably hurt a lot of you by keeping this all to myself. But it felt good to say it, felt good to say it all."

The story of Lauren Southern's fluctuating celebrity represents an interesting phenomenon of the far right. "It can be a profitable decision to go far to the right, where the audience is very accepting and gets excited about new personalities that come on the scene, especially young women," observes the journalist Jared Holt. "But because this audience is so toxic and hateful, going to that audience is sort of like your last stop on a media career."[9] The last part of Holt's statement may not necessarily be accurate, though, given how mainstream the far right has recently become, but his assessment does provide good insight into the culture of fandom surrounding far-right figures. Although becoming a microcelebrity is exciting, establishing a niche audience means keeping up with an appetite in producing content that is entertaining yet retains the same ideological message. At a certain point, influencers may shift the focus of their content, or new influencers will enter the scene, ready to take the helm. Within such a small field, competition for the spotlight is labor intensive and always "on demand."

There's an ethical conundrum with a book of this nature: Does writing about these women, their world, play into their strategy of mainstream exposure? Can revealing their efforts lead to more potential supporters seeking out their content when they perhaps wouldn't have otherwise? Indeed, the far right frequently toes the line that any media coverage, even if negative, is good for their cause because it enhances their visibility.

"I think it's good when they label people like me big bad monster because normal people are like, 'Who are you talking about?'" stated Lana Lokteff about media coverage in 2018. "I got a lot of messages from people after the press last year kept trying to call me the queen bee of white supremacy. I got a lot of emails from people that were like, 'I read those articles, I checked out your stuff, you actually make a lot of sense.' I was like, 'Hopefully, more people come.'"[10]

It's certainly a risk writing about far-right recruitment and communication, but one worth taking when grounded in context. By exposing how easy it is to enter the world of these women, scholars and journalists who write about them raise a red flag. This flag marks the joint responsibility of tech companies, government agencies, and civil society at large. A much-needed conversation about the multilayered and gendered response to countering the far right is still lacking when it comes to recognizing differing avenues for radicalization.

Risk isn't confined to giving these influencers a platform for exposure; it can also entail dangers to researchers' personal safety. When the PhD student Annie Kelly published an op-ed in the *New York Times* with a headline calling tradwives "the housewives of white supremacy," Ayla Stewart filmed a nearly two-hour livestream response because she was named in the piece.[11] While waiting for more viewers to join the livestream, Ayla began to read some of the comments in the chat box.

"Girl, give me a week and I'll rip this article to shreds," wrote Lacey Lynn. Ayla laughed: "I bet you will, and I'm looking forward to that." Further browsing through the comments, she exclaimed, "Oh, Blonde in the Belly of the Beast! Sweetheart, hello! I love you!"

She started to read Rebecca Hargraves's comment: "Have you seen a pic of Annie Kelly? She is hideous. No surprise. She doesn't want more dating-market competition." Ayla laughed again.

These influencers are constantly attacking the political left for not having the courage to engage in debate. But clearly there's hypocrisy at play when the far right fails to do the same and instead resorts to ad hominems.

"You're sweet, I will sling ad homs all day," wrote Rebecca in response. Ayla again laughed: "There is a place for every soldier in a war. We really are in a war against these people," she said. "Blonde, if you're going to be the ad hom girl, go with that, girl."

Throughout her career as an influencer, Rebecca has been very outspoken when the media criticizes far-right figures. For instance, upon release of the New York–based Data & Society Institute think tank report looking at the right-wing alternative ecosystem on YouTube (see chapter 2), the report's author, Rebecca Lewis, became the target of coordinated far-right hate campaigns seeking to discredit her. Rebecca Hargraves made an entire vlog criticizing the report, called the political left "desperate," and undertook a character assassination of Lewis.

"These media experts like Lewis, they study internet culture from afar. But they don't understand why it's so influential. Why memes speak louder than CNN pundits. Why we have millions, upon millions, of views and subscribers," scoffed Rebecca. "Part of that is they have a robotic inability to detect humor. Another part is that they aren't personable or likeable."[12] Ironically, Lewis's report precisely argues that the reason why the far right is so influential on YouTube is that creators employ branding tactics that make them seem relatable, authentic, and accountable to their audiences and position themselves as a hip counterculture. Lewis pinpointed exactly why influencers like Rebecca Hargraves are appealing.

By exploring in-depth the digital lives of these far-right women influencers, I demonstrate here that when you enter this world, you find a closed community of friendship, and that community becomes more insular when being constantly attacked for its opinions. It is a bubble that provides comfort and reassurance. Despite my intention to reveal what it's like to be a part of this community, although guided by intellectual curiosity, there is an underlying risk of harassment. The extremism researcher Julia Ebner told me about the backlash she experienced after going undercover with a fake identity for her book *Going Dark* (2020): "When I left white nationalist and alt-right groups, I was often targeted with harassment and hate campaigns. Sometimes the campaigns were merely nasty trolling campaigns, sometimes they were more serious and even included death threats against me and my colleagues," she elaborated. These experiences are unfortunately common for researchers in this field. Ebner continued, "As a woman, I also noticed that the extent and nature of the threats [against me were] often different from those against male researchers or journalists—they tended to be more intense, and threats were often sexual in nature."[13] The reality is that this type of harassment is quite common for female researchers and journalists.

Lana Lokteff devoted an entire video on Red Ice TV reacting to Seyward Darby's book *Sisters in Hate* (2020), personally attacking Darby for being childless and for deliberately "twisting" the facts about Lana's life.[14] She further accused Darby of promoting a biased, leftist agenda to undermine white housewives and white nuclear families, claiming that such lifestyles are not part of a white-supremacist objective—a claim that is false, as documented throughout Darby's book.

These far-right women influencers will claim that I have presented an inaccurate portrayal of them. "We're not white supremacists or Nazis," they will say. "We condemn extremists and being associated with those labels." However, the ideas and language that these women use *do* overlap with extremist elements. Notions such as "preservation of culture" and "Western civilization" have historically been euphemisms for race genocide. And being proud of your white ancestry and its legacy decontextualizes what it means to have been historically white and the privileges associated with it. As Darby summarizes in her book, "White nationalists are posing a challenge: If other groups can rally around their history, why not white people? This is a false equivalence, shorn of context, nuance, and power disparities."[15]

The information propagated by these women is sometimes blatantly false, as when Lacey Lynn stated that "the descendants of European countries built America. It is true that the West was built by Europeans."[16] In reality, slaves forcibly brought from Africa built an America stolen from Native peoples, tending to the fields and domestic labor in the master's household. Rebecca Hargraves didn't acknowledge this fact and dismissed the proposal to put abolitionist Harriet Tubman on the twenty-dollar bill: "The left is like, what random Black woman can I put on currency? Your people and your priorities, it's astonishing to me."[17] A well-known antislavery activist who founded the Underground Railroad to help enslaved people escape to freedom is here offensively categorized as a "random Black woman." Further, it was the successive arrivals of immigrants, not just Europeans, who later made novel and innovative contributions across industries and culture that shaped the United States. Across the West overall, much of the wealth that accumulated in Europe was financed through the exploitative practices of colonialism overseas, and the legacy remains visible across buildings and street names in capital cities today. This is not merely an interpretation of history. Living in a Western society means acknowledging the failures of the past and creating pathways for democratic inclusion in the present.

My aim is not to apologize for the ideas espoused by these far-right women influencers. Rather, I'm documenting the process that can unfold when someone becomes drawn into and remains within this world. When writing this book, I was constantly faced with reflecting on my own positionality. I considered myself immune from the messages and narratives of these far-right women influencers, but at times I could relate to the topics and ideas they frequently discussed. Many of them are close to my age, educated, and in committed heterosexual relationships. Part of their relatability stems from the unavoidable fact that the far right amplifies mainstream gender and sexuality norms, so what they say is a familiar refrain. As a cis, heterosexual person, I can easily assume certain roles for women and men as "natural" because those functions are still largely practiced in mainstream society every day. And although biracial, I benefit from passing as white and am provided with the same type of privilege afforded to these women in white-settler societies. What is rendered invisible to me demands constant recognition of its social reproduction.

Julia Ebner faced a similar experience when she went undercover with extremist groups. "I noticed that I found it harder to leave the female misogynist channels of the 'tradwives' because I was myself in a vulnerable stage of my life and probably more receptive to their propaganda," she told me. "That was strange to me because I considered myself a feminist and an expert on radicalization, so it really showed me that anyone could be drawn into extremist groups if the timing was right."

Ebner and I share a career dedicated to tracking and analyzing far-right radicalization, yet we both found ourselves drawn to the allure of these female-dominated far-right spaces. Ebner infiltrated the dark corners of the web, though, while I remained at the tip of the iceberg on mainstream platforms, which shows how easy it can be to slip into the vast recesses of online communities when the narratives are nearly indistinguishable. I argue that what makes these far-right women especially relatable is the medium through which they deliver their propaganda. By effectively exploiting the *publicness* of Instagram and YouTube in ways that audiences consume content on these platforms, their strategy is successful. Young far-right women influencers compellingly mix political and personal content presented in a familiar aesthetic for millennial and Gen Z viewers. Producing memes and interactive content to spread far-right ideology through easily digestible posts is a powerful metapolitical approach. Nonetheless, we must distinguish between a susceptible woman who is attracted to this community out of personal grievance and seeking empowerment, on the one hand, and the influencers in this book, on the other, who are literally profiting from and building careers in spreading far-right propaganda.

What if hypothetically the far right were to achieve its goals for society? At that point, will these far-right women influencers continue to have a voice, a de facto leadership in shaping society? If a far-right utopia were established, would these women still enjoy the visibility and power afforded to them now?

As Darby observes about Lana Lokteff, "It was hard to imagine Lana, who'd sought a spotlight for so much of her life, gladly disappearing into her home should a white ethno-state ever exist. I wondered if the pursuit of white nationalism—the struggle, as believers would call it—was the endgame for people like Lana."[18] As the most prominent women in the movement, these far-right influencers are attracted to the fame and status they receive as figureheads. Do they truly advocate for what they're saying, or do they just understand that using certain catchphrases will garner more attention and views? There is an underlying tension between authenticity and propaganda in these influencers' self-presentation online.

These women view themselves and a few others as the exceptions among women in general. "You and I are different kind of women in that we're more political. We ask questions," Lana told Darby during an interview. "That's not the norm for most women. They really do want to be beautiful, attract a guy, be taken care of, have their home, have their children."[19] Lana sees herself as an authoritative spokesperson for what most women want in life.

Brittany Sellner has similarly argued that most women are not well suited for politics because they are generally more emotional and sensitive than men, which places them in a position to be less effective. "[Political activism has] hardened me; I constantly have to be in fight-or-flight mode," she explained in a vlog in late 2018.[20] Lana has likewise stated that women "are too emotional for leading roles in politics" and should instead channel their "political power" in the domestic sphere.[21] Lauren Southern concurs. "Women should embrace our native spheres of influence. Biologically we are not as well built as men for the type of shallow, transactional relationships required for statecraft. On average, our calling is within the domestic realm, where we offer warmth and compassion to our families," she claimed in 2017.[22] She evidently doesn't see herself as an "average" woman, nor does she specify the criteria that determine whether a woman is an exception to the norm.

For mothers in particular, politics is not seen as an option. There are significant setbacks, Brittany claimed in late 2018, because "the brutal world of politics hardens women; . . . this makes it much more difficult for us to access our feminine and our nurturing side." Further, she added, "politics is extremely stressful," and if women are constantly stressed, "it will be much more difficult for us to care for our husband, for our children, and to care for our home if it is our intention to be a homemaker." For women in the far right, it is their biological duty to be a homemaker. Thus, Brittany warned that women being in politics can pose a significant risk: "A consistent role in politics will often keep us away from our loved ones, which could potentially strain our relationships with our husbands, our children, our family and friends."[23] Ironically, many of these far-right women influencers celebrated the electoral victory of the Italian far-right politician Giorgia Meloni as prime minister even though she is a mother who is not married to her child's father.

Influencers' paradoxical attitudes about women's "proper" roles can present at other times, such as when Lauren Southern appeared on a podcast hosted by Mikhaila Peterson (Jordan Peterson's daughter) in mid-2020, after she returned to political activism, and expressed completely opposite views on motherhood than she had before then: "There's this picture out there of women and mums, and that's all they are, and that's all they can do. And regrettably, I think, I maybe pushed this trope a little bit as well, sometimes, in my talking about traditional women and traditional families in older videos and speeches I've done."[24] In fact, Lauren had been voicing this "trope" of traditionalism for years, building her profile and profiting off this agenda. I suspect that Lauren herself changed the listing of her video titled "Return of the Traditional Woman," a speech she gave at California Polytechnic State University in 2017, to "unlisted," thus making it no longer searchable on YouTube. In fact, she has since 2020 removed several videos from her channel that are offensive or provocative, apparently attempting to clean up her (digital) image.

"I want to do something productive. I want to use my creative energy. And that's going to make me a better mother as well," Lauren continued on Mikhaila Peterson's podcast. "Not just being this person who's meek and stays at home all day and has no opinions on anything or hasn't created anything. No. Mums are multidimensional people." This is such a complete one-eighty it would almost be humorous if Lauren weren't a public far-right figure proclaiming traditional values and antifeminism. Acting through self-motivation, Lauren was trying to justify her own desire and passion for politics by now claiming suddenly that all mothers have multivaried interests.

Yet as Lauren also mentioned, "I even see people comment when I post on Instagram: 'Why are you on Instagram? Why are you back to doing documentaries? You should just be a mum.'" If influencers like Lauren have made repeated calls for women to take up their biological destiny and only be homemakers, are such comments really a surprise? Male critics say that these women should practice what they preach. Indeed, Lauren had long been called a hypocrite by those in the far right for not conforming to a trad lifestyle before getting married. In late 2017, she made a vlog titled "Why I'm Not Married," responding to these allegations. "I think it would be degenerate for me to get married right now without someone that I'm truly in love with and think could be a good father to my children," she stated. "In fact, I think that would be significantly worse for the Western world." She cited statistics of children who have been negatively affected by single parenthood. She reaffirmed the false narrative that "on average women and men are happy being in a marriage with kids. On average, women are happy being housewives."[25] Here, she justified her personal life choices in the vein of far-right ideology. Despite her claim of not having yet found the right man to have a family with, criticism was levied against her. Many called her a *tradthot*, a pejorative term referring to a single woman who claims to support traditional values simply to gain money and influence but who in reality doesn't get married and have children. Lauren became a symbol of the "tradthot" as her popularity grew.

The attack on Lauren was not the first time that sexist and misogynistic comments were levied against these women influencers by "allies" in the far right and manosphere. These women influencers have sometimes had to defend themselves against men's egregious behavior and comments, including in YouTube live chats. Sometimes they warn that such trolling won't be tolerated and that these men will be removed from the chat for it. Other times they respond with a snarky, emasculating comment meant to hurt a male viewer's ego. "I had spent so much time in my life standing up for men," Lauren stated in 2022. "And to have all of these red pill YouTubers, MGTOWS, MRAs [of the manosphere] make videos coming out just uncritically believing everything that had been said about me . . . that pissed me off."[26] Considering that these women influencers occupy a position in a movement that vehemently attempts to silence women's voices and views women as unequal to men, they probably should have expected this behavior from male viewers and "allies."

Perhaps this is why Lauren decided to create a separate Instagram account focused just on her homelife being a mother, thus segregating her audiences. Before doing so, she told her followers in an Instagram Story in August 2020, "So, because I'm going to be launching my next documentary very soon here, I was thinking of setting up another account just for my mum stuff. Because I feel like I've got this weird amalgamation of viewers where like 90 percent of them here are for politics, and I've just amassed like 10 percent that like my mum posting. So let me know if you would follow me to mum post on another page."[27] About an hour later, she created the "mom" Instagram account that she called "my personal blog." It accumulated more than 3,500 followers in the first hour.

Ultimately, there's a constant paradox in how these far-right women influencers must present themselves. "Lana, I realized," writes Darby, "faced competing audiences: racist men who were skeptical or disdainful of female strength, and racist women wary of a cause that might sideline them."[28] Lauren's decision to have separate Instagram accounts—presumably divided by gendered "interests"—reflects these competing audiences. On the one hand, these far-right women showcase their political activism, but on the other hand they promote the image of a comfortable and stable family as the foundation of their recruitment, radicalization, and propaganda narratives.

Sometimes the pressure to maintain celebrity within the far-right scene can take its toll, as expressed by one of the women who announced her departure. "I have been thinking a lot over the past several weeks, and I have made the difficult decision to leave politics," wrote Brittany Sellner in a Telegram post in June 2022. "I have really enjoyed making political content and doing political activism during the past five and a half years, and I'm extremely grateful to each and every one of you who watched my videos and especially those of you who supported me. It's been a very special time in my life that I'll never forget, and I ultimately hope that I have done some good with my work. I wish you all the best, and I once again cannot thank all of you enough."[29] Brittany then briefly removed all the videos on her YouTube channel (by changing the viewing settings to private)—although you could still find her videos posted on alt-tech platforms such as Odysee and BitChute—and her bio on her Instagram page. Although she had become less active in posting social media content over time, she was still regularly involved, and thus her rather quiet, public resignation was unexpected. Not only did Brittany rise to stardom on YouTube, but she had also married into the movement, and her husband continues to be a prominent far-right activist leader.

In some cases, though, attempting to leave the movement can have dire consequences. "Many alt-right groups make it hard to leave their channels by creating insider cultures that create strong group bonds and foster a feeling of belonging," Julia Ebner told me based on her experience of infiltrating far right networks. "These are the positive incentives, but they also work with negative incentives to keep members from leaving. In some channels, the risk was to get doxed or threatened after exiting." Although the far-right women influencers I feature here are unlikely to face such negative incentives, "exiting" the scene as a public figure presents its own complications for them in the most visible manner, and sometimes the desire for fame can draw them back in.

Indeed, four months later, in October 2022, Brittany deleted her resignation post on Telegram and replaced it with a new post advertising her latest YouTube video, "Sorry for Disappearing." "Honestly, the reason I didn't post [on YouTube] for so long was because for a while there I actually thought that I might have to be leaving YouTube for good due to the fact that things just got extremely busy in my life, particularly with taking care of my son," she told viewers in the vlog. "Ultimately, I ended up announcing on Telegram and Instagram that I was leaving YouTube [correction: Brittany had announced that she was "leaving politics," not just YouTube], which in hindsight wasn't wise. What I should have done instead is just let you all know that I simply needed a few months' break, which is something that I really did need, and I've put the last several months to very good use. So I genuinely apologize for just vanishing off the face of the earth without too much of an explanation, I mean, at least not here on YouTube. And I promise that if I ever need time off in the future, which who knows, I'm a mom now, so I might, then I will be clear about that; I'll post about it on YouTube instead of just disappearing."[30] And yet if she really did intend just to take a break, why did she remove all the videos on her YouTube channel, communicating a clear departure rather than a temporary "break"?

Brittany explained the reason for her return by showing a photo of her holding her baby son: "Fortunately, I now feel like I have finally acclimated to the rhythm of my new life and have time to make videos again." She continued, "While for a while there I thought perhaps I would be able to close the political chapter of my life without too much difficulty, in the end I was obviously completely wrong. I mean, look at me, here I am back on YouTube already after just five to six months. The truth is that I care very deeply about the myriad of issues that I've been discussing here on

YouTube and various other platforms for the past six years, I believe it's been, since I first started politics. And for whatever reason, God and you wonderful people have blessed me with a platform. And I think that it would be unwise and even a bit ungrateful if I squander that opportunity, particularly when there are still so many issues that I think are worth discussing, highlighting. So, for as long as I'm fortunate enough to have my YouTube platform—who knows how long this will be?—I am going to take advantage of it."

By framing her return as motivated by unselfish reasons ("God and you wonderful people"), Brittany obscured the fact that she enjoys being in the spotlight and commenting on far-right issues and even rejected her previous views of the primary importance of motherhood and its incompatibility with politics. How long Brittany continues to be successful in the online attention economy remains to be seen. The far-right milieu is a highly competitive space among thought commentators vying for the same fans.

As Kathleen Blee and Annette Linden conclude from studying far-right women, "In the end, the needs and ambitions of women activists never fit into right-wing extremist parties and organizations dominated by men."[31] And herein lie some ironic and inescapable facts for these far-right women influencers. They preach antifeminism but practice feminism. They view themselves as feminine figures yet adopt supposedly "masculine" traits such as assertiveness and leadership in propagating the movement. They paint an image of a far-right utopia, but they hope not to change their public lifestyle to achieve it. For as long as women in the far right continue to support a political ideology that designates women as submissive—under the false guise of choice—they will struggle to justify their own empowerment.

NOTES

INTRODUCTION: "A NEW CHAPTER"

1. I decided to refer to the far-right women of this book on a first name basis to capture the type of networked intimacy at the core of my argument about their relatability—that is, how their viewers see them—as well as to establish a more personal tone based on my experience researching them.
2. Lana Lokteff, with Brittany Pettibone (Sellner) and Tara McCarthy, "#VirtueOfTheWest: 5," March 8, 2017, https://www.youtube.com/watch?v=jmj0yhnziyE.
3. Crystal Abidin, "Communicative Intimacies: Influencers and Perceived Interconnectedness," *Ada: A Journal of Gender, New Media, and Technology* 8 (2015), https://adanewmedia.org/2015/11/issue8-abidin/.
4. Lauren Southern and Brittany Pettibone (Sellner), "Announcement!," August 8, 2017, https://www.youtube.com/watch?v=95CmPZtJJl0 (original link); alternative upload available here: https://www.bitchute.com/video/95CmPZtJJl0/.
5. Alice Marwick, Benjamin Clancy, and Katherine Furl, *Far-Right Online Radicalization: A Review of the Literature*, Bulletin of Technology and Public Life (Chapel Hill: Center for Information, Technology, and Public Life, University of North Carolina, 2022), https://assets.pubpub.org/9694oeej/31648241763479.pdf, 2.

6. Tama Leaver, Tim Highfield, and Crystal Abidin, *Instagram: Visual Social Media Cultures* (London: Polity, 2020), 111.

7. Rebecca Hargraves, "The Desperate Left | Data & Society Study," September 20, 2018, https://www.youtube.com/watch?v=PUd2RBEk9d0.

8. Lauren Southern (@laurencheriie), Instagram post, November 27, 2017, https://www.instagram.com/p/Bb-p7olnWx7/ .

9. Bobby Allyn, "The 'OK' Hand Gesture Is Now Listed as a Symbol of Hate," NPR, September 26, 2019, https://www.npr.org/2019/09/26/764728163/the -ok-hand-gesture-is-now-listed-as-a-symbol-of-hate.

10. Martin Patriquin, Mack Lamoureux, Alheli Picazo, and Evan Balgord, "The Racist Podcaster Who Started a Neo-Nazi Coffee Company to Fund White Nationalism," *Vice*, May 16, 2018, https://www.vice.com/en_us/article /59qb93/the-racist-podcaster-who-started-a-neo-nazi-coffee-company -to-fund-white-nationalism.

11. Cathrine Thorleifsson, email interview by the author, June 15, 2020.

12. See, for example, "Dear Cucks, Only One Kind of Nationalism Will Save the West," Red Ice TV, December 7, 2017, https://redice.tv/red-ice-tv/dear -cucks-only-one-kind-of-nationalism-will-save-the-west.

13. Ayla Stewart, "Ayla Stewart Responds, *New York Times* Anti Housewives Piece," June 2, 2018, https://www.youtube.com/watch?v=jo2Bx3w8r5s&t =5307s.

14. Lauren Chen, "The Need to Breed: Falling Birth Rates in the West," September 18, 2018, https://www.youtube.com/watch?v=jrrRM7H83P4&t =16s.

15. Seyward Darby, *Sisters in Hate: American Women on the Front Lines of White Nationalism* (New York: Little, Brown, 2020), 10.

16. Kathleen Blee, *Inside Organized Racism: Women in the Hate Movement* (Berkeley: University of California Press, 2002), 21.

17. Brittany Pettibone (Sellner) (@brittpettibone), "Back from a three-month Instagram ban with a photo of my beautiful mom and I," Instagram post, April 5, 2020, https://www.instagram.com/p/B-mUXaQhKp3/. Brittany was vague on social media about her three-month absence from Instagram but provides an explanation in a story/interview reported by a far-right media outlet. See Cassandra MacDonald (interview with Brittany Pettibone Sellner), "Instagram Forces Right-Wing Author Brittany Pettibone to Delete All Photos with Her Political Activist Husband—Including from Their Wedding," *The Gateway Pundit*, April 5, 2020, https://www .thegatewaypundit.com/2020/04/instagram-forces-right-wing-author -brittany-pettibone-delete-photos-political-activist-husband-including -wedding/.

18. Brittany Pettibone (Sellner), "Personal Q&A," August 22, 2017, https://www.youtube.com/watch?v=SBCtJ_rZzac.
19. Rebecca Hargraves, "My Red Pill Journey," August 12, 2017, https://www.youtube.com/watch?v=e8E3VjkSDqo.

1. THE ALT-RIGHT VERSUS THE FAR RIGHT

1. Lauren Chen, "What Is the Alt-Right? | Nationalism, Race & Supremacy," November 28, 2016, https://www.youtube.com/watch?v=ViF-uz9JOZI.
2. W. Carson Byrd and Matthew W. Hughey, "Born That Way? 'Scientific' Racism Is Creeping Back Into Our Thinking. Here's What to Watch Out For," *Washington Post*, September 28, 2015, https://www.washingtonpost.com/news/monkey-cage/wp/2015/09/28/born-that-way-scientific-racism-is-creeping-back-into-our-thinking-heres-what-to-watch-out-for/.
3. Ayla Stewart, "Ayla Stewart Is Not Alt Right," April 3, 2018, https://www.youtube.com/watch?v=fjr-vIPD8V4&t=1656s.
4. Kathleen Blee, *Inside Organized Racism: Women in the Hate Movement* (Berkeley: University of California Press, 2002), 97.
5. Lauren Chen, "What Do Muslims Really Believe?," June 27, 2016, https://www.youtube.com/watch?v=Af1pAmpCRs4&list=PLOhJRao9eBPPgYrfedyGvJ8OYkDD_84E_&index=17&t=0s; Lauren Chen, "I Enable Hate?," October 11, 2017, https://www.youtube.com/watch?v=fw1B66efXVE&t=52s.
6. Lauren Chen, "Immigration CRISIS: 'Take MORE Migrants' Says U.N.," June 22, 2019, https://www.youtube.com/watch?v=awuBkfTJZHA&list=PLOhJRao9eBPMqUyWaYrQL-1E5RPkb28BK&index=52.
7. Ben Zimmer, "The Origins of the 'Globalist' Slur," *The Atlantic*, March 14, 2018, https://www.theatlantic.com/politics/archive/2018/03/the-origins-of-the-globalist-slur/555479/.
8. J. M. Berger, *The Alt-Right Twitter Census: Defining and Describing the Audience for Alt-Right Content on Twitter*, VOX-Pol report (VOX-Pol Center for Excellence, 2018), https://www.voxpol.eu/download/vox-pol_publication/AltRightTwitterCensus.pdf.
9. Tamir Bar-On, "Richard Spencer and the Alt Right," in *Key Thinkers of the Radical Right: Behind the New Threat to Liberal Democracy*, ed. Mark Sedgewick (Oxford: Oxford University Press, 2019), 224–41.
10. George Hawley, *Making Sense of the Alt-Right* (New York: Columbia University Press, 2017), 3; Kathleen Blee, email interview by the author, July 27, 2020.

11. Dave Boddiger, "White Supremacists Disrupt DC Bookstore Discussion on Race and Politics," *Splinter,* April 28, 2019, https://splinternews.com/white-supremacists-disrupt-dc-bookstore-discussion-on-r-1834365211; Tom Jackman, "White Nationalists Interrupt Author at Politics and Prose," *Washington Post*, April 28, 2019, https://www.washingtonpost.com/local/public-safety/white-nationalists-interrupt-author-at-politics-and-prose/2019/04/27/d48012c6–692d-11e9–82ba-fcfeff232e8f_story.html. See also Jonathan M. Metzl, *Dying of Whiteness: How the Politics of Racial Resentment Is Killing America's Heartland* (New York: Basic, 2019).

12. Patrick Casey, "Building Upon Our Success: The Disbanding of AIM," November 2, 2020, https://web.archive.org/web/20201103002349/https://americanidentitymovement.com/2020/11/02/building-upon-our-success-the-disbanding-of-aim/

13. Anti-Defamation League, "Groyper Army and America First," March 17, 2020, https://www.adl.org/resources/backgrounders/groyper-army.

14. Cas Mudde, "The Populist Zeitgeist," *Government and Opposition* 39, no. 4 (2004): 543–44.

15. Duncan McDonnell, "Populist Leaders and Coterie Charisma," *Political Studies* 64, no. 3 (2016): 719–33; Benjamin Moffitt, *The Global Rise of Populism: Performance, Political Style, and Representation* (Stanford, CA: Stanford University Press, 2016).

16. Jason Stanley, *How Fascism Works: The Politics of Us and Them* (New York: Random House, 2018).

17. Hilary Pilkington, "'EDL Angels Stand Beside Their Men . . . Not Behind Them': The Politics of Gender and Sexuality in an Anti-Islam(ist) Movement," *Gender and Education* 29, no. 2 (2017): 240.

18. Sara R. Farris, *In the Name of Women's Rights: The Rise of Femonationalism* (Chapel Hill, NC: Duke University Press, 2017).

19. Jasbir K. Puar, *Terrorist Assemblages: Homonationalism in Queer Time* (Chapel Hill, NC: Duke University Press, 2017).

20. Pilkington, "'EDL Angels,'" 251.

21. Lauren Southern, "Asking Feminists: Women's Rights or Islam?," November 29, 2017, https://www.youtube.com/watch?v=PZHuFah0uds.

22. Robyn Riley, Instagram Story, accessed August 18, 2022, including quote from the study. Because Instagram Stories disappear after twenty-four hours, there is no permanent hyperlink available. However, I have collected screenshots of the Instagram Stories cited throughout the book.

23. Lauren Chen, "The Need to Breed: Falling Birth Rates in the West," September 18, 2018, https://www.youtube.com/watch?v=jrrRM7H83P4&t=211s.

24. José Pedro Zúquete, *The Identitarians: The Movement Against Globalism and Islam in Europe* (South Bend, IN: University of Notre Dame Press, 2018).

25. Blee, *Inside Organized Racism*, 25.
26. Blee, *Inside Organized Racism*, 67.
27. Brittany Pettibone (Sellner), "Leftist HYSTERIA Over My Idaho GOP Meeting," May 1, 2019, https://www.youtube.com/watch?v=2tVc6FiWg5M.
28. Rebecca Hargraves, "My Red Pill Journey," August 12, 2017, https://www.youtube.com/watch?v=e8E3VjkSDqo&t=233s.
29. Robyn Riley (@realrobynriley), Instagram posts, July 1, 2020, https://www.instagram.com/p/CCE0mXvAz6kkmorBbfSjf1NmAX-8yfsj9xZbkE0/; December 14, 2020, https://www.instagram.com/p/CIy0XnUAPEw_lr-oIExwK9x5aIyGleeFFAFuhU0/; June 5, 2020, https://www.instagram.com/p/CBEXf9fgcx3AFiSOPHV_O2ceRUfpac33XoeODc0/.
30. Blee, *Inside Organized Racism*, 9–10.
31. Brittany Pettibone (Sellner), "Personal Q&A," August 22, 2017, https://www.youtube.com/watch?v=SBCtJ_rZzac.
32. Lauren Southern, "Who Screwed Western Civilization? | Lauren Southern and Stefan Molyneux," December 21, 2016, https://www.youtube.com/watch?v=cqsmtvWzLnA&list=PLMNj_r5bccUw2CyB8kV7h3D01iP8eMiMA.
33. Robyn Riley, "Origin Story," August 1, 2018, https://www.youtube.com/watch?v=4GyAiJvRo_A.
34. Robyn Riley, "Rebel Revival #9: Life Updates and AMA," August 16, 2020, https://www.youtube.com/watch?v=ynHoE1S1INo&t=469s.
35. Seyward Darby, *Sisters in Hate: American Women on the Front Lines of White Nationalism* (New York: Little, Brown, 2020), 11, 98, 186.
36. Anti-Defamation League, "Michelle Malkin Is Attempting to Normalize White Supremacy," August 5, 2020, https://www.adl.org/blog/michelle-malkin-is-attempting-to-normalize-white-supremacy.
37. Lana Lokteff, "In Defense of America's European Roots," Red Ice TV, April 2, 2020, https://redice.tv/red-ice-tv/in-defense-of-americas-european-roots.
38. Lauren Chen, "The Problem with 'Token Minorities,'" September 23, 2018, https://www.youtube.com/watch?v=h1yG7RGPW9Y.
39. See Angela Nagle, *Kill All Normies: Online Culture Wars from 4chan and Tumbler to Trump and the Alt-Right* (New York: Zero Books, 2017).
40. Maura Conway, Ryan Scrivens, and Logan Macnair, "Right-Wing Extremists' Persistent Online Presence: History and Contemporary Trends," International Centre for Counter-Terrorism (ICCT) Policy Brief (2019), https://icct.nl/wp-content/uploads/2019/11/Right-Wing-Extremists-Persistent-Online-Presence.pdf. See also Bharath Ganesh, "Right-Wing Extreme Digital Speech in Europe and North America," in *Extreme Digital Speech: Contexts, Responses and Solutions*, ed. Bharath Ganesh and Jonathan

Bright, VOX-Pol report (VOX-Pol Network of Excellence, 2019), https://www.voxpol.eu/download/vox-pol_publication/DCUJ770-VOX-Extreme-Digital-Speech.pdf, 27–40.

41. Blee, *Inside Organized Racism*, 78.

42. Mike Wendling, *Alt-Right: From 4chan to the White House* (London: Pluto, 2018), 9.

43. Will Bedingfield, "How Telegram Became a Safe Haven for Pro-terror Nazis," *Wired*, March 1, 2020, https://www.wired.co.uk/article/hope-not-hate-telegram-nazis.

44. Julia Ebner, *Going Dark: The Secret Social Lives of Extremists* (London: Bloomsbury, 2020), 30.

2. DOWN THE RABBIT HOLE: MY RED PILL JOURNEY

1. Rebecca Hargraves, "The Desperate Left | Data & Society Study," September 21, 2018, https://www.youtube.com/watch?v=PUd2RBEk9d0&t=567s.

2. Jessie Daniels, *Cyber Racism: White Supremacy Online and the New Attack on Civil Rights* (Lanham, MD: Rowman & Littlefield, 2009), 70.

3. Julia Ebner, *Going Dark: The Secret Social Lives of Extremists* (London: Bloomsbury, 2020), 71.

4. Alexandra Minna Stern, *Proud Boys and the White Ethnostate: How the Alt-Right Is Warping the American Imagination* (Boston: Beacon Press, 2019), 103.

5. Ebner, *Going Dark*, 114.

6. Robyn Riley, "Origin Story," August 1, 2018, https://www.youtube.com/watch?v=4GyAiJvRo_A.

7. Rebecca Lewis, *Alternative Influence: Broadcasting the Reactionary Right on YouTube* (New York: Data & Society Institute, 2018), https://datasociety.net/wp-content/uploads/2018/09/DS_Alternative_Influence.pdf, 1.

8. Rebecca Lewis, " 'This Is What the News Won't Show You': YouTube Creators and the Reactionary Politics of Micro-celebrity," *Television & New Media* 21, no. 2 (2020): 201–17.

9. Theresa M. Senft, *Camgirls: Celebrity and Community in the Age of Social Networks* (New York: Peter Lang, 2008).

10. Tama Leaver, Tim Highfield, and Crystal Abidin, *Instagram: Visual Social Media Cultures* (London: Polity, 2020), 106.

11. Stern, *Proud Boys and the White Ethnostate*, 98.

12. Lauren Southern, "The WHOLE Truth," July 11, 2022, https://www.youtube.com/watch?v=dqzJmdlJx0k.

13. Ico Maly, "Metapolitical New Right Influencers: The Case of Brittany Pettibone," *Social Sciences* 9, no. 7 (2020): 12–13.
14. Maly, "Metapolitical New Right Influencers," 13.
15. Senft, *Camgirls*, 8.
16. Leaver, Highfield, and Abidin, *Instagram*, 111.
17. Penny Triệu and Nancy K. Baym, "Private Responses for Public Sharing: Understanding Self-Presentation and Relational Maintenance Via Stories in Social Media," in *Proceedings of the 2020 CHI Conference on Human Factors in Computing Systems* (New York: Association for Computing Machinery, 2020), 1–13.
18. Ebner, *Going Dark*, 145.
19. On BitChute, see Lizzie Dearden, "Inside the UK-Based Site That Has Become the Far Right's YouTube," *The Independent*, July 22, 2020, https://www.independent.co.uk/news/uk/home-news/bitchute-far-right-youtube-neo-nazi-terrorism-videos-a9632981.html.
20. Ebner, *Going Dark*, 145.
21. Chloe Havadas, "What's the Deal with Parler?," *Slate*, July 3, 2020, https://slate.com/technology/2020/07/parler-free-speech-twitter.html; Jack Nicas and Davey Alba, "Amazon, Apple and Google Cut Off Parler, an App That Drew Trump Supporters," *New York Times*, January 9, 2021, https://www.nytimes.com/2021/01/09/technology/apple-google-parler.html.
22. Jack Morse, "Police Are Worried About White Extremists Organizing on Gab Chat, Leaked Documents Show," Mashable, July 14, 2020, https://mashable.com/article/law-enforcement-documents-violent-white-extremists-encrypted-gab-chat/.
23. Eviane Leidig, "Odysee: The New YouTube for the Far-Right," *Global Network on Extremism & Technology Insights*, February 17, 2021, https://gnet-research.org/2021/02/17/odysee-the-new-youtube-for-the-far-right/.
24. Lauren Chen, "I Need You!," October 28, 2022, https://www.youtube.com/watch?v=AV8lEGB6NXQ.
25. Ebner, *Going Dark*, 145.
26. Rani Molla, "Why Right-Wing Extremists' Favorite New Platform Is so Dangerous," *Recode*, January 20, 2021, https://www.vox.com/recode/22238755/telegram-messaging-social-media-extremists.
27. Robyn Riley, "I Lost All My Friends in the Culture War," September 28, 2018, https://www.youtube.com/watch?v=PWmGi4MoFNc.
28. Rebecca Hargraves, "My Red Pill Journey," August 12, 2017, https://www.youtube.com/watch?v=e8E3VjkSDqo&t=233s.
29. Kathleen Blee, *Inside Organized Racism: Women in the Hate Movement* (Berkeley: University of California Press, 2002), 42.

30. Seyward Darby, *Sisters in Hate: American Women on the Front Lines of White Nationalism* (New York: Little, Brown, 2020), 98.
31. Riley, "Origin Story."
32. Stern, *Proud Boys and the White Ethnostate*, 102.
33. Bharath Ganesh, "What the Red Pill Means for Radicals," *Fair Observer*, June 7, 2018, https://www.fairobserver.com/world-news/incels-alt-right-manosphere-extremism-radicalism-news-51421/.
34. Rebecca Hargraves, "Living in Libtard USA," February 25, 2016, https://www.youtube.com/watch?v=Xm0l5hsykDc&t=84s.
35. Lacey Lynn, "Red Pilled: Losing Friends," February 20, 2019, https://www.youtube.com/watch?v=cfQgf2dZpGE.
36. Riley, "I Lost All My Friends in the Culture War."
37. Blee, *Inside Organized Racism*, 71.
38. Hargraves, "Living in Libtard USA."
39. Rebecca Hargraves, "Feminism Is for Idiots and Uglies," March 12, 2016, https://www.youtube.com/watch?v=52wGb7qt8Xg.
40. Rebecca Hargraves, "Will We Lose Our Platform? | YouTube Demonetization," March 28, 2017, https://www.youtube.com/watch?v=k_ZwsMg_Goo.
41. Robyn Riley (@realrobynriley), Instagram post, August 5, 2020, https://www.instagram.com/p/CDhHkLaAUsZeYWwXHPFwAg7mGS_u1ledv09vDw0/.
42. Nazanin Andalibi, Pinar Ozturk, and Andrea Forte, "Sensitive Self-Disclosures, Responses, and Social Support on Instagram: The Case of #Depression," in *Proceedings of the 2017 ACM Conference on Computer Supported Cooperative Work and Social Computing* (New York: Association for Computing Machinery, 2017), 1485–500, https://doi.org/10.1145/2998181.2998243.
43. Darby, *Sisters in Hate*, 203–4.
44. Darby, *Sisters in Hate*, 218.
45. Rebecca Hargraves, "How to Red Pill Women," May 10, 2017, https://www.youtube.com/watch?v=obdW1FRAn6A.
46. Lauren Chen, "A Chat with Roaming Millennial," April 4, 2017, https://www.youtube.com/watch?v=2NoBUvb_wJA.
47. Riley, "Origin Story."
48. Stern, *Proud Boys and the White Ethnostate*, 108.
49. Caleb Cain, interviewed for Kevin Roose, "One: Wonderland," *Rabbit Hole* (podcast series), *New York Times*, April 16, 2020, https://www.nytimes.com/2020/04/16/podcasts/rabbit-hole-internet-youtube-virus.html.

50. Caleb Cain, interviewed for Kevin Roose, "Two: Looking Down," *Rabbit Hole* (podcast), *New York Times*, April 23, 2020, https://www.nytimes.com/2020 /04/23/podcasts/rabbit-hole-internet-youtube-virus.html.
51. Caleb Cain, phone interview by the author, July 6, 2020.

3. FEMININITY NOT FEMINISM

1. Ayla Stewart, "Feminism—My History with It and My Rejection of It," September 12, 2015, https://www.youtube.com/watch?v=_5BCUTzzpQ.
2. Seyward Darby, *Sisters in Hate: American Women on the Front Lines of White Nationalism* (New York: Little, Brown, 2020), 101.
3. See Rebecca Lewis, "'This Is What the News Won't Show You': YouTube Creators and the Reactionary Politics of Micro-celebrity," *Television & New Media* 21, no. 2 (2019): 201–17.
4. Lauren Southern, "The WHOLE Truth," July 11, 2022, https://www.youtube .com/watch?v=dqzJmdlJx0k.
5. Brittany Pettibone (Sellner), "VICE: For Feminism to Succeed, We Must ABOLISH the Family," February 29, 2020, https://www.youtube.com/watch ?v=ZnD325BSP7I&t=10s.
6. Kathleen Blee, *Inside Organized Racism: Women in the Hate Movement* (Berkeley: University of California Press, 2002), 50.
7. Rebecca Hargraves, "Butch Broads and Soy Boys: What Happened to Millennials?," May 14, 2018, https://www.youtube.com/watch?v=_OS2KOwZ6xw.
8. Pettibone (Sellner), "VICE."
9. Gabriele Dietze and Julia Roth, "Right-Wing Populism and Gender: A Preliminary Cartography of an Emergent Field of Research," in *Right-Wing Populism and Gender: European Perspectives and Beyond*, ed. Gabriele Dietze and Julia Roth (Bielefeld, Germany: Transcript, 2020), 11.
10. Lauren Southern, "Millennials Are Being Set Up for Loneliness," October 15, 2017, https://www.youtube.com/watch?v=d35KqVLvZrM.
11. Molly Hayes and Colin Freeze, "Police Lay First Terrorism Charge for Toronto Case Involving Misogyny," *Globe and Mail* (Toronto), May 19, 2020, https://www.theglobeandmail.com/canada/article-police-lay-first -terrorism-charge-for-toronto-case-involving-misogyny/.
12. Moonshot, *Incels: A Guide to Symbols and Terminology* (London: Moonshot CVE, May 26, 2020), https://moonshotteam.com/resource/incels-a-guide -to-symbols-and-terminology/.
13. Eviane Leidig, "From Incels to Tradwives: Understanding the Spectrum of Gender and Online Extremism," *Impakter*, May 21, 2020, https://impakter

.com/from-incels-to-tradwives-understanding-the-spectrum-of-gender
-and-online-extremism/.

14. Lauren Chen, "Does Hook-Up Culture Create Incels? More Attacks Likely?
| Ep 180," May 21, 2020, https://www.youtube.com/watch?v=7dIy15z_Xf4
&t=543s.

15. Megan Kelly, Alex DiBranco, and Julia R. DeCook, *Misogynist Incels and Male
Supremacism* (Washington, DC: New America, 2021), https://www.new
america.org/political-reform/reports/misogynist-incels-and-male
-supremacism/.

16. Lauren Chen, "INCEL 'Ask Me Anything': Loneliness & Hating Women?
Response | Ep 110," December 1, 2019, https://www.youtube.com/watch
?v=aHMJQUl477Q.

17. Brittany Pettibone (Sellner), "The War on Men," October 5, 2019, https://
www.youtube.com/watch?v=pBjMuiIQxFg&t=570s.

18. Debbie Ging, "Alphas, Betas, and Incels: Theorizing the Masculinities of
the Manosphere," *Men and Masculinities* 22, no. 4 (2019): 638–57.

19. Alex DiBranco, email interview by the author, August 29, 2020; see also
Institute for Research on Male Supremacism (IRMS), https://www
.malesupremacism.org.

20. Darby, *Sisters in Hate*, 205.

21. Robyn Riley, "Rebel Revival #11: Hell World," January 16, 2021, https://
www.youtube.com/watch?v=CwPvccJkU0o&t=711s.

22. Anti-Defamation League, "Groyper Army and America First," March 17,
2020, https://www.adl.org/resources/backgrounders/groyper-army.

23. A. C. Thompson and Ford Fischer, "Members of Several Well-Known Hate
Groups Identified at Capitol Riot," *ProPublica*, January 9, 2021, https://www
.propublica.org/article/several-well-known-hate-groups-identified-at
-capitol-riot.

24. Robyn Riley and Rebecca Hargraves, "Motherland Live: w/ Roosh on the
Subversion of Family and Finding God," August 7, 2020, https://www
.youtube.com/watch?v=lHpq98orEW4.

25. Brittany Pettibone (Sellner), "Why Is Dating Becoming so Difficult?,"
August 10, 2018, https://www.youtube.com/watch?v=oDYQvAp6Ao4&t
=11s.

26. Brittany Pettibone (Sellner), "Why Many Men Are Hesitant to Approach
Women," August 24, 2018, https://www.youtube.com/watch?v=9f4ZJH
Hx0Qo.

27. Chen, "Does Hook-Up Culture Create Incels?"

28. Lauren Southern, "Return of the Traditional Woman—Cal Poly SLO,"
May 27, 2017, https://www.youtube.com/watch?v=HFW0z0Y5TR4&t=1s.

29. For a critical look at the study Lauren Southern refers to, see Daniel L. Carlson, Amanda J. Miller, Sharon Sassler, and Sarah Hanson, "The Gendered Division of Housework and Couples' Sexual Relationships: A Reexamination," *Journal of Marriage and Family* 78 no. 4 (2016): 975–95, https://doi.org/10.1111/jomf.12313.

30. Brittany Pettibone (Sellner), "Society Doesn't Care About Fathers Anymore," November 9, 2018, https://www.youtube.com/watch?v=D6atgUt4Z_4.

31. Rebecca Hargraves, "The Problem with Hormonal Birth Control," July 18, 2018, https://www.youtube.com/watch?v=YvvtaeYcnes.

32. Chris M. Herbst, " 'Paradoxical' Decline? Another Look at the Relative Reduction in Female Happiness," *Journal of Economic Psychology* 32, no. 5 (2011): 773–88, https://www.sciencedirect.com/science/article/pii/S0167487011000985?casa_token=5wi0evsO8eEAAAAA:pdShEnt5O6vLE5_S7clUE3AmGxCbO7Yp8F_RhRTcNKLW0GyD71E2ec7TZ4Bk_HoTDK-ZPXJung.

33. Lauren Southern, "What Every Girl Needs to Hear," May 6, 2017, https://www.youtube.com/watch?v=oxHIftZVfrQ&t=533s.

34. Marianne Bertrand, "Career, Family, and the Well-Being of College-Educated Women," *American Economic Review* 103, no. 3 (2013): 249–50.

35. Lauren Chen, "Dating 'UGLY' | Men vs. Women," February 7, 2019, https://www.youtube.com/watch?v=NtPHydvL2i0.

36. Norman P. Li, Jose C. Yong, William Tov, Oliver Sng, Garth J. Fletcher, Katherine A. Valentine, Yun F. Jiang, and Daniel Balliet, "Mate Preferences Do Predict Attraction and Choices in the Early Stages of Mate Selection," *Journal of Personality and Social Psychology* 105, no. 5 (2013): 757–76.

37. Chen, "Dating 'UGLY.' "

38. Ico Maly, "Metapolitical New Right Influencers: The Case of Brittany Pettibone," *Social Sciences* 9, no. 7 (2020): 17.

39. Francesca Tripodi, *Searching for Alternative Facts: Analyzing Scriptural Inference in Conservative News Practices* (New York: Data & Society Institute, 2018), https://datasociety.net/library/searching-for-alternative-facts/.

40. Maly, "Metapolitical New Right Influencers," 1.

41. Brittany Pettibone (Sellner), "Personal Q&A," August 22, 2017, https://www.youtube.com/watch?v=SBCtJ_rZzac; Brittany Pettibone (Sellner), "Interview | What Makes Us Girls," December 24, 2018, https://www.youtube.com/watch?v=CL1-_g9hS9E.

42. Brittany Pettibone (Sellner), "Why Young People Are so Unhappy," November 10, 2019, https://www.youtube.com/watch?v=PRXinPDhHuA.

43. Brittany Pettibone (Sellner), "Apparently, Abortion Is a 'Moral Good,' " September 24, 2019, https://www.youtube.com/watch?v=WRtJzkcJKWo.

44. Brittany Pettibone (Sellner) (@brittpettibone), Instagram post, October 12, 2019, https://www.instagram.com/p/B3hVlVPBrY4/.

45. "Poland Delays Abortion Block Amid Nationwide Protests," *Deutsche Welle*, November 4, 2020, https://www.dw.com/en/poland-delays-abortion-block-amid-nationwide-protests/a-55491323.

46. Robyn Riley, Instagram Story, accessed June 26, 2022.

47. Rebecca Hargraves, "What's Wrong on the Right?," June 24, 2019, https://www.youtube.com/watch?v=PG9isQ5VnQo.

48. Pew Research Center, "Religious Landscape Study," 2007/2014, https://www.pewforum.org/religious-landscape-study/; Pew Research Center, "In U.S., Decline of Christianity Continues at Rapid Pace," October 17, 2019, https://www.pewforum.org/2019/10/17/in-u-s-decline-of-christianity-continues-at-rapid-pace/.

49. Pew Research Center, "In U.S., Decline of Christianity Continues at Rapid Pace."

50. On Greene, see Jack Jenkins, "Republicans Mostly Mum on Calls to Make GOP 'Party of Christian Nationalism," *Washington Post*, August 19, 2022, https://www.washingtonpost.com/religion/2022/08/19/republicans-mostly-mum-calls-make-gop-party-christian-nationalism/. For more on this same idea, see Andrew L. White and Samuel L. Perry, *Taking America Back for God* (Oxford: Oxford University Press, 2020).

51. Lauren Chen, "The Need to Breed: Falling Birth Rates in the West," September 18, 2018, https://www.youtube.com/watch?v=jrrRM7H83P4&t=16s; Lacey Lynn, "The 1965 Red Pill," January 9, 2018, https://www.youtube.com/watch?v=EIDUHhMBYPg.

52. Robyn Riley, "I Lost All My Friends in the Culture War," September 28, 2018, https://www.youtube.com/watch?v=PWmGi4MoFNc.

53. Robyn Riley, "Rebel Revival #9: Life Updates and AMA," August 16, 2020, https://www.youtube.com/watch?v=ynHoE1S1INo&t=458s.

54. Robyn Riley, Instagram posts, October 1, 2020, https://www.instagram.com/p/CFyGezDgmuLiMTDaFBzrYCNcvlzwvn8rJqMZKY0/; October 11, 2020, https://www.instagram.com/p/CGN8woYAZEtAo2ZuVL9El7WGw61SJws1fYLBZE0/; and July 5, 2022, https://www.instagram.com/p/Cfo2UQyJaLkm3vI5ErFVbyxrl4fKxtGIT9DNQ80/?igshid=YmMyMTA2M2Y%3D.

55. Southern Poverty Law Center, "World Congress of Families Gathering in Tbilisi Showcases Anti-LGBT Rhetoric and Conspiracy Theories," June 1, 2016, https://www.splcenter.org/hatewatch/2016/06/01/world-congress-families-gathering-tbilisi-showcases-anti-lgbt-rhetoric-and-conspiracy.

56. Robyn Riley, Instagram Stories, accessed September 28 and October 25, 2022.

57. See, for example, Faith Goldy, "Degeneracy Is NOT Conservative (or Catholic)," October 31, 2019, https://www.youtube.com/watch?v=5kEQIO7C1EM.

58. Darby, *Sisters in Hate*, 109–11.

59. See, for example, Ayla Stewart, "{TradLife} Traditional Parenting and European Cultural Homeschooling: My Favorite Books," November 1, 2015, https://www.youtube.com/watch?v=Ke6sFHGBWSc&t=2755s.

60. Lauren Chen, "Our Marriage Class DISASTER | Ep 267," December 15, 2020, https://www.youtube.com/watch?v=xQK5YE77j20.

61. See, for example, Robert Chao Romero, *Brown Church: Five Centuries of Latina/o Social Justice, Theology, and Identity* (Downers Grove, IL: IVP Academic, 2020); and N. T. Wright, *Surprised by Hope: Rethinking Heaven, the Resurrection, and the Mission of the Church* (New York: Harper Collins, 2018).

62. Lana Lokteff, with Brittany Pettibone (Sellner) and Tara McCarthy, "#VirtueOfTheWest: 5," March 8, 2017, https://www.youtube.com/watch?v=jmj0yhnziyE.

63. Alexandra Minna Stern, *Proud Boys and the White Ethnostate: How the Alt-Right Is Warping the American Imagination* (Boston: Beacon Press, 2019), 105.

64. Riley, "Rebel Revival #9."

65. Robyn Riley, "Girl Talk #8: Brave the World on Improving Fertility, Dating Tips & Converting to Christianity," May 26, 2019, https://www.youtube.com/watch?v=FQ7S_4Pellg.

66. Jessie Daniels, *Cyber Racism: White Supremacy Online and the New Attack on Civil Rights* (Lanham, MD: Rowman & Littlefield, 2009), 69.

67. See Yannick Veilleux-Lepage, Alexandra Phelan, and Ayse D. Lokmanoglu, "Gendered Radicalisation and 'Everyday Practices': An Analysis of Extreme Right and Islamic State Women-Only Forums." *European Journal of International Security,* December 5, 2022, https://www.cambridge.org/core/journals/european-journal-of-international-security/article/gendered-radicalisation-and-everyday-practices-an-analysis-of-extreme-right-and-islamic-state-womenonly-forums/1C4E05907976274941A7CD240E62DC3F.

68. Lauren Chen, "Reddit's Women's Forum Is A FEMINIST CESSPOOL | Ep 199," July 4, 2020, https://www.youtube.com/watch?v=A9AKi0Tu1JA.

69. Melissa Block, "Accusations of 'Grooming' Are the Latest Political Attack—with Homophobic Origins," NPR, May 11, 2022, https://www.npr.org/2022/05/11/1096623939/accusations-grooming-political-attack-homophobic-origins.

70. Katrine Fangen and Inger Skjelsbæk, "Editorial: Special Issue on Gender and the Far Right," *Politics, Religion & Ideology* 21, no. 4 (2020): 411–15.

71. Brittany Pettibone (Sellner), "Fake Female Friendships," December 3, 2018, https://www.youtube.com/watch?v=TtSi3S6dU4w&t=122s.

72. Lacey Lynn, "Red Pilled: Losing Friends," February 20, 2019, https://www
.youtube.com/watch?v=cfQgf2dZpGE.

73. Robyn Riley (@realrobynriley), Instagram post, October 18, 2019, https://
www.instagram.com/p/B3vhN29BTp5jhlygswfhw7fGSSw8JlxVhsAwRc0
/?igshid=YmMyMTA2M2Y%3D.

74. Robyn Riley (@realrobynriley), Instagram post, July 19, 2020, https://www
.instagram.com/p/CC1tP9PA2KFDuWTR4mU7B5NJwCMTG8S-1Ejl_Y0/.

75. Pew Research Center, "An Examination of the 2016 Electorate, Based on
Validated Voters," August 9, 2018, https://www.pewresearch.org/politics
/2018/08/09/an-examination-of-the-2016-electorate-based-on
-validated-voters/.

76. "Of Course White Women Voted for Trump Again," *The Cut*, November 17,
2020, https://www.thecut.com/2020/11/many-white-women-still-voted
-for-trump-in-2020.html.

77. Riley, Instagram post, July 19, 2020.

78. Robyn Riley, Instagram Story, accessed July 13, 2020.

79. Brittany Pettibone (Sellner) and Martin Sellner, "3 Reasons Marriage Is a
Risk (and Why We Still Took It)," September 9, 2019, https://www.youtube
.com/watch?v=VPzBG3N-8P0.

80. Blee, *Inside Organized Racism*.

81. Brittany Pettibone (Sellner), "Do Women Fit Well in Politics?," November 28, 2018, https://www.youtube.com/watch?v=VKtldUgAM28.

82. Lokteff, with Pettibone (Sellner) and McCarthy, "#VirtueOfTheWest: 5."

83. Robyn Riley, "Bun in the Oven," September 25, 2019, https://www.youtube
.com/watch?v=zdVomMsy4TU.

84. Caleb Cain, phone interview by the author, July 6, 2020.

4. THE MAKING OF A TRADWIFE

1. Elora [Blonde Buttermaker], "How to Make Butter," March 15, 2017, https://
www.youtube.com/watch?v=-VAWwigPOFM.

2. Elora [Blonde Buttermaker], "Real Pumpkin Spice Creamer," October 25,
2018, https://www.youtube.com/watch?v=26fP5moCIk4.

3. Cynthia Miller-Idriss, *Hate in the Homeland: The New Global Far Right* (Princeton, NJ: Princeton University Press, 2020), 70, 76.

4. Miller-Idriss, *Hate in the Homeland*, 70.

5. Robyn Riley (@realrobynriley), Instagram post, November 22, 2019,
https://www.instagram.com/p/B5J5M9IgwWf3U17MRUeGjsgt
-sInV0okT0IC_Y0/.

6. Robyn Riley, Instagram Stories, accessed October 31, November 3, and November 11, 2020; January 26 and February 16, 2022.

7. Seyward Darby, *Sisters in Hate: American Women on the Front Lines of White Nationalism* (New York: Little, Brown, 2020), 152–53.

8. "'Submitting to My Husband Like It's 1959': Why I Became a TradWife," *BBC Stories*, January 17, 2020, https://www.youtube.com/watch?v=ZwT-zYo4-OM; Annie Kelly, "The Housewives of White Supremacy," *New York Times*, June 1, 2018, https://www.nytimes.com/2018/06/01/opinion/sunday/tradwives-women-alt-right.html; Hadley Freeman, "'Tradwives': The New Trend for Submissive Women Has a Dark Heart and History," *The Guardian*, January 27, 2020, https://www.theguardian.com/fashion/2020/jan/27/tradwives-new-trend-submissive-women-dark-heart-history.

9. Julia R. DeCook, "Memes and Symbolic Violence: #Proudboys and the Use of Memes for Propaganda and the Construction of Collective Identity," *Learning, Media and Technology* 43, no. 4 (2018): 485–504.

10. Darby, *Sisters in Hate*, 153.

11. Alena Kate Pettit, "About," *The Darling Academy* (blog), https://www.thedarlingacademy.com/about/.

12. Caitlin Ann Huber [Mrs. Midwest], "Shop My Life!," *Mrs. Midwest* (blog), https://www.mrsmidwest.com/shop.

13. Caitlin Ann Huber [Mrs. Midwest], "SIMPLE Beauty Secrets to Level-Up Your Look . . . ‖ Go a Step Beyond Makeup," April 25, 2022, https://www.youtube.com/watch?v=U-H-iTfVY5o.

14. Mrs. Midwest merchandise is made available through the personalized merchandise platform Spring.

15. Caitlin Ann Huber [Mrs. Midwest], Instagram Story, accessed November 28, 2022.

16. Juliana Stewart, "Here's Why I Decided to Become a #TradWife," *Evie Magazine*, April 27, 2020, https://www.eviemagazine.com/post/heres-why-i-decided-to-become-a-tradwife/.

17. Juliana Stewart, "The Difference Between a Strong Masculine Man and an Abusive One," *Evie Magazine*, August 14, 2020, https://www.eviemagazine.com/post/the-difference-between-a-strong-masculine-man-and-an-abusive-one/.

18. Caitlin Ann Huber [Mrs. Midwest], "The 5 Keys to Fun & Productive Homemaking!," May 24, 2020, https://www.youtube.com/watch?v=ui-CaWYp9No&t=225s.

19. Lillian [Postmodern Mom] and Juliana Stewart, "Guest Interview on a Podcast: Ladies Let's Chat—Single Income!," June 4, 2020, https://www.youtube.com/watch?v=xeF_fzg0-iU.

20. Cynthia Loewen, "TRADITIONAL WIVES?," March 16, 2020, https://www
    .youtube.com/watch?v=t8xUATPDuCU.
21. "Are Traditional Wives Betraying Feminism?," *Jeremy Vine Show*, with
    guests Felipe and Lillian [Postmodern Mom], February 4, 2020, https://
    www.youtube.com/watch?v=sk-81oM6JVQ.
22. Lillian [Postmodern Mom], "A Day in the Life of a #Tradwife," May 12, 2020,
    https://www.youtube.com/watch?v=JIVIUkBKEyA&t=113s.
23. Brittany Pettibone (Sellner), "My Baby Boy Is Finally Here!," November 27,
    2021, https://www.youtube.com/watch?v=KmbE1Eaz0jI.
24. Caitlin Ann Huber [Mrs. Midwest], "How I Handle Criticism for Being Tra-
    ditional . . .," April 20, 2020, https://www.youtube.com/watch?v=PM0
    FCzGCG6k.
25. Alena Kate Pettitt, "Why Does the Media Hate Traditional Housewives?,"
    The Darling Academy (blog), July 23, 2020, https://www.thedarlingacademy
    .com/articles/traditional-family-values-and-trad-wives/.
26. Alena Kate Pettitt, "What Is a Trad Wife?," *The Darling Academy* (blog),
    March 10, 2020, https://www.thedarlingacademy.com/articles/what-is-a
    -trad-wife/.
27. Alena Kate Pettitt, Facebook Page post, May 16, 2020, https://www
    .facebook.com/permalink.php?id=1093864314021359&story_fbid
    =3747301785344252. For the interview, see Emilie Stendahl, "Traditionella
    Fruar ger Extremismen en Städad Front," *Expo*, May 5, 2020, https://expo
    .se/2020/05/traditionella-fruar-ger-extremismen-en-städad-front.
28. Loewen, "TRADITIONAL WIVES?"
29. Daisy Cousens, "Tradwives Make Feminists Jealous," February 13, 2020,
    https://www.youtube.com/watch?v=rBa9ZKLw-qw.
30. Darby, *Sisters in Hate*, 156.
31. Ashley Mattheis, "#TradCulture: Reproducing Whiteness and Neo-fascism
    Through Gendered Discourse Online," in *Routledge Handbook of Critical Stud-
    ies in Whiteness*, ed. Shona Hunter and Christi van der Westhuizen (Lon-
    don: Routledge, 2021), 96.
32. Darby, *Sisters in Hate*, 155.
33. Darby, *Sisters in Hate*, 107, 120.
34. Ayla Stewart, "{TradLife} Traditional Parenting and European Cultural
    Homeschooling; My Favorite Books," November 1, 2015, https://www
    .youtube.com/watch?v=Ke6sFHGBWSc&t=2755s.
35. Kathleen Blee, *Inside Organized Racism: Women in the Hate Movement* (Berke-
    ley: University of California Press, 2002), 127.
36. Lauren Southern, "Millennials Are Being Set Up for Loneliness," Octo-
    ber 15, 2017, https://www.youtube.com/watch?v=d35KqVLvZrM.

37. Rebecca Hargraves and Brittany Pettibone (Sellner), "Brittany Sellner on Patriotism, America and Motherhood," May 7, 2021, https://www.youtube .com/watch?v=APJIYanhMaA&t=506s.

38. Robyn Riley, Instagram Story, accessed September 8, 2022.

39. Mattheis, "#TradCulture," 94, 98.

40. Robyn Riley, Instagram Story, accessed March 29, 2022.

41. Caleb Cain, phone interview by the author, July 6, 2020.

42. See "Mrs. Midwest Reddit and Twitter," imgur (image-hosting service), December 24, 2019, https://imgur.com/a/dLgkZFc; "Mrs. Midwest Likes White Supremacist Content," imgur (image-hosting service), April 12, 2020, https://imgur.com/a/4BleLbh; Caitlin Ann Huber [Mrs. Midwest], "20 'Things' I Recommend," *Mrs. Midwest* (blog), July 5, 2019, https://www .mrsmidwest.com/post/20-things-i-recommend.

43. Caitlin Ann Huber [Mrs. Midwest], "The Art of Femininity, with Feminine Homemaker Caitlin Ann Huber | MSGA #7," January 24, 2019, https://www .youtube.com/watch?v=pQRicwhOrr0&feature=youtu.be.

44. Donald Trump, tweet, Twitter, August 17, 2020, https://twitter.com /realDonaldTrump/status/1293517514798960640.

45. Alana Semuels, "White Flight Never Ended," *The Atlantic*, July 30, 2015, https://www.theatlantic.com/business/archive/2015/07/white-flight -alive-and-well/399980/.

46. Lacey Lynn (@laceylaurenlynn), Instagram page, https://www.instagram .com/laceylaurenlynn/.

47. Lacey Lynn, "The 1965 Red Pill," January 9, 2018, https://www.youtube .com/watch?v=EIDUHhMBYPg.

48. Lacey Lynn, "Phyllis Schlafly: From Another Traditionalist Perspective," October 25, 2017, https://www.youtube.com/watch?v=B3Sfh-GycMk&t=67s.

49. Lynn, "Phyllis Schlafly."

50. Lacey Lynn, "Eagle Forum Council 2017 Review," September 27, 2017, https://www.youtube.com/watch?v=0Njl5MpLrvU.

51. Lynn, "Phyllis Schlafly."

52. Lacey Lynn, "Tag Along! Eagle Forum Meeting!," March 31, 2018, https:// www.youtube.com/watch?v=09kuiaJ4w7s&t=346s.

53. Lacey Lynn, "*Mrs. America* Review | Phyllis," May 5, 2020, https://www .youtube.com/watch?v=eLCgT2aWf3k.

54. Ayla Stewart, "Trump Won! It's Morning in America Again!," November 9, 2016, https://www.youtube.com/watch?v=Ashd6x-neNQ&t=1s.

55. Darby, *Sisters in Hate*, 173.

56. Lacey Lynn, "Finding Traditionalism (My Journey)," June 5, 2017, https:// www.youtube.com/watch?v=hSUYHc7O0Ig.

57. Lacey Lynn, "Red Pilled: Losing Friends," February 20, 2019, https://www
    .youtube.com/watch?v=cfQgf2dZpGE.

58. Darby, *Sisters in Hate*, 102.

59. Brittany Pettibone (Sellner), "Housewives Are Lazy?," August 7, 2017,
    https://www.youtube.com/watch?v=8SlN8K4_Kbc&t=1s.

60. Lana Lokteff, with Brittany Pettibone (Sellner) and Tara McCarthy, "#Vir-
    tueOfTheWest: 5," March 8, 2017, https://www.youtube.com/watch?v
    =jmj0yhnziyE.

61. Darby, *Sisters in Hate*, 187.

62. Robyn Riley, Instagram Story, accessed December 10, 2020; Robyn Riley,
    "The Rebel Revival #6: Trump at Rushmore + Insta AMA," July 5, 2020,
    https://www.youtube.com/watch?v=DTmdrEwTtCo.

63. Caitlin Ann Huber [Mrs. Midwest] (@mrs.midwest), Instagram post,
    August 7, 2020, https://www.instagram.com/p/CDmIhxxAZxN/.

64. Isabel Slone, "Escape Into Cottagecore, Calming Ethos for Our Febrile
    Moment," *New York Times*, March 10, 2020, https://www.nytimes.com/2020
    /03/10/style/cottagecore.html.

65. Robyn Riley (@realrobynriley), Instagram post, April 20, 2020, https://
    www.instagram.com/p/B_Lvbh6ADHsM8XfmYMx9VAhRP8wb0erNGp5
    XcM0/.

66. Robyn Riley and Colin Robertson [Millennial Woes], "Millenniyule 2020:
    Robyn Riley," December 19, 2020, https://altcensored.com/watch?v
    =Pegr7ZGUILQ.

67. Robyn Riley, "Bun in the Oven," September 25, 2019, https://www.youtube
    .com/watch?v=zdVomMsy4TU.

68. Darby, *Sisters in Hate*, 153.

69. Robyn Riley, "I'm Starting a New Channel: Motherland," January 14, 2020,
    https://www.youtube.com/watch?v=xFB61AoU6A4.

70. Rebecca Hargraves and Robyn Riley, "Motherland Live: Blonde Butter-
    maker on Homebirth and Prenatal Nutrition," March 6, 2020, https://
    www.youtube.com/watch?v=HNjhdfBDxYE.

71. Rebecca Hargraves and Robyn Riley, "Motherland Live: Birth and Post-
    partum Anxiety," May 29, 2020, https://www.youtube.com/watch?v=ADXalq
    w0iKA&list=PLSlzFQi5c_hkb22tU2anIuAX73jLLvyFi&index=2&t=0s.

72. Ashley Mattheis, "Shieldmaidens of Whiteness: (Alt) Maternalism and
    Women Recruiting for the Far/Alt-Right," *Journal for Deradicalization* 17
    (2018): 143.

73. Robyn Riley (@realrobynriley), Instagram post, December 13, 2019,
    https://www.instagram.com/p/B5_00gxAgrek6AjpFr66zjwcVPW72sJDh
    LfmNo0/.

74. Rebecca Hargraves and Robyn Riley, "Motherland Live: Rebecca's Birth Story," June 15, 2020, https://www.youtube.com/watch?v=Ji9cvfD9vV4.

75. Robyn Riley, with Rebecca Hargraves, "Girl Talk #18 with Blonde: Trying to Conceive, Pregnancy and New Life Direction," December 15, 2019, https://www.youtube.com/watch?v=Q_VyuWadk4E&list=PLZrRcekQdiqClmbGI_hKplMmJDesXFBqu&index=2.

76. Rebecca Hargraves and Robyn Riley, "Motherland Live: Prepping for SHTF w/ a Family," January 26, 2021, https://www.youtube.com/watch?v=lW4NuCo9VxM.

77. Robyn Riley, Instagram Story, accessed August 12, 2022.

78. Lauren Chen, "HEALTHIER to Get Pregnant in Your 30s Than Your 20s? Anti-natalism | Ep 160," April 5, 2020, https://www.youtube.com/watch?v=E9w-br2pKmk.

79. Lauren Chen (@thelaurenchen), " 'Noms,' " Instagram Story Highlight, n.d., https://www.instagram.com/stories/highlights/17946092182049658/.

80. Annie Lowrey, "Millennials Don't Stand a Chance," *The Atlantic*, April 13, 2020, https://www.theatlantic.com/ideas/archive/2020/04/millennials-are-new-lost-generation/609832/.

81. Chen, "HEALTHIER to Get Pregnant in Your 30s Than Your 20s?"

82. Chen, "HEALTHIER to Get Pregnant in Your 30s Than Your 20s?"

83. Lauren Chen, "The Need to Breed: Falling Birth Rates in the West," September 18, 2018, https://www.youtube.com/watch?v=jrrRM7H83P4&t=16s.

84. Stewart, "{TradLife} Traditional Parenting."

85. Rebecca Hargraves, "The Problem with Hormonal Birth Control," July 18, 2018, https://www.youtube.com/watch?v=YvvtaeYcnes.

86. Eva Vlaardingerbroek, Instagram Story, accessed July 31, 2022.

87. Robyn Riley, Instagram Story, accessed January 11, 2021.

88. Instagram, "Keeping People Informed, Safe, and Supported on Instagram," March 24, 2020, https://about.instagram.com/blog/announcements/coronavirus-keeping-people-safe-informed-and-supported-on-instagram/.

89. Southern, "Millennials Are Being Set Up for Loneliness."

90. Lokteff, with Pettibone (Sellner) and McCarthy, "#VirtueOfTheWest: 5."

91. Robyn Riley, "Rebel Revival #9: Life Updates and AMA," August 16, 2020, https://www.youtube.com/watch?v=ynHoE1S1INo.

92. See, for example, Elizabeth M. Lusk, Matthew J. Taylor, John T. Nanney, and Chammie C. Austin, "Biracial Identity and Its Relation to Self-Esteem and Depression in Mixed Black/White Biracial Individuals," *Journal of Ethnic & Cultural Diversity in Social Work* 19, no. 2 (2010): 109–26.

93. Trenette Clark Goings, Emily Butler-Bente, Tricia McGovern, and Matthew O. Howard, "Prevalence and Correlates of Substance Use in Black, White, and Biracial Black-White Adolescents: Evidence for a Biracial Intermediate Phenomena," *American Journal of Orthopsychiatry* 86, no. 5 (2016): 527–39.

94. Robyn Riley, Instagram Story, accessed June 8, 2020.

95. Riley, "Bun in the Oven."

96. For example, Ayla Stewart, Instagram posts, November 7, 2020, https://www
.instagram.com/p/CHTeWPqg-7Y/; June 23, 2020, https://www.instagram
.com/p/CBwOAhIA4ir/; January 5, 2019, https://www.instagram.com/p
/BsQ85klA3bP/.

97. Lacey Lynn (@laceylaurenlynn), Instagram posts, October 14, 2019,
https://www.instagram.com/p/B3m0vv3gfl1/, and September 17, 2019,
https://www.instagram.com/p/B2hZtPcgPSb/.

98. Mattheis, "Shieldmaidens of Whiteness," 131.

99. On white women at the forefront of resistance to integration, see Glen
Jeansonne, *Women of the Far Right: The Mothers Movement and World War II*
(Chicago: University of Chicago Press, 1996); and Elizabeth Gillespie McRae,
Mothers of Massive Resistance: White Women and the Politics of White Supremacy (Oxford: Oxford University Press, 2018).

100. Blee, *Inside Organized Racism*, 127.

101. Ayla Stewart, Instagram Story, accessed January 27, 2022.

102. Elora [Blonde Buttermaker], "Blonde Buttermaker: After Hours—Women's
Self Defense Corset Holster," February 20, 2017, https://redice.tv/red-ice
-tv/blonde-buttermaker-after-hours-womens-self-defense-corset
-holster (no longer available).

103. Caitlin Dickerson, "Anxiety About Muslim Refugees Is Stoked Online by
the Far-Right Media," *New York Times*, January 28, 2017, https://www
.nytimes.com/2017/01/28/us/anxiety-about-muslim-refugees-is-stoked
-online-by-the-far-right-media.html.

5. CROWDSOURCING HATE

1. On shield-maidens, see Ashley Mattheis, "Shieldmaidens of Whiteness:
(Alt) Maternalism and Women Recruiting for the Far/Alt-Right," *Journal
for Deradicalization* 17 (2018): 128–62.

2. Maxine Bedat, "How to Decipher 'Sustainable Fashion' in 2020," *Harper's
Bazaar*, December 11, 2019, https://www.harpersbazaar.com/fashion
/designers/a30185938/sustainable-fashion-explained/.

3. Lana Lokteff, "Lana's Llama: Non Toxic Clothing & The," Red Ice TV, November 6, 2015, https://redice.tv/red-ice-radio/lanas-llama-non-toxic -clothing-and-the.

4. Lauren Chen, "Female Dating Strategy!? Reddit Review | Ep 112," December 8, 2019, https://www.youtube.com/watch?v=YjK216nbRd8&t=165s.

5. Garnuu, "Our Impact," n.d., https://garnuu.com/pages/our-impact.

6. Sarah Banet-Weiser, *Empowered: Popular Feminism and Popular Misogyny* (Durham, NC: Duke University Press, 2018). See the Garnuu pages "Our Impact," "The Cycle," and "Ambassador" at https://garnuu.com/.

7. Garnuu (@garnuu), Instagram page, June 12, 2022, https://www.instagram .com/p/Cetn5X3uXD7/.

8. Cynthia Miller-Idriss, *Hate in the Homeland: The New Global Far Right* (Princeton, NJ: Princeton University Press, 2020), 74.

9. Rebecca Hargraves and Robyn Riley, "Motherland Live: Prepping for SHTF w/ a Family," January 26, 2021, https://www.youtube.com/watch?v =lW4NuCo9VxM.

10. Robyn Riley, Instagram Story, accessed November 11, 2020.

11. Hargraves and Riley, "Motherland Live: Prepping for SHTF w/ a Family."

12. Robyn Riley, Instagram Stories, accessed August 28, September 28, and September 30, 2022.

13. Robyn Riley, "The Rebel Revival #2: The Overton Window Has Shifted, Lets [*sic*] Talk About It," June 4, 2020, https://www.youtube.com/watch?v =rDyx31hOyD0.

14. Faith Goldy, "Gun Grab = Secession?," May 5, 2020, https://www.youtube .com/watch?v=1DydQC2k1tc.

15. Brittany Pettibone (Sellner), "The Prisoners Are in Love with Their Prison," January 21, 2022, https://www.youtube.com/watch?v=hRzKH YwbfzI.

16. Brittany Pettibone (Sellner) (@brittpettibone), Instagram post, January 8, 2022, https://www.instagram.com/p/CYeg3hzM58Q/.

17. Hargraves and Riley, "Motherland Live: Prepping for SHTF w/ a Family."

18. Miller-Idriss, *Hate in the Homeland*, 85.

19. Cynthia Miller-Idriss, email interview by the author, July 28, 2020.

20. Amy B. Wang, "Swastika Shirts Pulled After Backlash: 'Fashion Can't Reclaim This Symbol from Hate,'" *Washington Post*, August 8, 2017, https://www .washingtonpost.com/news/morning-mix/wp/2017/08/08/a-design -studio-tried-to-reclaim-the-swastika-by-putting-it-on-t-shirts-it -didnt-end-well/; "Extremist Content Online: White Supremacist T-Shirts Found on Teespring," Counter Extremism Project, August 19, 2019, https:// www.counterextremism.com/press/extremist-content-online-white

-supremacist-t-shirts-found-teespring; Christopher Ruvo, "Teespring Sells, Then Removes, Apparel Glorifying Dylann Roof," Advertising Specialty Institute, April 25, 2018, https://www.asicentral.com/news/news letters/promogram/april-2018/teespring-sells-then-removes-apparel -glorifying-dylann-roof/.

21. For an article on the far right's use of this phrase, see Anti-Defamation League, "It's Okay to Be White," https://www.adl.org/education/references /hate-symbols/its-okay-to-be-white.

22. Karl Spracklen, "Nazi Punks Folk Off: Leisure, Nationalism, Cultural Identity and the Consumption of Metal and Folk Music," *Leisure Studies* 32, no. 4 (2013): 415–28.

23. On Julius Evola, see Anna Momigliano, "The Alt-Right's Intellectual Darling Hated Christianity," *The Atlantic*, February 21, 2017, https://www .theatlantic.com/international/archive/2017/02/julius-evola-alt-right /517326/.

24. PhilosophiCat, "Traditional Woman's Path to Heroism," January 23, 2019, https://www.youtube.com/watch?v=2LTr-MGrvm0; PhilosophiCat, "Traditional Man's Path to Heroism," March 29, 2019, https://www.youtube .com/watch?v=y_XUN1HOl2c.

25. Lana Lokteff, with PhilosophiCat, "How to Talk to Normies & Agitators Posing as Alt-Right Men," *Radio 3Fourteen* (podcast), May 3, 2017, https:// redice.tv/radio-3fourteen/how-to-talk-to-normies-and-agitators -posing-as-alt-right-men; Robyn Riley, with PhilosophiCat, "Girl Talk #13: PhilosophiCat on the Path to Heroism, Evola & Tradition," July 7, 2019, https://www.youtube.com/watch?v=HDwEgvY1YHU&t=240s.

26. Benjamin R. Teitelbaum, *Lions of the North: Sounds of the New Nordic Radical Nationalism* (Oxford: Oxford University Press, 2017), 119, 103 (quote from Mattias Karlsson).

27. Cathrine Thorleifsson, "The Swedish Dystopia: Violent Imaginaries of the Radical Right," *Patterns of Prejudice* 53, no. 5 (2019): 515–33.

28. Lauren Chen, "Sweden's Fall: The Cost of Altruism," March 13, 2017, https://www.youtube.com/watch?v=AvRov5IweJ8.

29. Lauren Southern, "The Nightmare of Mass Immigration," May 19, 2017, https://www.youtube.com/watch?v=OePRY9gkTSU.

30. Rebecca Hargraves, "What Will It Take for Europeans to Push Back?," February 19, 2017, https://www.youtube.com/watch?v=ISK7jvxuz-I.

31. Lokteff, with PhilosophiCat, "How to Talk to Normies."

32. Lokteff, with PhilosophiCat, "How to Talk to Normies."

33. Brittany Pettibone (Sellner), "SURPRISE: I Wrote a Book for Girls," December 11, 2018, https://www.youtube.com/watch?v=2d2Gkqzs24Q.

34. Ayla Stewart, "{TradLife} Traditional Parenting and European Cultural Homeschooling; My Favorite Books," November 1, 2015, https://www.youtube.com/watch?v=Ke6sFHGBWSc&t=2755s.

35. Brittany Pettibone (Sellner), "LAUNCH DAY: What Makes US Girls," December 18, 2018, https://www.youtube.com/watch?v=vFNToXPm9Eg.

36. Lauren Southern, "If You Don't Raise Your Kids, Someone Else Will," November 17, 2020, https://www.youtube.com/watch?v=prSJDnh2Gsg.

37. Lauren Southern, Instagram Story, accessed December 19, 2021.

38. Brittany Pettibone (Sellner) (@brittpettibone), Instagram post, May 5, 2020, https://www.instagram.com/p/B_zcPFDh__S/ (archived at https://archive.is/JBLgA); Brittany Pettibone (Sellner), "A Personal Interview," October 11, 2020, https://www.youtube.com/watch?v=LBBnfutYZwI.

39. Robyn Riley (@realrobynriley), Instagram post, June 17, 2020, https://www.instagram.com/p/CBg15TRAbv0jyhKRpuLN3eXRMWPEtz6IydbFuk0/.

40. Robyn Riley, "The Rebel Revival #5: White People Are Cancelled," June 28, 2020, https://www.youtube.com/watch?v=PY4lusY6VXw.

41. Robyn Riley, Instagram Story, accessed June 25, 2020.

42. "About Us," *Evie Magazine*, https://www.eviemagazine.com/about/.

43. Faith Moore, "It's Okay to Aspire to Motherhood Over a Career," *Evie Magazine*, March 8, 2019, https://www.eviemagazine.com/post/its-okay-to-aspire-to-motherhood-over-a-career/.

44. *Evie Magazine* (@eviemagazine), Instagram page, https://www.instagram.com/eviemagazine/.

45. Carolynne Cantila, "5 Health Benefits of Orgasms (They're Not Just for Fun)," *Evie Magazine*, March 20, 2020, https://www.eviemagazine.com/post/5-health-benefits-of-orgasms-theyre-not-just-for-fun/.

46. Robyn Riley, Instagram Story, accessed August 18, 2020. Article in reference: Robyn Riley, "You Don't Need a Perfect Man. You Need a Man with Potential," *Evie Magazine*, August 14, 2020, https://www.eviemagazine.com/post/you-dont-need-a-perfect-man-you-need-a-man-with-potential/.

47. Robyn Riley, "Rebel Revival #9: Life Updates and AMA," August 16, 2020, https://www.youtube.com/watch?v=ynHoE1S1INo&t=469s.

48. Robyn Riley, Instagram Story, accessed November 19, 2020.

49. Alice E. Marwick, "Instafame: Luxury Selfies in the Attention Economy," *Public Culture* 27, no. 1 (2015): 157.

50. Zeynep Tufekci, "'Not This One': Social Movements, the Attention Economy, and Microcelebrity Networked Activism," *American Behavioral Scientist* 57, no. 7 (2013): 849, emphasis in original.

51. Marwick, "Instafame," 140.

52. Rebecca Lewis, *Alternative Influence: Broadcasting the Reactionary Right on YouTube* (New York: Data & Society Institute, 2018), https://datasociety.net/wp-content/uploads/2018/09/DS_Alternative_Influence.pdf, 28.

53. Nancy Baym, "Connect with Your Audience! The Relational Labor of Connection," *Communication Review* 18, no. 1 (2015): 16.

54. Casey Michel, " 'This Is All We've Got': Young White Supremacists Are Down to Their Last Fundraising Platform," *Think Progress*, March 19, 2018, https://archive.thinkprogress.org/makersupport-and-white-supremacists-729a273afb9c/.

55. Lauren Southern, "What Is Crypto-currency?," June 6, 2017, https://www.youtube.com/watch?v=G1JtJLRuqgo.

56. Lauren Chen, "Are Cryptocurrencies a SCAM? | What You Should Know," May 31, 2018, https://www.youtube.com/watch?v=smqJk2g5x_w.

57. Hargraves and Riley, "Motherland Live: Prepping for SHTF w/ a Family."

58. Robyn Riley, Instagram Story, accessed January 12, 2021.

59. Lana Lokteff and Bre Faucheux, "Lana Lokteff | How Women Can Course Correct | 27Crows Radio," February 27, 2018, https://www.youtube.com/watch?v=dMyTy8QKLfA.

60. See Lauren Southern's Bitcoin ledger at https://www.blockchain.com/btc/address/1JLM6GJwaPdNv4dM8K5KkcFHeziXXXMGKT.

61. Lauren Southern, "The WHOLE Truth," July 11, 2022, https://www.youtube.com/watch?v=dqzJmdlJx0k.

62. Brooke Erin Duffy and Urszula Pruchniewska, "Gender and Self-Enterprise in the Social Media Age: A Digital Double Bind," *Information, Communication & Society* 20, no. 6 (2017): 843–59.

6. FROM PROTESTS TO PARLIAMENTS

1. Lauren Southern, "European Parliament on Right-Wingers Banned from UK," March 14, 2018, https://www.youtube.com/watch?v=odGiYJdFtE0.

2. Lauren Southern, "The WHOLE Truth," July 11, 2022, https://www.youtube.com/watch?v=dqzJmdlJx0k.

3. Southern, "European Parliament on Right-Wingers Banned from UK."

4. Cas Mudde, *The Far Right Today* (Cambridge: Polity, 2019).

5. Lauren Southern (@laurencheriie), Instagram post, March 14, 2018, https://www.instagram.com/p/BgTIqDQHQ-b/.

6. Lauren Southern (@laurencheriie), Instagram post, March 11, 2018, https://www.instagram.com/p/BgKk02FH00R/.

7. "European Parliament: Facts and Figures," briefing, April 2019, https://www.europarl.europa.eu/RegData/etudes/BRIE/2019/635515/EPRS

_BRI(2019)635515_EN.pdf; "European Election Results—2019—European Union, Results by Political Group—Constitutive Session," July 2, 2019, https://www.europarl.europa.eu/about-parliament/en/in-the-past/previous-elections.

8. Duncan McDonnel and Annika Werner, *International Populism* (London: Hurst, 2019).

9. Lauren Southern and Brittany Pettibone (Sellner), "What Happened in Australia? With Lauren Southern," August 16, 2018, https://www.youtube.com/watch?v=j8EkdouvVuo.

10. Seyward Darby, *Sisters in Hate: American Women on the Front Lines of White Nationalism* (New York: Little, Brown, 2020), 185.

11. Alexandra Minna Stern, *Proud Boys and the White Ethnostate: How the Alt-Right Is Warping the American Imagination* (Boston: Beacon Press, 2019), 101.

12. Lauren Southern, "Changing My Mind on Immigration—My EU Speech," February 3, 2019, https://www.youtube.com/watch?v=UlM-bkGg08I&t=13s. Lauren writes in the video description that it is "a re recording of the actual speech at the EU." So we can assume that a recording of the speech on location was not possible, and she filmed herself redelivering it, but she reassures her viewers that "there were no changes to the speech etc." At the end of the video, though, she includes a recording of the press briefing from the European Parliament, so, indeed, it is verifiable.

13. Lauren Southern (@laurencheriie), Instagram post, January 9, 2018, https://www.instagram.com/p/BdtYOcNnkld/.

14. Southern, "The WHOLE Truth."

15. Lauren Southern (@laurencheriie), Instagram post, August 23, 2018, https://www.instagram.com/p/Bmzj5oFH2uh/.

16. Lauren Southern, "Why I left, and Why I'm Back," June 19, 2020, https://www.youtube.com/watch?v=2YhyNqXWqiU.

17. Southern, "Why I Left."

18. Lauren Southern, "CROSSFIRE IS OUT!," December 30, 2020, https://www.youtube.com/watch?v=q0KF4oL1KS4.

19. Lauren Southern and Brittany Pettibone (Sellner), "Defend Europe Alps Mission," April 22, 2018, https://www.youtube.com/watch?v=WIJpl3pVtSM.

20. Brittany Pettibone (Sellner), "IT'S ME: BARBIE FIANCÉ," September 25, 2018, https://www.youtube.com/watch?v=MSTfQIB6Ecg.

21. Brittany Pettibone (Sellner), "Why It's Hard to Make Girlfriends," August 1, 2017, https://www.youtube.com/watch?v=7vOzxpbn_dE.

22. Julia Ebner, *Going Dark: The Secret Social Lives of Extremists* (London: Bloomsbury, 2020), 40.

23. Lauren Southern (@laurencheriie), Instagram post, July 19, 2017, https://www.instagram.com/p/BWvVWI7Hm5h/.

24. Lisa Firestone, "Why Millennials Are so Lonely," *Psychology Today*, September 18, 2019, https://www.psychologytoday.com/us/blog/compassion-matters/201909/why-millennials-are-so-lonely.

25. Lauren Southern, "Berkeley 'Free Speech Week,'" September 24, 2017, https://www.youtube.com/watch?v=5GCEkz5wd3w.

26. German Lopez, "The Far Right's 'Free Speech Week' at UC Berkeley, Explained," *Vox*, September 21, 2017, https://www.vox.com/policy-and-politics/2017/9/21/16333260/free-speech-week-uc-berkeley.

27. Brittany Pettibone (Sellner), "Right-Wing Movements: America Versus Europe," October 2, 2017, https://www.youtube.com/watch?v=DF6HHYcbmMg.

28. Southern, "Berkeley 'Free Speech Week.'"

29. Lauren Southern, "Return of the Traditional Woman—Cal Poly SLO," May 27, 2017, https://www.youtube.com/watch?v=HFW0z0Y5TR4&t=2s.

30. Ebner, *Going Dark*, 46.

31. Cynthia Miller-Idriss, "Why Does the Far Right Love Fred Perry? Mainstream Fashion Is Its New Camouflage," *The Guardian*, August 29, 2019, https://www.theguardian.com/commentisfree/2019/aug/29/far-right-fred-perry-mainstream-fashion-camouflage-brands.

32. Andrew Hartman, *A War for the Soul of America: A History of the Culture Wars* (Chicago: University of Chicago Press, 2015).

33. See Francesca Bolla Tripodi, *The Propagandists' Playbook: How Conservative Elites Manipulate Search and Threaten Democracy* (New Haven, CT: Yale University Press, 2022), 30.

34. Mark Memmott, "GOP Students' Race-Based Bake Sale Sparks Controversy at Berkeley," NPR, September 26, 2011, https://www.npr.org/sections/thetwo-way/2011/09/26/140809070/gop-students-race-based-bake-sale-sparks-controversy-at-berkeley?ft=1&f=1001&sc=tw&utm_source=twitterfeed&utm_medium=twitter&t=1587639742125.

35. Anti-Defamation League, "Turning Point USA," February 14, 2019 (updated January 25, 2023), https://www.adl.org/resources/backgrounders/turning-point-usa; Brendan Joel Kelley, "Turning Point USA Accused of 'Boosting Their Numbers with Racists' by Long-Established Conservative Student Group," Southern Poverty Law Center, June 15, 2018, https://www.splcenter.org/hatewatch/2018/06/15/turning-point-usa-accused-'boosting-their-numbers-racists'-long-established-conservative.

36. Jim Dickinson, "Is This a Turning Point in the Campus Culture Wars?," *Wonkhe*, March 2, 2020, https://wonkhe.com/blogs/is-this-a-turning-point-in-the-campus-culture-wars/.

37. "WATCH: Trump Addresses Turning Point USA's Teen Student Summit," July 23, 2019, https://www.youtube.com/watch?v=Y2kHkZccf_Y.

38. Turning Point USA (@turningpointusa), Instagram page, https://www
.instagram.com/turningpointusa/.
39. Makena Kelly, "Turning Point Is Quietly Building the Next Generation of
Conservative Influencers," *The Verge*, January 5, 2022, https://www
.theverge.com/2022/1/5/22868483/turning-point-charlie-kirk
-republican-influencers-instagram-today-is-america.
40. Lauren Southern, "The Identity Politics of Turning Point USA," May 18,
2018, https://www.youtube.com/watch?v=I2f3MRQiyFo.
41. For the announcement, see Lauren Chen (@thelaurenchen), Instagram
post, September 28, 2022, https://www.instagram.com/p/CjBv7vzpox5/.
42. Brittany Pettibone (Sellner) and Martin Sellner, "Right-Wing Movements:
America Versus Europe," October 2, 2017, https://www.youtube.com
/watch?v=DF6HHYcbmMg.
43. Brittany Pettibone (Sellner) and Martin Sellner, "The Full Story: Why We
Were Banned from the U.K.," March 12, 2018, https://www.youtube.com
/watch?v=4glysfmgOC0; Brittany Pettibone (Sellner) and Martin Sellner,
"Generation Identity Facing Prison," May 15, 2018, https://www.youtube
.com/watch?v=RV_walFCEfk; Brittany Pettibone (Sellner) and Martin
Sellner, "VERDICT: Generation Identity Trial," July 27, 2018, https://www
.youtube.com/watch?v=t1pRw_gTnWY.
44. Brittany Pettibone (Sellner), "My Fiancé Has Been BANNED from the USA,"
March 30, 2019, https://www.youtube.com/watch?v=pWarECxIcaU.
45. Brittany Pettibone (Sellner) and Martin Sellner, "Reunited in Exile,"
May 11, 2019, https://www.youtube.com/watch?v=fPJaug5rAbY.
46. Brittany Pettibone (Sellner), "The Crazy Reason Why I'm Being Investi-
gated by Austrian Police," July 15, 2019, https://www.youtube.com
/watch?v=SnseOqBGiU0.
47. Brittany Pettibone (Sellner) and Martin Sellner, "VICTORY: Two House
Raids Against Us Declared ILLEGAL," December 17, 2019, https://www
.youtube.com/watch?v=e7ffQIDQnh0&t=215s.
48. Pettibone (Sellner) and Sellner, "VICTORY."
49. Brittany Pettibone (Sellner), "Leftist HYSTERIA Over My Idaho GOP Meeting," May 1, 2019, https://www.youtube.com/watch?v=2tVc6FiWg5M&t
=344s.
50. United Nations Population Division, "Executive Summary [of *Replacement
Migration*]," 2001, https://www.un.org/en/development/desa/population
/publications/pdf/ageing/replacement-es.pdf.
51. Daniela Craveiro, Isabel Tiago de Oliveira, Maria Sousa Gomes, Jorge Mal-
heiros, Maria João Guardado Moreira, and João Peixoto, "Back to Replacement Migration," *Demographic Research* 40 (2019): 1323–44, https://www
.demographic-research.org/volumes/vol40/45/40-45.pdf.

52. Jacob Davey and Julia Ebner, *"The Great Replacement": The Violent Conse-quences of Mainstreamed Extremism* (London: Institute for Strategic Dia-logue, 2019), https://www.isdglobal.org/wp-content/uploads/2019/07/The-Great-Replacement-The-Violent-Consequences-of-Mainstreamed-Extremism-by-ISD.pdf.

53. Rick Noack, "Christchurch Endures as Extremist Touchstone, as Investi-gators Probe Suspected El Paso Manifesto," *Washington Post*, August 6, 2019, https://www.washingtonpost.com/world/2019/08/06/christchurch-endures-extremist-touchstone-investigators-probe-suspected-el-paso-manifesto/; Dustin Jones, "What Is the 'Great Replacement' and How Is It Tied to the Buffalo Shooting Suspect?," NPR, May 16, 2022, https://www.npr.org/2022/05/16/1099034094/what-is-the-great-replacement-theory?t=1661622741071.

54. Brittany Pettibone (Sellner), "What Makes a Great Woman?," October 23, 2019, https://www.youtube.com/watch?v=kMj11pLGkaU&t=188s.

55. Lauren Southern and Brittany Pettibone (Sellner), "Who Is Aleksandr Dugin?," June 8, 2018, https://www.youtube.com/watch?v=8nzUMsN0l58.

56. Bharath Ganesh, "Reintroducing Dugin to the Alt-Right: Lauren Southern and Brittany Pettibone's Recent Interview," *Centre for Analysis of the Radi-cal Right Insight* (blog), June 18, 2018, https://www.radicalrightanalysis.com/2018/06/18/reintroducing-dugin-to-the-alt-right-lauren-southern-and-brittany-pettibones-recent-interview/.

57. Brittany Pettibone (Sellner), "What Most Russian Women Think of Femi-nism," July 3, 2018, https://www.youtube.com/watch?v=P9LJx70KWuE.

58. Max de Haldevag, "A Glamorous Young Russian Nationalist Is Leading Her Country's Love Affair with Trump and Le Pen," *Quartz*, March 24, 2017, https://qz.com/941383/maria-katasonova-the-glamorous-young-russian-nationalist-leading-her-countrys-love-affair-with-trump-and-le-pen/.

59. On feminism in Russia, see Daniel Ofman and Indra Ekmanis, "After Decades in the Shadows, Russia's Feminists Grab Their Spotlight," *The World*, June 5, 2019, https://www.pri.org/stories/2019-06-05/after-decades-shadows-russias-feminists-grab-their-spotlight.

60. Lauren Southern and Brittany Pettibone (Sellner), "Crazy Things That Happened to Us in Russia," June 26, 2018, https://www.youtube.com/watch?v=JIoyhG9D9Tc&t=353s.

61. Lauren Southern, Instagram Story, accessed March 21, 2022.

62. Brittany Pettibone (Sellner), "The Tommy Robinson Interview That Got Me Banned from the U.K.," March 14, 2018, https://www.youtube.com/watch?v=WnQ3pmDjfkc&t=1968s.

63. Brittany Pettibone (Sellner), "A Chat with Tommy Robinson," October 27, 2017, https://www.youtube.com/watch?v=6GAi4jiZQB4&t=585s.

64. See, for example, Philipp Bovernmann, "Zweifelsfreie Zweifel," *Süddeutsche Zeitung*, November 24, 2019, https://www.sueddeutsche.de/politik /leugner-des-klimawandels-zweifelsfreie-zweifel-1.4695188.

65. Brittany Pettibone (Sellner), "Fighting for Germany (with Naomi Seibt)," June 20, 2019, https://www.youtube.com/watch?v=9N0Y-9tqIbs.

66. Darby, *Sisters in Hate*, 136, 139.

67. See, for example, Lacey Lynn and Lana Lokteff, "My Appearance on Red Ice/*Radio 3 Fourteen*," August 21, 2018, https://www.youtube.com/watch ?v=v8Rn34qOSZ8; Lana Lokteff, with Ayla Stewart, Bre Faucheux, PhiloSophiCat, and Kirsten Lauryn, "Debunking the Claim That Nationalism Is Hostile Towards Women," Red Ice TV, November 30, 2017, https://redice .tv/radio-3fourteen/debunking-the-claim-that-nationalism-is-hostile -towards-women; Lana Lokteff, with Elora [Blonde Buttermaker], Bre Faucheux, and Rebecca Hargraves, "Femininity in the Modern World," Red Ice TV, April 10, 2017, https://redice.tv/radio-3fourteen/femininity-in-the -modern-world.

68. Brittany Pettibone (Sellner), "#120db: What the #MeToo Movement Ignores," February 4, 2018, https://www.youtube.com/watch?v=4QJ3wYi _Fug; Brittany Pettibone (Sellner), "What It's Like to Be a Right-Wing Woman in Europe," October 18, 2017, https://www.youtube.com/watch?v =12I-tmhRg1M&t=540s.

69. Brittany Pettibone (Sellner), with Thaïs d'Escufon, "Fighting for France (with Thaïs d'Escufon)," August 3, 2021, https://www.youtube.com/watch ?v=-ykn8KbuWo4&t=107s.

70. Thaïs d'Escufon, Instagram Story, accessed March 15, 2022.

71. Brittany Pettibone (Sellner), Instagram posts, December 31, 2021, https:// www.instagram.com/p/CXbs8jpsdgT/, and January 28, 2023, https://www .instagram.com/p/Cn9oz0ZI-9m/.

72. Gabriella Elgenius and Jens Rydgren, "Frames of Nostalgia and Belonging: The Resurgence of Ethno-nationalism in Sweden," *European Societies* 21, no. 4 (2019): 583–602.

73. "Sweden's Violent Crime Surge Could Be Linked to 'Extreme' Immigration Policies," *Fox News*, June 12, 2021, https://www.youtube.com/watch?v =0sa2ciindUg.

74. Eva Vlaardingerbroek (@EvaVlaar), tweet, Twitter, April 23, 2022, https:// twitter.com/EvaVlaar/status/1517873138675159041; Eva Vlaardingerbroek (@EvaVlaar), tweet, Twitter, April 6, 2022, https://twitter.com /EvaVlaar/status/1511657101671768069.

75. Brittany Pettibone (Sellner), with Eva Vlaardingerbroek, "Fighting for the Netherlands (with Eva Vlaardingerbroek)," November 12, 2022, https://www.youtube.com/watch?v=NteBYYuSbrM.

7. COUNTERING THE FAR RIGHT

1. Brittany Pettibone (Sellner), "IT'S ME: BARBIE FIANCÉ," September 25, 2018, https://www.youtube.com/watch?v=MSTfQIB6Ecg.
2. Brittany Pettibone (Sellner), "We Are All Being Lied To," July 28, 2020, https://www.youtube.com/watch?v=HMKDI0jrHmI.
3. Rebecca Hargraves, "Don't Be Evil | Oh Really, Google?," August 27, 2017, https://www.youtube.com/watch?v=IwggrnlyYGo.
4. Rebecca Hargraves, "Black Pigeon Speaks on Society & the Future of the West," January 22, 2021, https://www.youtube.com/watch?v=nzPTBvuIAV4.
5. Robyn Caplan, *Content or Context Moderation? Artisanal, Community-Reliant, and Industrial Approaches* (New York: Data & Society Institute, 2018), https://datasociety.net/wp-content/uploads/2018/11/DS_Content_or_Context_Moderation.pdf, 4.
6. Lauren Chen, "BANNED: Big Tech PURGES Conservatives | Ep 195," June 25, 2020, https://www.youtube.com/watch?v=-nv-VeHvj_k.
7. Southern Poverty Law Center, "Proud Boys," n.d., https://www.splcenter.org/fighting-hate/extremist-files/group/proud-boys.
8. Alan Feuer, "Did the Proud Boys Help Coordinate the Capitol Riot? Yes, U.S. Suggests," *New York Times*, February 5, 2021, https://www.nytimes.com/2021/02/05/nyregion/proud-boys-capitol-riot-conspiracy.html; "Proud Boys: Canada Labels Far-Right Group a Terrorist Entity," *BBC News*, February 3, 2021, https://www.bbc.com/news/world-us-canada-55923485.
9. Nicola Slawson and Jim Waterson, "Katie Hopkins Permanently Removed from Twitter," *The Guardian*, June 19, 2020, https://www.theguardian.com/media/2020/jun/19/katie-hopkins-permanently-removed-from-twitter.
10. Chen, "BANNED."
11. Lauren Chen, "HEALTHIER to Get Pregnant in Your 30s Than Your 20s? Anti-Natalism | Ep 160," April 5, 2020, https://www.youtube.com/watch?v=E9w-br2pKmk.
12. Paul M. Barrett and J. Grant Sims, *False Accusation: The Unfounded Claim That Social Media Companies Censor Conservatives* (New York: New York University, 2021), https://bhr.stern.nyu.edu/bias-report-release-page.

13. Megan Squire, email interview by the author, July 14, 2020.

14. Richard Rogers, "Deplatforming: Following Extreme Internet Celebrities to Telegram and Alternative Social Media," *European Journal of Communication* 35, no. 3 (2020): 213–29.

15. Rebecca Hargraves, with Lana Lokteff, "Red Ice on Community Building & Resilience," July 8, 2021, https://www.youtube.com/watch?v=jG1qDR5u FbY&t=405s.

16. Cassandra MacDonald (interview with Brittany Pettibone Sellner), "Instagram Forces Right-Wing Author Brittany Pettibone to Delete All Photos with Her Political Activist Husband—Including from Their Wedding," *The Gateway Pundit*, April 5, 2020, https://www.thegatewaypundit.com /2020/04/instagram-forces-right-wing-author-brittany-pettibone -delete-photos-political-activist-husband-including-wedding/.

17. Robyn Riley, Instagram Story, accessed July 8, 2020.

18. Ayla Stewart, "Ayla Stewart Responds, *New York Times* Anti Housewives Piece," June 2, 2018, https://www.youtube.com/watch?v=jo2Bx3w8r5s&t =5307s.

19. Gabriel Weimann and Natalie Masri, "Research Note: Spreading Hate on TikTok," *Studies in Conflict & Terrorism,* June 2020, https://doi.org/10.1080 /1057610X.2020.1780027; Sarah Manavis, "How the Alt-Right Is Pivoting to TikTok," *New Statesman*, April 27, 2020, https://www.newstatesman.com /science-tech/social-media/2020/04/how-alt-right-pivoting-tiktok -tommy-robinson-britain-first.

20. Taylor Hatmaker, "More Universities Are Banning TikTok from Their Campus Networks and Devices," *TechCrunch,* January 20, 2023, https://tcrn.ch /3Wjbb7a.

21. Julia Alexander, "The Yellow $: Comprehensive History of Demonetization and YouTube's War with Creators," *Polygon*, May 10, 2018, https://www .polygon.com/2018/5/10/17268102/youtube-demonetization-pewdiepie -logan-paul-casey-neistat-philip-defranco.

22. Original video now deleted but titled "Ad Friendly Makeup Tutorial" and published on June 12, 2017. Fan video uploaded at https://www.youtube .com/watch?v=oyndAr7jJN4&t=64s.

23. Lauren Southern, "We Let Hate Win. #London," June 4, 2017, https://www .youtube.com/watch?v=vvTdEzw8upQ&t=227s.

24. Rebecca Hargraves, "Twitter | Censorship, Suspensions & the Future," November 30, 2017, https://www.youtube.com/watch?v=gRPE1krJ5jQ.

25. Rebecca Hargraves, "Will We Lose Our Platform? | YouTube Demonetization," March 28, 2017, https://www.youtube.com/watch?v=k_ZwsMg _Goo.

26. Brittany Pettibone (Sellner), "Support My Work," personal website, January 25, 2021, https://web.archive.org/web/20210125125446/https://brittpettibone.com/support/; Jack Hadfield, "EXCLUSIVE: Lauren Southern Taking First Steps to Sue Patreon," *National File*, July 31, 2020, https://nationalfile.com/exclusive-lauren-southern-taking-first-steps-to-sue-patreon/.

27. Rebecca Hargraves (@blonde_beast1), Instagram post, October 30, 2020, https://www.instagram.com/p/CG_B9BxAAPtIvTLFrARXtUwsbopiOd_A_nkPds0/.

28. Hargraves, "Will We Lose Our Platform?"

29. Lauren Chen, "Why MEN Like YOUNGER Women: The TRUTH About AGING & Dating," August 13, 2019, https://www.youtube.com/watch?v=Ux-WKpjzs38&t=111s.

30. Lauren Chen, "INCEL 'Ask Me Anything': Loneliness & Hating Women? Response | Ep 110," December 1, 2019, https://www.youtube.com/watch?v=aHMJQUl477Q.

31. Emillie de Keulenaar, Anthony Glyn Burton, and Ivan Kisjes, "Deplatforming, Demotion and Folk Theories of Big Tech Persecution," *Fronteiras-estudos midiáticos* 23, no. 2 (2021): 120.

32. Bharath Ganesh, "The Ungovernability of Digital Hate Culture," *Columbia Journal of International Affairs*, December 19, 2018, https://jia.sipa.columbia.edu/ungovernability-digital-hate-culture.

33. Robyn Riley, Instagram Stories, accessed June 26 and August 19, 2022.

34. Tama Leaver, Tim Highfield, and Crystal Abidin, *Instagram: Visual Social Media Cultures* (London: Polity, 2020), 22–25, my emphasis.

35. Brooke Erin Duffy and Colten Meisner, "Platform Governance at the Margins: Social Media Creators' Experiences with Algorithmic (In)visibility," *Media, Culture & Society* 45, no. 2 (2022), https://doi.org/10.1177/01634437221111923, 14, emphasis in original.

36. Bharath Ganesh and Jonathan Bright, eds., *Extreme Digital Speech: Contexts, Responses and Solutions*, VOX-Pol report (VOX-Pol Center for Excellence, 2020), https://www.voxpol.eu/download/vox-pol_publication/DCUJ770-VOX-Extreme-Digital-Speech.pdf; see also Marguerite Borelli, "Social Media Corporations as Actors of Counter-Terrorism," *New Media & Society*, online, August 8, 2021, https://doi.org/10.1177/14614448211035121.

37. John Gallacher, "Automated Detection of Terrorist and Extremist Content," in *Extreme Digital Speech*, ed. Ganesh and Bright, 60–61.

38. Savvas Zannettou, "'I Won the Election!': An Empirical Analysis of Soft Moderation Interventions on Twitter," in *Proceedings of the Fifteenth International AAAI Conference on Web and Social Media 2021*, ed. Ceren Budak,

Meeyoung Cha, Daniele Quercia, and Lexing Xie (Palo Alto, CA: AAAI, 2021), 865–76, https://doi.org/10.1609/icwsm.v15i1.18110.

39. Robyn Riley, Instagram Story, accessed December 19, 2021.

40. Sarah T. Roberts, *Behind the Screen: Content Moderation in the Shadows of Social Media* (New Haven, CT: Yale University Press, 2019).

41. Zoey Reeve, "Human Assessment and Crowd Sourced Flagging," in *Extreme Digital Speech*, ed. Ganesh and Bright, 67–79.

42. Tarleton Gillespie, *Custodians of the Internet: Platforms, Content Moderation, and the Hidden Decisions That Shape Social Media* (New Haven, CT: Yale University Press, 2018), 6.

43. Robert Gorwa, "The Platform Governance Triangle: Conceptualising the Informal Regulation of Online Content," *Internet Policy Review* 8, no. 2 (2019): 1–22.

44. Valentine Crosset, "Removing and Blocking Extremist Content," in *Extreme Digital Speech*, ed. Ganesh and Bright, 83–84.

45. Gillespie, *Custodians of the Internet*, 30.

46. White House, "Executive Order on Preventing Online Censorship," May 28, 2020, https://trumpwhitehouse.archives.gov/presidential-actions/exe cutive-order-preventing-online-censorship/.

47. Shirin Ghaffary, "Trump's Executive Order on Social Media Is Legally Unenforceable, Experts Say," *Vox*, May 28, 2020, https://www.vox.com /recode/2020/5/28/21273878/trump-executive-order-twitter-social -media-section-230-free-speech-implications.

48. Lauren Chen, "Trump SLAMS Social Media Censorship in Executive Order," May 31, 2020, https://www.youtube.com/watch?v=Rump-XOGNS0.

49. Shirin Ghaffary, "Most Americans Think Social Media Companies Are Censoring People," *Vox Recode*, August 19, 2020, https://www.vox.com /recode/2020/8/19/21373960/social-media-companies-censor-political -bias-trump-pew-study; Casey Newton, "The Real Bias on Social Networks Isn't Against Conservatives," *The Verge*, April 11, 2019, https://www .theverge.com/interface/2019/4/11/18305407/social-network -conservative-bias-twitter-facebook-ted-cruz.

50. Hargraves, "Don't Be Evil." See also Anti-Defamation League, "ADL Applauds Google and YouTube in Expanding Initiative to Fight Online Hate," August 1, 2017, https://www.adl.org/news/press-releases/adl -applauds-google-and-youtube-in-expanding-initiative-to-fight-online -hate.

51. Hargraves, "Don't Be Evil."

52. Robyn Riley, with Lauren Chen, "Girl Talk #7: Lauren Chen on Censorship & the Family VS Career Choice," May 19, 2019, https://www.youtube.com /watch?v=FSCp9mrHnoY.

53. Duffy and Meisner, "Platform Governance at the Margins," 4.
54. Ryan Mac and Craig Silverman, "'Mark Changed the Rules': How Facebook Went Easy on Alex Jones and Other Right-Wing Figures," *Buzzfeed News*, February 21, 2021, https://www.buzzfeednews.com/article/ryanmac/mark-zuckerberg-joel-kaplan-facebook-alex-jones.
55. U.S. Senate, "Wyden, Booker and Clarke Introduce Algorithmic Accountability Act of 2022 to Require New Transparency and Accountability for Automated Decision Systems," press release, February 3, 2022, https://www.wyden.senate.gov/news/press-releases/wyden-booker-and-clarke-introduce-algorithmic-accountability-act-of-2022-to-require-new-transparency-and-accountability-for-automated-decision-systems.
56. Kate Coyer, "Informal Counter-Narratives," in *Extreme Digital Speech*, ed. Ganesh and Bright, 104.
57. Jigsaw, "GOOGLE IDEAS BECOMES JIGSAW," *Medium*, February 17, 2016, https://medium.com/jigsaw/google-ideas-becomes-jigsaw-bcb5bd08c423#.fz3pt7rcg.
58. Vidhya Ramalingam, email interview by the author, July 23, 2020.
59. Clark Hogan-Taylor, phone interview by the author, August 7, 2020.
60. Bharath Ganesh, "Evaluating the Promise of Formal Counter-Narratives," in *Extreme Digital Speech*, ed. Ganesh and Bright, 90.
61. Coyer, "Informal Counter-Narratives," 105.
62. Ganesh, "Evaluating the Promise of Formal Counter-Narratives," 93.
63. Kurt Braddock, "Vaccinating Against Hate: Using Attitudinal Inoculation to Confer Resistance to Persuasion by Extremist Propaganda," *Terrorism and Political Violence* 34, no. 2 (2022): 240–62.
64. Andrew Guess, Jonathan Nagler, and Joshua Tucker, "Less Than You Think: Prevalence and Predictors of Fake News Dissemination on Facebook," *Science Advances* 5, no. 1 (2019): eaau4586.
65. Huw Davies, "Digital Literacy vs the Anti-human Machine: A Proxy Debate for Our Times?," in *Extreme Digital Speech*, ed. Ganesh and Bright, 111.
66. danah boyd, "You Think You Want Media Literacy . . . Do You?," *Points: Data & Society* (blog), March 9, 2018, https://points.datasociety.net/you-think-you-want-media-literacy-do-you-7cad6af18ec2.
67. Francesca Bolla Tripodi, *The Propagandists' Playbook: How Conservative Elites Manipulate Search and Threaten Democracy* (New Haven, CT: Yale University Press, 2022), 100.
68. Lauren Southern, Instagram post, May 30, 2018, https://www.instagram.com/p/BjaUPGan01L/.
69. YouTube, Creator Awards, n.d., https://www.youtube.com/creators/awards/.

70. YouTube, "Community Guidelines," n.d., https://www.youtube.com/about/policies/#community-guidelines.

71. Lauren Southern, "Paris Train Station Overwhelmed with Migrants," July 16, 2017, https://www.youtube.com/watch?v=G8LGX8o2fw8; Southern, "We Let Hate Win."

72. Lauren Southern, "PATREON BANNED MY ACCOUNT??," July 22, 2017, https://www.youtube.com/watch?v=rtImwK5TI4g, quoting Patreon.

73. ContraPoints [Natalie Wynn], "Incels | ContraPoints," August 17, 2018, https://www.youtube.com/watch?v=fD2briZ6fB0; ContraPoints [Natalie Wynn], "Gender Critical | ContraPoints," March 31, 2019, https://www.youtube.com/watch?v=1pTPuoGjQsI; ContraPoints [Natalie Wynn], "Decrypting the Alt-Right: How to Recognize a F@scist | ContraPoints," September 1, 2017, https://www.youtube.com/watch?v=Sx4BVGPkdzk&t=813s.

74. ContraPoints [Natalie Wynn], "Decrypting the Alt-Right."

75. See Coyer, "Informal Counter-Narratives," 98–109.

76. Eisellety (@eisellety), Instagram post, June 24, [no year], https://imgur.com/a/FVMtXxC.

77. Abbie Richards, https://www.tiktok.com/@tofology; Leonie [FrauLöwenherz], https://www.tiktok.com/@frauloewenherz.

78. Barbara Sprunt, "The White House Is Turning to TikTok Stars to Take Its Message to a Younger Audience," NPR, October 9, 2022, https://www.npr.org/2022/10/09/1127211983/the-white-house-is-turning-to-tiktok-stars-to-take-its-message-to-a-younger-audi.

79. Ian Cobain and Nadda Osman, "UK Counter-Terror Programme Targeted BAME Women Using Instagram Influencers," *Middle East Eye*, June 9, 2020, https://www.middleeasteye.net/news/uk-prevent-stoosh-bame-women-instagram-influencers.

80. Benjamin Lee, "Countering Violent Extremism Online: The Experiences of Informal Counter Messaging Actors," *Policy & Internet* 12, no. 1 (2020): 67, 83, 79.

81. Benjamin Lee, email interview by the author, July 20, 2020.

82. Coyer, "Informal Counter-Narratives," 100.

83. Elizabeth Pearson, email interview by the author, August 26, 2020.

84. Seyward Darby, *Sisters in Hate: American Women on the Front Lines of White Nationalism* (New York: Little, Brown, 2020), 155.

85. Sarah K. Papworth, Janna Rist, Lauren Coad, and Eleanor J. Milner-Gulland, "Evidence for Shifting Baseline Syndrome in Conservation," *Conservation Letters* 2, no. 2 (2009): 93.

86. David Roberts, "The Scariest Thing About Global Warming (and COVID-19)," *Vox*, July 7, 2020, https://www.vox.com/energy-and-environment

/2020/7/7/21311027/covid-19-climate-change-global-warming-shifting
-baselines.

87. Rebecca Hargraves, "How Women Can Provide Value Again," January 14,
2018, https://www.youtube.com/watch?v=VQ3Xdb-wvBs.

88. Betty Friedan, *The Feminine Mystique* (New York: Norton, 1963).

89. For the Chase & Sanborn add, see image 30523402 in the Advertising
Archives, https://www.advertisingarchives.co.uk/detail/20141/1/Mag
azine-Advert/Chase-and-Sanborn; for the Mornidrine ad, see *Canadian
Medical Association Journal* 81 , no. 1 (1959): 59, https://www.ncbi.nlm.nih
.gov/pmc/articles/PMC1830735/pdf/canmedaj00808-0002.pdf.

CONCLUSION: "I'VE TAKEN THE REAL-LIFE PILL"

1. Lauren Southern (@laurencheriie), Instagram post, January 30, 2020,
https://www.instagram.com/p/B76_b_QgoCu/.

2. Lauren Southern, "Why I Left, and Why I'm Back," June 19, 2020, https://
www.youtube.com/watch?v=2YhyNqXWqiU.

3. Lauren Southern (@laurencheriie), Instagram post, July 16, 2020, https://
www.instagram.com/p/CCt8nRaAzEA/.

4. Robyn Riley, "The Rebel Revival #4: The Abandonment of Personal
Responsibility," June 20, 2020, https://www.youtube.com/watch?v=I9Q
_fmRiLys.

5. This livestream was later posted as "Lauren Southern & Nick Fuentes
Squash Beef??? | Debate w/ Destiny, Nick Fuentes, Lauren Southern,"
August 12, 2022, https://www.youtube.com/watch?v=RlTnYi9iAzE.

6. Lauren Southern, "Online Cancel Culture Is Fostering 'Mass Hatred,'"
July 18, 2020, https://www.youtube.com/watch?v=DpYbjdB-_qc; Lauren
Southern, articles for *Spectator*, https://www.spectator.com.au/author
/lauren-southern/.

7. Lauren Southern and Randall Evans, *Executive Disorder* (podcast series),
streamed beginning in 2020, https://www.listennotes.com/podcasts
/executive-disorder-lauren-southern-and-6d4TcMoGLrC/.

8. Lauren Southern, "The WHOLE Truth," July 11, 2022, https://www.youtube
.com/watch?v=dqzJmdlJx0k.

9. Jared Holt quoted in Anna Silman, "We Thought We Knew Faith, Until We
Didn't," *The Cut*, November 9, 2018, https://www.thecut.com/2018/11/faith
-goldy-toronto-white-nationalist-poster-girl.html.

10. Lana Lokteff and Bre Faucheux, "Lana Lokteff | How Women Can Course
Correct | 27Crows Radio," February 27, 2018, https://www.youtube.com
/watch?v=dMyTy8QKLfA.

11. Annie Kelly, "The Housewives of White Supremacy," *New York Times*, June 1, 2018, https://www.nytimes.com/2018/06/01/opinion/sunday/tradwives -women-alt-right.html; Ayla Stewart, "Ayla Stewart Responds, *New York Times* Anti Housewives Piece," June 2, 2018, https://www.youtube.com /watch?v=jo2Bx3w8r5s&t=5307s.

12. Rebecca Hargraves, "The Desperate Left | Data & Society Study," September 21, 2018, https://www.youtube.com/watch?v=PUd2RBEk9d0&t=567s.

13. Julia Ebner, email interview by the author, July 14, 2020.

14. Lana Lokteff, "I'm in a Book Called *Sisters in Hate*. It's All Lies!," Red Ice TV, September 2, 2020, https://redice.tv/red-ice-tv/im-in-a-book-called -sisters-in-hate-its-all-lies.

15. Seyward Darby, *Sisters in Hate: American Women on the Front Lines of White Nationalism* (New York: Little, Brown, 2020), 151.

16. Lacey Lynn, "The 1965 Red Pill," January 9, 2018, https://www.youtube .com/watch?v=EIDUHhMBYPg.

17. Robyn Riley and Rebecca Hargraves, "Motherland Live: Prepping for SHTF w/ a Family," January 26, 2021, https://www.youtube.com/watch?v=lW4Nu Co9VxM.

18. Darby, *Sisters in Hate*, 243–45.

19. Lana Lokteff quoted in Darby, *Sisters in Hate*, 218.

20. Brittany Pettibone (Sellner), "Do Women Fit Well in Politics?," November 28, 2018, https://www.youtube.com/watch?v=VKtldUgAM28.

21. Lana Lokteff quoted in Darby, *Sisters in Hate*, 238.

22. Lauren Southern, "Return of the Traditional Woman—Cal Poly SLO," May 27, 2017, https://www.youtube.com/watch?v=HFW0z0Y5TR4&t=2s.

23. Pettibone (Sellner), "Do Women Fit Well in Politics?"

24. Mikhaila Peterson, "The Mikhaila Peterson Podcast #11—Lauren Southern," July 14, 2020, https://www.youtube.com/watch?v=uG9Ughixo4o.

25. Lauren Southern, "Why I'm Not Married," November 23, 2017, https:// www.youtube.com/watch?v=P-UKPpmQlys&t=1s.

26. Southern, "The WHOLE Truth."

27. Lauren Southern, Instagram Story, accessed August 18, 2020.

28. Darby, *Sisters in Hate*, 240.

29. Brittany Pettibone (Sellner), Telegram post, June 4, 2022, https://imgur .com/a/mtxZAt4.

30. Brittany Pettibone (Sellner), "Sorry for Disappearing," October 7, 2022, https://www.youtube.com/watch?v=U76N64CMRJ8.

31. Kathleen M. Blee and Annette Linden, "Women in Extreme Right Parties and Movements: A Comparison of the Netherlands and the United States," in *Women of the Right: Comparisons and Interplay Across Borders* (University Park: Pennsylvania State University Press, 2012), 107.

INDEX